MW01628319

Procurement Project Management Success

Achieving a Higher Level of Effectiveness

Diana L. Lindstrom

ISBN-13: 978-1-60427-089-1

Printed and bound in the U.S.A. Printed on acid-free paper
10 9 8 7 6 5 4 3 2 1

Library of Congress Cataloging-in-Publication Data

Lindstrom, Diana L., 1955-
Procurement project management success : achieving a higher level of effectiveness / by Diana L. Lindstrom.
pages cm
Includes index.
ISBN 978-1-60427-089-1 (hardcover : alk. paper) 1. Industrial procurement. 2. Project management. 3. Business logistics. I. Title.
HD39.5.L56 2013
658.7'2--dc23

2013033270

Direct all inquiries to J. Ross Publishing, Inc., 300 S. Pine Island Road, Suite #305, Plantation, FL, 33324.

Phone: (954) 727-9333
Fax: (561) 892-0700
Web: www.jrosspub.com

To my husband, Jay, who has persevered with all my life choices.
You have been by my side in sickness and in health, for richer or poorer,
through all the days of our life together.

CONTENTS

FOREWORD

There are two methods of learning that I consider to be most powerful. One of those methods is learning from our mistakes. The other is learning from an expert who can show us the path to success. In my career as a procurement practitioner and leader, I did both.

Very early in my procurement career, a supplier decided to discontinue pursuing doing business with an employer of mine because I made a mistake and pushed this supplier too hard in a scenario that was not conducive to strong-arm negotiation tactics. It was an unpleasant experience, but an important lesson learned.

A short time later, I participated in intensive training and was fortunate to have great mentors who helped me to learn the professional procurement role quite well, including, for example, the art of negotiating. From then on, by applying the principles and techniques learned during the training and the guidance gained from my mentors, I was often able to set aggressive—seemingly impossible—negotiation targets and, through diligent effort, persuade suppliers to agree to the terms that I was seeking for my employers.

By getting into the habit of applying newly gained knowledge of what to do and what not to do as soon as possible, I have greatly improved my retention of knowledge and effectiveness. This practice has enabled me to rise up through the procurement ranks of my employers and to achieve an amazing amount of success in my career as a procurement practitioner and leader.

Since transitioning to my current role as president and chief procurement officer of the Next Level Purchasing Association (NLPA), this trend of career success has continued. Under my leadership, this relatively new organization has experienced year-after-year explosive growth and attained international recognition as one of the procurement profession's foremost authoritative bodies.

There are two common threads that I attribute to my success previously as a professional procurement practitioner and leader and currently as the head of the NLPA. The first is the knowledge I gained from intensive training and having some great mentors in purchasing and supply management and utilizing project management best practices. The second is quickly and effectively applying what I learn on a daily basis.

In today's evermore challenging business environment—particularly in procurement—you cannot just "wing it" and expect to succeed. You must have a multi-component plan. You must have structure. You have to know what your tasks are, what your dependencies are, what your constraints are, what your risks are, what your resources are, what your deadlines are, and more. Additionally, if you want to become truly successful in procurement today, then project management best practices must absolutely be a part of your arsenal.

For many—perhaps you—this evolving procurement environment with accelerating complexity requiring the use of project management best practices is new, uncharted territory and a bit scary. There is a lot that you need to know and learn. I suspect that you like many other procurement professionals may have been worrying about the thought of learning these applicable best practices via the painful method—by making mistakes. Well, there is good news. It is in the form of this new book entitled *Procurement Project Management Success: Achieving a Higher Level of Effectiveness* by Diana Lindstrom.

As you will read in the *About the Author* section of this text, Diana Lindstrom is an expert in both procurement and project management. Most importantly to you, she is an expert in employing project management best practices in procurement. She, like the great mentors I was fortunate enough to have, demonstrates through her book the ability to explain to others the seemingly complex in a manner that is easy to understand and apply. Diana is an expert in the truest sense of the word and a great mentor.

This desk reference will give you an advantage. Instead of learning from your mistakes, you can now learn what to do from an expert with years of highly successful practical experience as well as what not to do using the guidance she provides based on the lessons learned from various real projects. You can learn how to manage your procurement projects perfectly without the need to "repair" things done wrong. This customized-to-procurement application of project management best practices is the first proven framework on the market.

Procurement Project Management Success is a desk reference that gives you a comprehensive approach for utilizing project management practices in your procurement work. Step-by-step instructions guide you around the myriad pitfalls and landmines that can lead to project-threatening, and potentially career-killing, mistakes.

At the NLPA, we utilize our expertise and lessons learned to provide real-world advice to procurement professionals like you to help you succeed. This unique guide by Diana Lindstrom embodies that same spirit of education. I wish it had been available in the early days of my procurement career.

As you read this book, try to absorb every principle that Diana teaches. Take a minute to realize that while you are learning how to succeed in the new procurement world via the best method—learning from an expert—too many of your peers will be learning the hard way. By applying the project management best practices you are going to read about, you will be well-positioned for success in your procurement career and beyond. I hope that this valuable book plays a significant part in you becoming the next expert to show others the path to success.

Charles Dominick
President & Chief Procurement Officer
Next Level Purchasing Association
Lead Author of *The Procurement Game Plan: Winning Strategies and Techniques for Supply Management Professionals*
http://www.NextLevelPurchasing.com

PREFACE

This book is a result of discussions with many supply management and supply chain professionals about what they want to know and then use in their everyday work. The overwhelming single point was "techniques commonly used in project management." While not everyone used the exact term "project management," the basic ideas of planning, scheduling, budgeting, tracking, and managing all aspects of a procurement were mentioned often.

Why would anyone want to learn new techniques for doing work? Simply put, to be more successful. Success can be defined in many different ways. Some people look at success as the simple measurement of how much money they can make each year. Other people measure success by how good they feel about what they are doing. Yet others use a combination of measurements that include money, feelings, free time, etc. Correctly using project management techniques will positively impact all measurements of success.

Many books are written every year about project management. And many books are written about procurement. The idea that is missing in these books is the combination of both—procurement *and* project management. The intent of this book is to relay information about the project management techniques and tools that are applicable to most procurements.

Many books are written in hard-to-understand language or language that uses very specialized terminology. While specialized terminology is necessary in some instances, it makes learning more difficult. This how-to book uses language that is easy to understand. We will examine theories as needed, but focus on exactly what is needed to get the work done successfully. This book also focuses on specific people and situations, including:

- Procurement professionals who want to incorporate project management techniques
- Procurement managers/executives who want to provide their employees with new tools

- Adult continuing education instructors of procurement courses
- College professors and instructors of purchasing, supply management, and supply chain management who are interested in upgrading the courses they teach with project management tools and techniques
- Students who are interested in a procurement career
- People who want to move from buying to procurement
- People who find themselves assigned to do a procurement with no prior experience
- Accidental project managers who are suddenly thrown into a project
- Project managers who have never done a procurement or wish to improve their skills in this area

Procurement professionals often find that they have a high hurdle to clear. In many companies, other business units in the company will do almost anything to avoid using a procurement professional in a purchasing effort. This comes from a long history of inadequate communication and a lack of knowledge of the specific needs of the business unit. Using project management techniques changes all that. Project management techniques *require* good communications with all stakeholders. Every person that the procurement touches is included as a stakeholder—from the planning phase all the way through until the goods or services are under contract. All of these stakeholders have input that matters to the procurement.

Project management techniques *require* a schedule to be developed. During development of the schedule, all stakeholders are consulted. This technique assists the procurement professional in showing stakeholders exactly what needs to be done for an ethical and legal procurement. The schedule also serves as the basis for educating other people in the company about what is involved in making a procurement and how long it takes. The project management technique of developing a schedule makes communications stronger between procurement and other business units. The schedule also helps keep the procurement professional on track—meeting milestone deadlines and getting the procurement completed on time.

Not all project management techniques are discussed in this book. Some do not apply to procurements at all. Others would only apply to very complex procurements. Taking the middle road—using the techniques that apply to the majority of procurements—allows this book to focus on exactly how to apply the techniques needed.

It is my hope that this book will provide the information needed by so many procurement professionals to make their contributions even more valuable to their organizations, add value to the current body of knowledge, and help all those with procurement responsibilities to achieve a higher level of effectiveness and success.

ACKNOWLEGMENTS

As usual in most undertakings, there is a team of people behind the scenes. I want to thank each and every person who has touched this project.

Charles Dominick served as my inspiration. Besides my boss at Qwest, Charles was the only professional I knew who saw, and understood, the importance of incorporating project management tools into supply chain management.

Donna Johnson gave her generous support by reviewing the manuscript. With many years of experience in supply chain management, Donna provided wonderful ideas and suggestions.

Drew Gierman, my Publisher, Carolyn Lea, my Editor, and the entire publishing team at J. Ross Publishing provided support and expertise with a soft hand.

ABOUT THE AUTHOR

Diana Lindstrom has more than 25 years of experience as an electrical engineer and project manager working in electrical power and facilities management, design, construction, and maintenance. As a former certified Project Management Professional (PMP®), she managed projects ranging from small designs in electrical system transmission substations to large construction projects in various industries.

She decided to take a break from this career to try something else for a while that would enhance her current skill set and became a paralegal primarily drafting and supporting litigation of contracts. Upon achieving her objective and having gained considerable procurement experience writing specifications, using win-win negotiating to obtain contract work, and actually performing simple to fairly complex procurements previously as a project manager, Diana became interested in developing a new career in supply management. She was interested in finding a position that would give her the opportunity to apply most, if not all, of the knowledge and skills she had acquired over the years.

Diana was hired by a major telecommunications company with the specific intention of bringing her project management knowledge into the procurement department. She held the position of strategic sourcing manager, which was fairly broad in scope. In this role her average procurement was $100 million spend per year. The largest was $250 million spend per year. Utilizing her legal training and negotiations skills, along with her project management skills, she implemented programs that saved the telecommunications company many millions of dollars each year.

Following her career as an electrical engineer, project manager, paralegal, and supply management professional, Diana became a certified life coach (CTACC) and founded Los Lobos Consulting, a firm specializing in executive coaching. During this period she coached executives, corporate attorneys, project managers, and both new and experienced procurement professionals. She also developed and taught a project management course in an adult continuing education program at the University of New Mexico, Los Alamos, when she worked for Los Alamos National Laboratories.

After four years of honorable service in the United States Navy, Diana earned her Bachelor of Science in Electrical Engineering from San Diego State University. She earned her Project Management Professional (PMP®) certification from the Project Management Institute. She has been a member of the Project Management Institute (PMI), Institute of Electrical and Electronics Engineers (IEEE), and National Fire Protection Association (NFPA) and continues to be a member of the Institute of Supply Management (ISM). She is now semi-retired and spends her time working with people who are searching for new ways to be successful, as well as writing and speaking on various topics.

Free value-added materials available from the Download Resource Center at www.jrosspub.com

At J. Ross Publishing we are committed to providing today's professional with practical, hands-on tools that enhance the learning experience and give readers an opportunity to apply what they have learned. That is why we offer free ancillary materials available for download on this book and all participating Web Added Value™ publications. These online resources may include interactive versions of material that appears in the book or supplemental templates, worksheets, models, plans, case studies, proposals, spreadsheets and assessment tools, among other things. Whenever you see the WAV™ symbol in any of our publications it means bonus materials accompany the book and are available from the Web Added Value™ Download Resource Center at www.jrosspub.com.

Downloads available for *Procurement Project Management Success: Achieving a Higher Level of Effectiveness* consist of an actual schedule and budget, a procurement plan, and a Request for Proposals (RFP) for Case Example 2: Janitorial Services from Chapter 3. These downloads may be used as templates for the user's procurements. Also included are step-by-step instructions for creating a Gantt chart in a Microsoft Excel spreadsheet for Mac.

Schedule Budget: The spreadsheet is a combined schedule and budget for Case Example 2 that displays procurement team information, including direct and indirect costs for each person; every WBS, task description, predecessor, owner, role, start date, finish date, effort, duration, labor costs, and percent complete; and the procurement milestones in bold for the entire row of each milestone. This spreadsheet is the major tool to use to manage and communicate any procurement. It can easily be used as a template to help create schedules and budgets. Especially useful is easy access to the cell equations that are needed to complete a budget.

Procurement Plan: The document is the actual procurement plan for Case Example 2. Using the tools and techniques described in the chapters, this procurement plan is a guide that may be used for completing a procurement. This plan may be also be used in a presentation to management for obtaining approvals for the strategy and timing of a procurement. The plan includes the Statement of Work (SOW), procurement milestones, goal of the procurement, success metrics for the procurement, preliminary cost estimate, preliminary estimated date of completion, the members of the procurement team, assumptions about the procurement, constraints to the procurement, milestone schedule and budget, the communication plan, change control, and the risk management plan. This document can easily be used as a template for any procurement to help create procurement plans.

Request for Proposals: The document is the actual RFP for Case Example 2. The RFP includes every major component needed to receive relevant proposals: the invitation, table of contents, overview of the request, timeline and events, general instructions for responding the request, proposal stipulations and requirements, insurance requirements, the proposal evaluation process, specialized services to be performed, proposal reply page, proposal contents, signature page, and attachments. The attachments include a sample contract, deviation form, notice of non-participation form, how to access IRS Form W-9, and a contractor sign-in log. Although the RFP is very specific for janitorial services, it can be used for any type of procurement. The template can be used as a template for any RFP, as well as to support a procurement team in uncovering the information needed to provide an ethical, legal procurement.

A Gantt Chart in MS Excel for Mac: Step-by-step instructions describe how to create a Gantt chart in a Microsoft Excel spreadsheet. Several websites offer similar instructions for creating a Gantt chart in MS Excel for Windows, but this is the only instruction sheet currently available for MS Excel for Mac. Although MS Excel is not the easiest tool to use to create a Gantt chart, its charting capabilities can be finessed to produce an acceptable Gantt chart. This Gantt chart can be used to communicate the baseline schedule when the procurement begins and to update the schedule as the procurement progresses. Although the Gantt chart created using these instructions is for the Case Example 2 schedule, the instructions can be used to create a Gantt chart for any procurement.

CHAPTER 1

FIRST THINGS FIRST

Procurements are purchases of materials, products, or services in a business environment. This concept translates to everyday life as well. We all buy things. Most of us buy services at some point in our lives. Let's look at a case example that is common for most people in the United States. We will watch a family that shops for a car.

CASE EXAMPLE 1: SHOPPING FOR A CAR

Bill and Sheila needed to buy a vehicle for their sixteen-year-old daughter, Abby. Their decision to buy a vehicle took quite some time—their daughter's safety was first in their minds. Now that the decision to buy the vehicle had been reached, they started looking at different makes and models. The first requirement, safety, ruled out several models. Abby would not be getting a Ford Mustang, a Dodge Charger, a Chevrolet Corvette, or many other vehicles. Next they looked at body styles—SUV, minivan, sedan, and pickup. They could not see a sixteen-year-old girl driving a minivan or a SUV. That left a sedan or pickup. They did not need a pickup because Bill already drove one. So a sedan it would be.

Doing their research online, Bill and Sheila started with a trusted site. This site had reports on all types of vehicles. The reports included safety, reliability, fuel consumption, and comfort as the metrics, along with the technical specifications for each vehicle. The site also provided guidance on pricing of each vehicle and which vehicles provided the best value for the money.

After they narrowed down the choices, Bill and Sheila visited car dealerships. They still had to decide if they would buy a new sedan or a used sedan, so they went to both types of dealers. They also looked in the local newspaper for ads for both new and used vehicles. With ongoing conversations between each other, and with their daughter, they decided to buy a new car. The major factors influencing their decision were safety, reliability, and value. With car loan interest rates very low, and prices for new vehicles quite reasonable, they decided that this new car would last their daughter at least through college and probably several more years after that.

Still looking for the best possible value, Bill thought about a hybrid car. Sure it would save on gas costs over the life of the vehicle, but what would that life be? Five years? Ten years? More? What about repairing or replacing the batteries? Bill decided to do research to find out about hybrids. Here is some of what he found online:

> ***Pros:*** great gas mileage (ranges from about 42 to over 60 miles per gallon); very quiet while running on batteries; good reliability; good durability; great braking; good interior style; smooth ride; good cargo capacity; good power train performance
>
> ***Cons:*** sluggish handling (steering); high price; slow acceleration; too quiet (cannot hear engine running); not enough leg room; poor driving position reduces visibility; not recommended for towing; high maintenance costs

With these findings, Bill talked with Sheila and Abby, and they all decided to do test drives. The conflicting ratings of the quietness and power train performance would be decided during the drives, as well as the driving position and comfort level for Abby.

They decided to test drive a Toyota Prius first. At the dealership, there was only one Prius available. All three went on the test drive, with Abby driving out of the dealership. The salesman rode in the back seat and answered questions as she drove. Bill and Sheila found the Prius to be very different from the vehicles that they had driven all their lives. It was very quiet without the gas engine running. They had to agree with the online comments that the steering was less responsive than they were used to, but Abby did not have any problems with it. Secretly Sheila was very happy that the car did not have the pep that sports cars have—Abby would be safer. When they arrived back at the dealership, the salesman invited them into his office to talk about the car.

Before they went to the dealership, all three had decided that they would do the test drive only. They did not want to buy the car right now. There were other cars to look at and test drive before their decision could be made.

Inside the dealership office, the salesman pointed out that there was only the one Prius at the dealership. He said that they never kept a Prius on the lot for more than two days, and this one had arrived the day before. No other dealers had a Prius on their lots right now, either. If they wanted a Prius without a wait, they would need to make a decision now.

Bill and Sheila looked at each other, then at Abby, and Bill stood up. Sheila asked, "What kind of deal can we get on this Prius?"

The salesman responded, "Do you have a trade-in?"

"No. And we're not ready to proceed with this right now, are we?" Bill said as he looked at Sheila.

"But, honey, we're here now and we all like the car. Does it hurt to find out more?" Sheila looked at the salesman.

Bill sat down. Abby touched her mother's arm and said, "Mom, we need to go. We're looking at some other cars now, remember?"

Sheila looked surprised and then gathered her belongings. She stood up and extended her hand to the salesman. "Perhaps you can give us a card. We'll call you when we make a decision."

The salesman stood and shook hands with Sheila and Bill. Then he handed Sheila his business card. "I hope you folks hurry with your decision. That Prius won't be here tomorrow."

After two weeks of test drives and getting answers to their questions, the family was ready to make a decision. They decided that despite the high initial price of the Toyota Prius, it was the best choice for their daughter. They called the salesman at the Toyota dealership to find out if he had a Prius on the lot. He did not, but suggested that they could order one and it would be there within three weeks. They agreed with his suggestion and went to the dealership to negotiate. The salesman met all three of them at the door of the dealership and escorted them to his office. After bringing in an extra chair, the salesman sat behind his desk.

The salesman started the negotiation. "For the model you folks looked at, the Prius C, which trim did you decide on?"

Bill answered, "We want the C 3."

"Uhh!" Everyone looked at Abby, the source of the noise. Abby rolled her eyes.

"That's what you and Mom want. I want the C 2," Abby said and crossed her arms.

"What do you mean, you want the C 2? We discussed this and decided on the C 3." Bill squinted his eyes, but maintained his calm.

"You mean you and Mom decided. I couldn't get a word in edgewise," said Abby.

"Okay," the salesman interrupted. "We can look at both models again and see all the options. Here are the brochures." He handed Bill two glossy brochures.

Sheila took the brochures from Bill and laid them on the desk so that all three of them could see. She opened them up side by side.

"Honey," she said, "we just want the safest car for you. That's our main concern."

"Yeah, but I want something that's fun. Something that my friends will like," Abby said as she scooted forward in her chair to see the brochures. "See, the C 2 has so much more fun stuff. And it's safe, isn't it?" She looked at the salesman.

"Of course it's safe," he answered. "It's a Toyota." The three adults smiled at that.

"Okay, let's go through it all again," Bill conceded.

They went through the various base and option specifications. They compared how the two models were alike and how they differed. The salesman answered questions as they came up. The three members of the family discussed the pros and cons of each model.

And they did not reach a conclusion. Parents wanted the C 3 and teenager wanted the C 2. At this point the salesman spoke up.

"If she were my teenager, I'd go with the C 3. It does have more safety features … now let me talk," he said and held up his hand, "and fewer entertainment features. Those features can be a distraction—especially with friends in the car."

Abby crossed her arms, sat back in her chair, and looked away from the adults. It was a full power huff.

Bill and Sheila looked at each other for a few seconds, and then Bill spoke. "Honey, we really want your first car to be as safe as possible. That includes reliability, which Toyota has, and safety features. We also want to spend as little as possible to get those things. But you'll have this car for a long time, we hope, and you need to be happy with it. So we'll get the Prius C 2."

No one has ever seen a happier teenage girl. Abby jumped up and hugged her parents. Then she kept on jumping and clapping her hands. "Thank you, thank you, thank you! I'll take really good care of it and I'll be careful. I promise!"

"Okay, okay," the salesman was grinning. "Why don't you go out to the waiting area while your folks and I finalize this?" He rose and walked around his desk to open the door for her. As he seated himself again, he started typing on the computer. "So, you want the Prius C 2. We need to get specific with the options that you want. Here's the list again and we'll go through it, item by item. Okay?"

"Sure." Bill sat back and let Sheila look at the brochure.

Supply chain/purchasing/procurement affects everyone.

Everyone purchases something. In this case, it is one of the major purchases that families make. Looking at the case example, we see that the family did their research before they made a decision. We also see that the family made some strategic and tactical errors in how they approached this procurement. As we continue in this book, we will use this case example to illustrate key points about procurement.

WHAT IS A PROCUREMENT?

Consider some definitions of a procurement:

BusinessDictionary.com: Procurement is "the act of obtaining or buying goods and services."

Susan Ward (*About.com* Guide): "Procurement is the sourcing and purchasing of goods and services for business use."

The *Collins Dictionary:* Procurement is "the act of getting or providing."

Broken down, all of these definitions include:

- Sourcing
- Purchasing
- Goods and services

Our case example shows a personal procurement, and it is exactly like a commercial or business procurement. While it sounds simple—"let's buy a car for our daughter"—procurement often becomes complex very quickly as it did in our case example.

The most complex procurements often involve:

- Determining a specific need
- Defining standards
- Developing specifications
- Researching where to get goods or services (sourcing)
- Researching viability of companies that provide the goods or services
- Analyzing value, including in-house versus outsourced costs
- Developing the procurement strategy, including compete or non-compete
- Locating financing
- Negotiating price and various other requirements
- Executing the contract (purchasing)
- Putting the contract in place
- Administering the contract
- Managing inventory and stores
- Managing disposals and other related functions

Do you see how many of these activities were involved in our case example?

As you can see, procurement is a major part of any company's strategy. The amount of money that a company pays for goods and services must be less than the profit it makes. For example, if an electronics company spends more for the raw materials to build a television than it charges the consumer, that company will not survive for very long. But if the company negotiates lower pricing for its raw materials, then it increases its profit margin and becomes a money making machine.

Next we will find out what a project is.

WHAT IS A PROJECT?

Consider some definitions of a project:

Project Management Book of Knowledge (PMBOK® Guide), The Project Management Institute (2003): "A project is a temporary endeavor undertaken to create a unique product or service."

The Complete Idiot's Guide to Project Management, 2nd Edition, Macmillan/ Alpha (2000) by Sunny and Kim Baker: "A project is a sequence of tasks with a beginning and an end that is bounded by time, resources, and desired results."

Project Management: A Systems Approach to Planning, Scheduling, and Controlling, 6th Edition, Van Nostrand Reinhold (1997), by Harold Kerzner, Ph.D.: "A project can be considered to be any series of activities and tasks that:

- Have a specific objective to be completed within certain specifications
- Have defined start and end dates
- Have funding limits (if applicable)
- Consume resources (i.e., money, people, equipment)"

Breaking down these definitions of a project, we have:

- Defined beginning
- Unique product or service
- Sequence of tasks (interdependent activities)
- Defined ending

Looking at our case example, it has a defined beginning ("let's buy Abby a car"), a unique product (the car), a sequence of tasks (doing the research, making decisions on requirements for the car, and negotiating), and a defined ending (driving the car home).

Projects range from very simple to extremely complex. Everyday activities can be perceived as projects. For example, cooking spaghetti at home is a project. It has a defined beginning (when you decide to cook), a unique product (cooked spaghetti), a sequence of interdependent activities (getting the pot before pouring the water), and a defined ending (ready-to-eat spaghetti).

Let's get complicated now. If a restaurant's primary product is spaghetti and meatballs, then cooking spaghetti becomes a business process, not a project. We will talk about business processes in the next section.

Very complex projects include space exploration and interstate highways. In space exploration, there are the challenges of determining where to go, how to get there, how to survive while there, and how to get back. In each of these challenges, there can be several projects that span years. Every rocket, every space capsule, every space suit, and every space vehicle include at least one project. The space vehicles include a project for every major system within the vehicle. Every major system includes projects for materials development to withstand the rigors of space travel.

You are probably familiar with the term *program*. While *program* is often used interchangeably with the term *project*, a program is defined as "another name for recurring projects." Examples of programs are producing a monthly newsletter, publishing the annual report, and producing the half-time show of the Superbowl. While each individual endeavor is a project, the endeavor is done over and over again. Each time the endeavor has a unique project plan and a unique product. The newsletter is produced every month, so it is recurring. It is a project every month because it will have variations in the plan and in the end product each month. Programs are predictable, but each recurring project involves a new plan and a unique final product.

Many examples of programs are found in the aerospace industry and in the military. Designing and building a jet aircraft is a program—similar projects over and over again. New tanks, rocket launchers, drones, ships, submarines, jet fighters, bombers, etc. are all examples of programs in the military. Programs happen predictably, but each cycle involves a new plan and a unique end product.

Now that we know about projects and programs, how is a project different from a business process?

WHAT IS A BUSINESS PROCESS?

In this book, we define a *business process* as "an ongoing work effort." A business process does not produce a unique product, nor does it have a defined beginning and ending.

Using the example of a restaurant that specializes in spaghetti and meatballs, cooking spaghetti becomes a business process. The product is not unique nor does it have a defined beginning and end—producing edible spaghetti many times within a span of several hours. In this simple example, several large pots of spaghetti are boiling at the same time in order to produce the final dish.

Here is another example of project versus process. You are a procurement professional. You have been assigned the task of setting up a new office building for your company. This task is on top of your everyday work—emails, telephone calls, reports, etc. It is obvious that setting up a new office building is different from your day-to-day activities. But what exactly is it that makes the job of setting up a new office building a project and your daily work a process?

Both the project to set up a new office building and the everyday work of procurement involve similar activities such as making telephone calls, writing reports, and going to meetings. But projects have different goals from ongoing, day-to-day activities. You do a project *only once*, and when the project is completed, *something exists that never existed before*. In this case, you will have new offices in a different building.

Other processes in business include assembly lines in manufacturing, the systems used to produce fuel in a refining plant, or the systems required to turn fuel into electrical energy in a power plant. Each of these processes leads to the company's primary product, i.e., motor vehicles, gasoline, and electricity. None of these products is unique. None of these processes has a defined beginning and ending. At least the shareholders and employees hope there is no defined ending.

Here is a list of everyday processes that most people do:

- Answer a telephone
- Read and respond to email
- Attend meetings
- Order office supplies
- Write a weekly report

Here is a list of projects:

- Writing and publishing a book
- Producing an annual report
- Hiring a new employee
- Producing the half-time show at the Superbowl

See how the items in the lists are different? You will note that the everyday processes are also used within a project. When you are part of a project team, either as the leader or as a team member, you will still answer the telephone, read and respond to email, attend meetings, etc. As a member of the project team, you will also do work specific to the project. In our case, you will either lead the procurement project or be the procurement SME (subject matter expert) for a different project. More about that in the next section, *How Is Procurement a Project?*

Within every business, there are operational processes. Buying—equipment, materials, services—is one of the major processes every business requires. So procurement is part of an operational process, and each procurement is a project. How is *a procurement* the same as *a project*?

HOW IS PROCUREMENT A PROJECT?

Look at our definition of a project. Does a procurement meet all the criteria for a project (Table 1-1)?

- Does a procurement have a defined beginning? Looking at our examples, they all have a specific time when they started.
- Does a procurement have a unique product or service? The executed contract is the final product of a procurement.
- Does a procurement have a sequence of tasks? Yes, it does (an overview of those tasks is listed earlier in this chapter under the section titled, *What Is a Procurement?*).
- Does a procurement have a defined ending? The last signature on the contract is the defined ending of a procurement. (All activities after that are contract administration. While contract administration may be part of a procurement professional's job, it is not part of the procurement.)

Table 1-1. Procurement Is a Project

Defined beginning?	Yes: when first determined that goods or services are required
Unique product or service?	Yes: the executed contract for goods or services
Sequence of tasks?	Yes
Defined ending?	Yes: as soon as the contract is executed or at the termination date of the contract, depending on your company's definition of procurement

There is a process to performing a procurement, just like there is a process to managing a project. The activities and tasks involved in a procurement can be iterative, i.e., they can be repeated. The same is true for projects.

Another concept is that a procurement may be part of a larger project. As such, it is managed by both the procurement professional as an SME and the project manager of the overall project. An example of this is a project to build a prototype nondestructive assay machine. This project requires the procurement of parts, materials, and labor. One specialized material is the lead shielding required to minimize radiation scatter. One of the parts is manufactured only in France and has a six-month lead-time with a cost of $100,000 (includes shipping and handling). The project also requires subcontracting design engineers to create the machine that the physicists will develop. This is not a simple project, nor is it a simple procurement. We can think of the procurement part of the project as a *subproject*, just like the design *subproject*, and the manufacturing *subproject*.

Now that we know a procurement, no matter how simple or complex, is a project, we need to learn how to manage projects.

WHAT IS PROJECT MANAGEMENT?

Consider some definitions of project management:

Project Management Book of Knowledge Guide (PMBOK®), The Project Management Institute (2003): "... the application of knowledge, skills, tools, and techniques to project activities in order to meet or exceed stakeholder needs and expectations from a project."

The Complete Idiot's Guide to Project Management, 2nd Edition, Macmillan/Alpha (2000), by Sunny and Kim Baker: "... a discipline of combining systems, techniques, and people to complete a project within established goals of time, budget, and quality."

Project Management: A Systems Approach to Planning, Scheduling, and Controlling, 6th Edition, Van Nostrand (1997), by Harold Kerzner, Ph.D.: "... designed to make better use of existing resources by getting work to flow horizontally as well as vertically within the company."

Project management can be traced back to the earliest efforts of humans. Records indicate that the earliest great building was the Greek Island House built in 3000 BC. Think about other great buildings—Stonehenge, Solomon's Temple, The Great Wall of China, all of the Egyptian pyramids, the Mayan and Incan pyramids, etc. These great buildings were projects that had to be managed, albeit not the way we manage projects now. First there were the designers of the buildings—the people who came up with the ideas and then figured out how to make them happen. Then there were the workers—thousands of people, often over several generations. Along with the workers came hundreds of suppliers who provided everything from food and water for the workers, to transportation of materials, to mining and cutting the building materials. Also there were skilled laborers who finished the stone or wood, laid it so that it would not collapse, cut doors and/or windows into it, painted, carved, and/or sculpted the decorative touches, and did everything else to make it a finished product. Think about the massive effort it took to manage a multigenerational project. Of course, managing a project that included slave labor and unlimited funds was very different from what we need in order to manage a project today. There were no computers or systems for maintaining plans, budgets, schedules, or resource loading in those ancient times.

In the modern era in the United States, project management started as a method to perform complex Department of Defense (DoD) and National Aeronautics and Space Administration (NASA) projects. Over time, the U.S. federal government, specifically DoD, General Services Administration (GSA), and NASA, has developed a very strict regulation for procurement, including subcontracting, called the Federal Acquisition Regulation (FAR). DoD added some regulations to the FAR known as the Defense Federal Acquisition Regulation Supplement (DFARS), Procedures, Guidance, and Information (PGI). These are some of the procurement and standards requirements procurement professionals use when they work for the federal government. (DoD and NASA also have very rigorous requirements for projects in research and development (R&D), design, testing, production, etc.) Many procurement professionals in corporate America use these requirements as a reference for what they do and how they do it, although each corporation has its own set of rules and requirements.

Because corporate America has run up against a highly competitive world market, we have to do more with less. We face tighter budgets, less time, fewer people, and smaller inventories. You will deal with this, along with decreasing natural resources. It is procurement's job to make the company profitable despite all these challenges.

Doing more with less requires a different perspective or paradigm. Processes have to become more efficient. People have to have several skills instead of just one. Interdepartmental cooperation becomes paramount to effectively conduct business. Quality and customer satisfaction are integral to market share. Many businesses are moving to project management as the way to deal with these requirements, and procurement departments are using project management skills, tools, and techniques to become successful.

PROJECT MANAGEMENT PROCESSES

Project management consists of processes. A *process* is "a series of actions that bring about a specific result." Our previous discussion on the difference between a project and a process becomes very important here. The project is unique, but how we manage the project is not. Each procurement is unique, but how we get to the executed contract is not. It is a group of processes that create the map leading to successfully completing procurements.

Project management processes describe and organize the work of the project. In order to be able to replicate success, we need to communicate exactly what we did and how we did it. The processes do that for us.

Within the project management processes are product-oriented processes. These are the processes that describe and organize the work of the product—the end goal of the project. In procurement the product is the executed contract. So the product-oriented processes are the activities required to find competitors, do a competition, negotiate an agreement, draft the agreement, have it reviewed, and obtain final approval (signatures). The final process is delivering the executed contract to every party involved, including the employees who will be managing the contract administration. Other professions will use a different set of product-oriented processes. One of the most documented product-oriented processes is software development.

PROCESS GROUPS

According to the PMBOK, five process groups are found within project management. Each process group is linked by the results of the previous group. The result of one process becomes the *input* to another process. The result can also be referred to as the *output* of that process. The processes are

- Initiating
- Planning
- Executing
- Controlling
- Closing

Looking at the process diagram in Figure 1-1, we see that each process can have more than one input and more than one output. As the project progresses, each individual process will provide input for other processes. This is the iterative property of project management. For example, the executing process will often create a new, or unexpected, piece of the project that will require modification of one or more of the plans created in the planning process.

Procurement does not need to utilize all five processes in order to be successful, unless the procurement is extremely complicated. Generally, we can combine the initiating process with the planning process and the executing process with the controlling process. That leaves us with three processes that describe and organize the work of the procurement—planning, executing, and closing. We will, however, discuss all five of the processes in order to become familiar with the project management terminology, tools, and techniques.

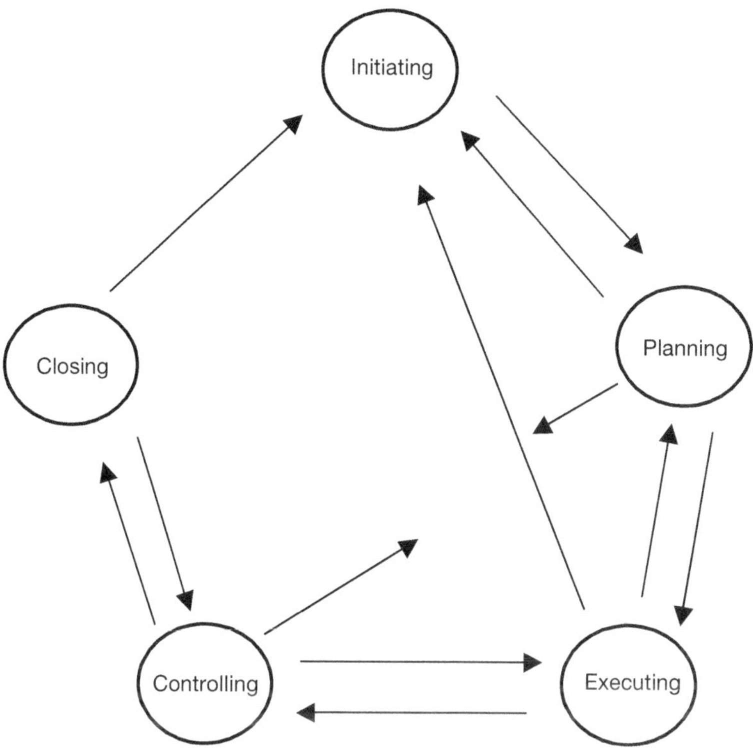

Figure 1-1. Process diagram.

Initiating

Initiating is the process of beginning the project. This is the time to get the organization to commit to the project/procurement. A commitment by the organization is required in order to begin the procurement. While some planning may be done during the initiating process, so that management knows what is being committed, the detailed planning will be completed during the planning process. In procurement, the strategy to be used to complete the procurement is the most important output of the initiating phase.

Procurement strategy consists of the what, why, who, how, and how much:

- What is the procurement?
- Why does the organization need this procurement? Savings? New materials? Outsourcing?
- Who will be involved in the procurement?
- How will the procurement be carried out?
- How much will the contract cost? Annual costs? Monthly costs?

Many organizations have a procurement plan that requires answers to these questions, at a minimum. If you find that your organization does not require that these questions be answered, it would be a good idea to go ahead and make your own document that answers all of these questions.

Planning

To have a successful procurement, the planning process is the most important. This importance comes from the fact that you will be doing something that has never been done before. You will get an executed contract to provide goods or a service that is unique from any other contract in place now. There is an old axiom used by carpenters: "measure twice, cut once." When something has to be done correctly the first time, planning is required.

The final output of the planning process is the project plan—we call it the procurement plan. We will discuss planning in depth in Chapter 3.

The schedule is the time frame for completing the procurement and is included in the procurement plan. We will discuss all aspects of scheduling in Chapter 4.

Executing

Executing is when the actual work of the procurement/project is done. The executing process includes the following:

- Project/procurement plan execution: doing the work that the plan lays out
- Scope verification: making sure the scope is defined and includes everything that meets the needs of the company
- Quality assurance: making sure the quality requirements are captured
- Team development: bringing the members of the team up to date on the plan and their part in it
- Information distribution: sending out plans and reports to stakeholders
- Solicitation: sending out a Request for Proposal (RFP), Request for Information (RFI), etc.
- Source selection: evaluating proposals, doing cost analysis and comparisons, deciding on the source
- Negotiation: working with the potential vendor to finalize all terms and conditions, especially pricing and delivery
- Contract finalization: getting the required signatures of all parties
- Contract administration: assigning the person responsible to manage the contract

Controlling

The controlling process consists of maintaining regular measurements of the project/procurement in order to identify variances from the plan. This is the time when change control happens.

In the procurement plan, there will be a process for making scope changes in the procurement. Although we will discuss this process in detail in Chapter 6, *Communications*, following a process for all scope changes is very important. Every change that is made will impact the entire procurement. This caution cannot be said strongly or often enough. *Every change that is made will impact the entire procurement.* Changes usually impact the schedule for the procurement to be completed, the price of the goods or services, and the costs associated with completing the procurement.

By maintaining regular measurement of the plan, you will be able to take preventive action when you see a possible problem developing. For example, if the date for releasing the RFP will not be met, you will know it early enough to communicate that fact with all the stakeholders. While communicating does not get the RFP out on time, it does help to keep people calm when they know ahead of time that there is a problem and what you are doing to deal with it.

Other aspects of the controlling process include:

- Schedule control
- Cost control
- Quality control
- Performance reporting
- Risk response control

We will discuss the controls that are needed as we talk about each of these areas later in this book.

Closing

The closing process involves finalizing the procurement/project files. Most companies already have procedures in place for storage of procurement files, especially where contracts are kept. This is usually an administrative duty. It is important for the successful completion of the procurement.

The closing process is the time for putting together the *lessons learned*. Your company may call it something else, but lessons learned is a document where all successes and all challenges that the procurement/project manager had are preserved for sharing with others. The types of successes to document in lessons learned include:

- Meeting or exceeding the estimated schedule
- Using people and/or other resources effectively

- Meeting or exceeding the estimated costs for the procurement
- Meeting or exceeding the requested savings in annual spend for this product or service
- Everything else that made the procurement successful

The types of challenges to document in lessons learned include:

- Not having the scope for the product or service well defined
- Lack of information on the competitors' finances/stability
- Surprises in negotiations
- Unforeseen risks
- Lack of cooperation of stakeholders
- Bottlenecks encountered for getting authorizations/signatures
- Anything else that caused either delay or substandard quality in the procurement

Customizing Process Interactions

When we talk about processes, it is important to understand that not all of the processes listed in this chapter will be necessary for all procurements or projects. As stated before, procurements often combine processes in order to be successful.

One example of a process interaction that will not be necessary is the closing to initiating process shown in Figure 1-1. Unless you have a program (repeating projects) or a project that is so large it has to be completed in stages, you will not use a closed procurement file to initiate a new procurement. Do not confuse using a closed procurement file as a resource with using it to initiate a new procurement. In the rare circumstance when you would initiate a new procurement using a closed procurement file, you will use the information there *exactly* as it is. Changes for the new procurement will come in the planning process.

Customizing all of the process interactions is one of the learned skills that successful procurement/project managers utilize. So what defines a successful procurement manager?

WHAT LEADS TO BEING A SUCCESSFUL PROCUREMENT MANAGER?

What leads to an individual being a successful procurement manager? This is a huge question. Entire books, actually volumes of books, address this subject in depth. Information on the skills and personal traits of successful managers can be found everywhere, including the American Management Association, www.

amanet.org. We will briefly skim the skills and personal traits that the most successful managers have.

Professional Management Skills

Successful procurement management combines both science and art. Managers need to learn how to manage exceptions and risks because there are always surprises in every procurement. Dealing with people effectively is the most important art any manager can have, particularly procurement managers who do negotiations regularly. Many skills combine into the art of dealing with people. Of these, eight important ones are valued in all managers, at all levels of the business:

- Team building
- Leadership
- Conflict resolution
- Technical expertise
- Planning
- Effective communications
- Sincere interest in the professional growth of team members
- Commitment

Effective communicator. Note that almost all of these skills involve communicating with other people. Managers who communicate well, and understand the viewpoint of the people they deal with, are the most successful. When managers are successful, the business is successful. An effective management style is characterized by:

- Giving clear direction
- Assisting in problem solving
- Facilitating group decisions
- Handling interpersonal conflict
- Facilitating the integration of new members into the team
- Planning
- Eliciting commitments
- Communicating clearly
- Presenting the team to higher management

Again, all of these management styles are the product of effectively communicating with other people. Many business experts call these the "soft" skills, but they are the most necessary skills to develop in order to be successful in any position.

Personal Traits

Successful managers also have certain personal traits, including experience, flexibility, acceptance of change, innovative thinking, initiative, enthusiasm, persuasiveness, organization, and discipline. One more trait that is very important to success is persistence: "If at first you don't succeed, try, try again" (T. H. Palmer, *Teacher's Manual*, 1840). Temper Palmer's advice with this definition: "Insanity: doing the same thing over and over again, and expecting different results" (Albert Einstein).

Persistence. Being persistent does not include doing the exact thing over and over again. Being persistent means that you do not give up on something important and that you use different strategies, tactics, or techniques to get it accomplished. Thomas Edison is a good example of how that works. When he was interviewed by a young reporter who asked if he felt like a failure because he was still working on an incandescent light bulb that would work and last a reasonable amount of time, Edison said, "Young man, why would I feel like a failure? And why would I ever give up? I now know definitively over 9,000 ways that an electric light bulb will not work. Success is almost in my grasp." It took over 10,000 attempts, but Edison succeeded in inventing the incandescent light bulb.

Other Management Skills

Conflict-resolution. Whenever we work with other people, we will need to use conflict-resolution skills. An old saying goes something like, "When there is more than one person in a room, there is politics." Honest people can have honest disagreements, even in the professional setting of a business. Resolving these disagreements, also called conflicts, is a skill that every manager must develop. Conflict is fundamental to complex task management. Schedule conflicts, budgetary conflicts, and personnel conflicts arise often. These conflicts may be beneficial. They can produce involvement of the people working on the procurement, and they can produce new information. Conflict can also enhance the competitive spirit of those involved. Imagine the challenge that one person issues to the rest of the team—"Let's see who can get the meeting minutes published within six hours of the meeting." Will other teammates rise to the challenge? Is it more likely that meeting minutes will be published more quickly than usual? The answer to both questions is yes. In our culture, competition and challenges are very motivating. (We will discuss conflict resolution more in Chapter 5, *Communications*.)

Technical. Every manager requires some technical skills. Procurement professionals are no different. Some of the technical skills that a good procurement manager needs include:

- Working knowledge of contract law
- Complete knowledge of the company's procurement process(es)
- Computer technology used to track the procurement process: research, analysis, Request for X (RFX), bids, negotiations, signatures, etc.
- Specific markets, customers, and requirements
- Market trends and evolutions in the area of expertise of the manager
- Knowing the people involved in the market area of expertise

Planning. Planning skills are necessary for all people in all areas of life. In business, planning skills are very important. Some of the skills required for successful planning are information processing, communication, resource negotiations, and securing commitments. We will discuss these ideas more fully in Chapter 3, *Planning.*

Administrative. Administrative skills are vital for procurement professionals. The only way to measure how well we do our jobs is shown through our administrative skills, which include:

- Staffing (Chapter 2)
- Cost versus value concerns (Chapter 2)
- Planning (Chapter 3)
- Scheduling (Chapter 4)
- Reporting all metrics (Chapter 5)
- Budgeting (Chapter 6)

Every profession requires the management skill of building support at all levels of the business, however, no procurement or project can succeed without the support of upper management. We will discuss how important it is to know where your procurement sits on the priority list for your company. We will discuss this in detail in Chapter 3, *Planning.*

Organizational. Organizational skills are part and parcel of building support from management. "Organization" refers to your business unit and the business unit(s) you support as a procurement professional. If you are working for a small- or medium-sized company, it means your entire company. To have organizational skills, you need to know your organization inside and out. More than knowing the organizational chart, this means that you must also know the reporting relationships of everyone. You know each person's responsibilities. You understand how to work within the organization (how to get work done) as well as how the organization works with others (suppliers). You know the lines of authority and when to use them. If you are a new employee in a company, part of your job is to learn all of the aspects of your organization.

Entrepreneurial. Finally, every good manager needs entrepreneurial skills. Procurement professionals need entrepreneurial skills in order to succeed. Even the largest multinational companies need employees who understand the purpose of the business (to make money) and how to support that purpose. Entrepreneurial skills include taking a general manager's perspective (the big picture view), understanding profit, understanding customer satisfaction (company customers as well as internal business unit customers), future growth of the company, and cultivation of related market activities.

It can take a lifetime to develop all of the skills mentioned in the sections above. Some people have more natural talent in certain areas than others. Everyone works to build these skills throughout their careers. The earlier you know what you need to learn, the sooner you can start learning. "Bite off" one skill at a time. Plan your learning approach using mentors, including your manager. Decide what skills make the most sense to begin learning, usually these are basics such as contract law or the specific processes used in your procurement department, and start there.

Specific Procurement Management Skills

Now that we know what skills are required to be a successful manager of anything, what specific skills are needed to be a successful procurement manager? Charles Dominick and Soheila R. Lunney share a list of procurement management skills in their book, *The Procurement Game Plan: Winning Strategies and Techniques for Supply Management Professionals*, 2012 (J. Ross Publishing):

- Purchasing fundamentals
- Analysis and spreadsheets
- Contract law
- Project management
- Purchasing best practices
- Sourcing
- Negotiation
- Leadership
- International business
- Financial acumen
- Supplier relationship management

Having these skills will make you an SME (subject matter expert) in procurement.

Let's now briefly look at what each of these skills entails:

- Purchasing fundamentals: gathering necessary information, setting a purchase strategy, developing a Request for X (RFX), sending the RFX, evaluating suppliers, choosing suppliers, negotiating terms and conditions, executing the contract, and implementing the agreement

Some of the information in the remainder of this listing was gleaned from a course titled *Fundamentals of Purchasing*, which was developed by George L. Harris for the American Management Association:

- Analysis and spreadsheets: deciding what needs to be analyzed and expert use of spreadsheets to do the analysis
- Contract law: knowing the fundamentals of contract law within the United States (or your country) and keeping up with court rulings and judgments as they are made (federal and state)
- Project management: knowing the skills and techniques that lead to successful projects (procurements)
- Purchasing best practices: knowing what the best companies in the world do
- Sourcing: finding the potential suppliers for the goods or services required
- Negotiation: the process of getting the best deal for your company
- Leadership: the ability to guide, influence, or direct people
- International business: understanding the differences in cultures, language, currency, etc. in other countries
- Financial acumen: understanding your company's financial needs, reports, etc., understanding financial reports of any company in order to evaluate the viability of the potential supplier
- Supplier relationship management: knowing the skills and techniques to maintain a professional and ethical relationship with suppliers

TERMINOLOGY

Some terminology used by procurement professionals already reflects the influence of project management. Table 1-2 contains words and phrases used often in project management.

Table 1-2. Project Management Terms

Term	Definition
Activity	A specific project task
Audit	A formal and detailed examination of the progress, costs, operations, results, or some other aspect of work
Baseline plan	The initial approved plan
Buying the job	An unusually low bid designed to get the work "no matter what"
Contingency	An amount of time and/or money set aside in case things do not go as planned; in risk, an alternative to avoid or mitigate a risk
Cost-benefit analysis	An analysis, stated as a ratio, used as one evaluation criteria for a proposed course of action
Critical path	The sequence of tasks that determines the minimum schedule for a project
Deliverables	The clearly defined results, goods, or services produced as a result of the project
Duration	An amount of time allowed to complete a task; not the amount of time to actually do the task (see Effort)
Effort	The amount of work (in hours or workdays) actually required to complete a task
Facilitator	A person who makes it easier for other people to accomplish objectives
Float	The amount of time for a task to be scheduled without affecting other tasks; the difference between the duration available for a task and the effort required to complete it; also known as slack
Functional management	The departments of a business organization representing individual disciplines such as engineering, marketing, purchasing, accounting, etc.
Go/no-go indicator	Any monitoring or observation that allows a manager to decide whether to move forward with a project or task
Lag	The amount of time after one task is started before the next task can be started
Loading	The amount of time individual resources are available for project work
Material Requirements Planning (MRP)	An approach for materials planning and ordering based on known or expected demand, lead times, and existing inventories

Table 1-2. Project Management Terms (Continued)

Term	Definition
Milestone	A clearly identifiable point in a project that summarizes the completion of an important set of tasks; used to summarize important events in a project for managers
One-on-ones	Meetings between only two people
Padding	Adds extra time or money to estimates in case of changes or delays; a type of contingency
Pro forma	Projected or anticipated; usually applied to financial data such as balance sheets and income statements
Project management process	The five phases of initiating, planning, executing, controlling, and closing as defined by PMI
Resource leveling	Spreading the work among qualified employees to avoid overtime and/or missing deadlines
Risk analysis	An evaluation of the probability that an outcome will be the desired one; usually compares two or more conditions
Rush charges	Charges that are applied by outside vendors when goods are needed quickly
Scope	The magnitude of the effort required to complete a project
Scope creep	The process of changing the work of a project; implies the changes are not managed or controlled
Situational management	Matching management style to specific needs of a situation
Stakeholders	People who have any interest in the end results of a project
Statement of Work (SOW)	Details the work to be completed on the project
Subcontract	Delegates tasks or subprojects to contractors or other organizations
Subtasks	Steps that are conceptually related; necessary to complete a task
Task	A cohesive unit of work on a project; trackable on its own; may include subtasks
Trade-off	Deciding that one aspect of a project can change in order to enhance another aspect
Win-win negotiation	Both parties are better off after the negotiation is concluded
Work Breakdown Structure (WBS)	A basic project listing that documents and describes all the work that must be done to complete the project; forms the basis for budgeting, scheduling, network diagramming, and work assignments

SUMMARY

In this chapter we have defined what a procurement is, what a project is, and how a procurement is actually a project. We talked about business processes and how every procurement follows a process, but is not a process on its own. Project management and how to be a successful manager were discussed, including listing the many skills involved. Finally, we listed some interesting terminology used by procurement professionals that reflects the influence of project management. In Chapter 2, we will discuss initiating a procurement.

This book has free material available for download from the Web Added Value™ resource center at *www.jrosspub.com.*

CHAPTER 2

STARTING

We now know what procurement and project management are, so we can start discussing using project management techniques to make procurements successful.

PRIORITIZING

Time is the only coin of your life. It is the only coin you have, and only you can determine how it will be spent. Be careful lest you let other people spend it for you.
—Carl Sandburg

To be successful at anything that you do, setting your priorities is key. To set your priorities, you must know what your goals are. This is true for both business and personal success. Often our business, personal, and spiritual goals are intertwined. Separating them can be difficult.

Determine your goals. Goals are the targets we want to reach. Goals can be thought of as aims or intentions, something that we want to achieve. In more formal business settings, a goal is defined as "an observable and measureable end result having one or more objectives to be achieved within a more or less fixed timeframe" (*BusinessDictionary.com*). A goal is also defined as "the end toward which effort is directed" (*Merriam-Webster.com*). According to the business definition of a goal, it must be *observable* and *measureable*. One business goal might be to show 5% more profit next quarter than in the same quarter one year ago. Another goal might be to manufacture 10% more units this year than last year. And yet another example of a business goal could be to complete a new software program and have it ready to sell on March 15 of next year. In procurement our goals are often tied to savings, e.g., "Our goal is to save 50% of annual spend by competing a contract for services." Personal goals are often just as observable and measureable. Losing weight, stopping smoking, or drinking alcohol less often are all examples of goals. Then there are the more spiritual goals that people have. Although not as measureable, these goals are often just as observable as personal or business goals. One spiritual goal might be to treat people more kindly. Another spiritual goal might be to meditate every day. Let's use the example of a goal to treat people more kindly. How could we do that? Some steps to reaching this goal could be to:

- Volunteer at a soup kitchen
- Volunteer at the American Red Cross
- Give a granola bar to the next homeless person you see
- Smile at a person using a wheelchair
- Open a door for someone to walk through
- Stop before you yell at your child or significant other
- Smile at a newly hired person in the office
- Ask if a co-worker needs some help when you have extra time
- Offer to sit in on a negotiation strictly as an observer and then share what you thought with your co-worker

There are many, many ways to treat people more kindly. You decide exactly what you plan to do in order to achieve your goal.

Have a plan. Putting together a plan, whether on paper or just in your head, is the second step to determining your priorities. Putting together a plan is an iterative process because you will also make plans after you determine your priorities. Going back and forth between planning and setting priorities will move you forward.

Prioritizing means "to put something first, second, third, etc." We each have only twenty-four hours in a day and sixty minutes in each hour. No one has figured out a way to add more minutes to an hour or more hours to a day. So we have to decide how we use those minutes and hours. That is prioritizing.

Priority Matrix

The matrix in Figure 2-1 shows one method that can be used for prioritizing. This matrix is called the Priority Matrix. You see that the matrix has four boxes (or quadrants) and four priorities.

DO NOW	PLAN TO DO
PRIORITY A • Emergencies • Crisis issues • Demands from customers • Planned tasks or project work now due • Meetings and appointments • Reports and other submissions • Staff issues or needs Subject to confirming the importance and the urgency of these tasks, do these tasks now. Prioritize according to their relative urgency	**PRIORITY B** • Developing change, direction, strategy • Planning, preparation, scheduling • Research, investigation, designing, testing • Networking, relationship building • Thinking, creating, modeling, designing • Systems and process development • Anticipation and prevention These tasks are critical to success. Plan time slots and personal space for these tasks.
REJECT AND EXPLAIN	**RESIST AND CEASE**
PRIORITY C • Trivial requests from others • Someone else's emergencies • Interruptions and distractions • Pointless routines or activities • Accumulated, unresolved trivia Wherever possible, reject and avoid these tasks sensitively, yet immediately.	**PRIORITY D** • "Comfort" activities • Email, instant messaging • Daydreaming, doodling, overly long breaks • Reading irrelevant material • Embellishment and overproduction These tasks are nonproductive/ demotivational. Schedule or cease these tasks altogether.

Figure 2-1. Priority matrix. (Based on the work of Stephen Covey in *7 Habits of Highly Effective People*, Free Press, 1990.)

Do Now - Priority A

The box on the upper left side is the DO NOW quadrant and is labeled Priority A. Most often the activities that fit in this quadrant are not planned, but nonetheless they are things that we must do (or address) immediately. Things always come up unexpectedly in our day. Dealing with them is often referred to as "fighting fires." Some examples are emergencies, crisis issues, demands from customers, staff issues or needs, and more. When you have confirmed the importance and urgency of these tasks, do them now, but you need to decide which ones to do first, based on their relative urgency. For example, let's say client X emails you that the report you have scheduled to do later in the week is needed NOW. Then client Y calls to say that she needs all of the bookkeeping files for her accountant NOW. How do you prioritize one of these tasks over the other?

- First, get more information from client X. Ask client X about the reason for the change in schedule for the report. What caused the change? Are there alternatives to needing the entire report immediately?
- Then get more information from client Y. Why does she need those bookkeeping files right now? Be specific with your questions. Drill down to the actual reason to see if there are other options to get the client what she needs.
- When you have all of the information, you can prioritize one task or the other.

Let's say client X convinces you that the entire report needs to be completed today and client Y actually does need the files right away. *Do the easiest first.* Assuming the bookkeeping files for client Y are ready, go ahead and send them first—prioritize client Y to position 1. Then finish the report for client X and send it—you prioritize client X to position 2. Neither client needs to know your priorities. As long as you complete the work as promised, how you prioritize clients and their requests is your business. *Note*: Your boss needs to know what you are prioritizing and why. Your boss may need you to prioritize differently based on knowledge or experience that he has.

What do you do if too many tasks are in the DO NOW quadrant? Simple—delegate them. Delegation can be done formally or informally. Formal delegation is assigning work to a person who reports to you. Informal delegation is asking a co-worker to help you out. In either case, make sure the person doing the work understands exactly what needs to be done and exactly when it needs to be done. Be accessible to that person in case there are any questions along the way.

Your goal when you place tasks in the DO NOW quadrant is to move them from this quadrant to the PLAN TO DO quadrant, the next quadrant to the right. When you move tasks from the DO NOW quadrant to the PLAN TO DO quadrant, you gain control over your schedule. (We will discuss the PLAN TO DO quadrant a little later.)

Reject and Explain - Priority C

The REJECT AND EXPLAIN quadrant, in the lower left, is labeled Priority C. This is the hardest area to prioritize for many people. These are the activities and tasks that *appear* to be urgent, but they are not important to your goals: trivial requests from others, someone else's emergencies, interruptions and distractions, pointless routines or activities, and anything else that does not advance your goals.

Numerous examples of REJECT AND EXPLAIN are found in every workplace. Quite often, bosses are the worst offenders. "I need it ***now***!" How often do you hear that? And how often does it turn out that the boss does not need it at all?

The next offender is the internal business partner (IBP), also known as the client or the customer. IBPs make the same demand as the boss—"I need it ***now***." And IBPs often do not need it either.

How do you deal with the activities that you assign to this quadrant? The title of the quadrant—REJECT AND EXPLAIN—describes the basic strategy for dealing with these tasks. Fundamentally, you need to learn how to say, "No." Say it politely and diplomatically, and you will not only do less work, but you will also create a better relationship with the person making the demand. Some examples of a diplomatic "no" include:

- "I wish I could be of more help to you, but I can't go into the depth you need right now. Here are some resources that you might find helpful."
- "I need to check my schedule and get back with you."
- "Okay, Boss. What other work do you want me to drop so that I can get on that right now?"

Every time you tell someone that you will get back to him or her, make a note of it in your calendar. And then do it. Keep your promises, and your credibility goes up every time.

What do you do if you feel guilty when you do not attend to someone else's needs? Remember that saying "no" does not reject the person who asked. Saying "no" only refuses the request. You are the only advocate for your own best interests. Do you want to work for your own promotion or do you want to work to get someone else promoted? You have to decide.

Saying "no" politely and diplomatically is a skill. You can learn and then practice any skill, so this one is no different. Here is an idea on how to improve this skill: create a list of comfortable responses. Then brainstorm with trusted co-workers or friends and create a list of more responses.

Resist and Cease - Priority D

The lower right quadrant, RESIST AND CEASE, labeled Priority D, lists activities that are not important to reaching your goals. They are not urgent to you—or anyone else. These activities are nonproductive and can actually be demotivational. Taking a short break from work is a good idea, but taking a short break that turns into an entire afternoon of getting nothing done is not. Activities such as daydreaming, doodling, reading irrelevant material, and playing computer games are obvious time wasters. Other activities are not so obvious, e.g., constantly checking email, instant messages (IMs) and texts, and embellishment or overproduction of your work. Embellishment or overproduction means doing *much more* than is necessary. While we all want to exceed expectations, there is a time when doing more actually gets us less. It is called the Law of Diminishing Returns. Sometimes there is a fine line between "good enough" and "too much." Check with your boss, or more experienced co-workers, to see where that line is in your organization.

All of the activities that you list in the RESIST AND CEASE quadrant need to be either stopped or scheduled. For example, taking a break can be scheduled. Checking email, IMs, and texts can be scheduled—believe it or not! Playing computer games for ten minutes can be scheduled. Other activities can be stopped. Daydreaming, doodling, and reading irrelevant material at work can all be stopped. The goal with the RESIST AND CEASE quadrant is to keep it empty.

From a book by Jim Collins, *Good to Great: Why Some Companies Make the Leap ... and Others Don't* (HarperBusiness), we find an idea for creating a "Stop Doing" list. As individuals, we can evaluate exactly what we do, and how we do it, so that we can be as efficient and effective as possible. Your company might have processes in place that help, but most do not. Some questions to ask when creating a Stop Doing list include:

- Does this task add value or generate positive results?
- Am I the most qualified person to do this task or could someone else do it faster and better?
- If I did not have to do this task, what would I choose to spend that time on?
- What impact would that have on my goals?

The real secret behind a Stop Doing list is to stop doing the specific activities that keep you from your goals.

Plan to Do – Priority B

The final quadrant we will discuss is the upper right box, PLAN TO DO, labeled Priority B. PLAN TO DO is the most important quadrant to your success. You should spend most of your time on the tasks in this quadrant. Some of the activities to list in this quadrant are strategy development, planning, scheduling, research, networking, thinking, system and process development, anticipation and prevention (risk management), etc. These activities are critical to your success.

To accomplish activities in the PLAN TO DO quadrant, you need to plan time slots that minimize interruptions. You will also need to make sure you have personal space in order to complete these activities. You use your brainpower as well as your time to complete the PLAN TO DO tasks. Interruptions take away from your ability to concentrate and do your best work. Some ways to avoid interruptions are to close your email, turn off your cell phone, let voice mail answer landline calls, close your door, etc.

Nothing in the PLAN TO DO quadrant is urgent, but everything in it needs to be scheduled. Most of these activities will have deadlines that you must meet. (We will discuss scheduling your procurement in Chapter 4, *Scheduling*. All of the techniques that we cover in Chapter 4 apply to scheduling the Priority B tasks listed in Figure 2-1.)

Prioritizing Methods

Some techniques to use that will help you prioritize include:

- Allow enough time to get things done: plan for interruptions, driving time, etc.
- Schedule time for yourself during your most productive time of the day.
- Do not multi-task. You need to focus on one thing at a time.
- At the end of each day, create tomorrow's to-do list, prioritize it, and then go home.

Prioritizing is a technique to use to increase your chances of being successful at anything that you do—as true for your procurements as it is for your life. Figure 2-2 is an example of a schedule that has been prioritized using our priority codes of A, B, C, and D.

As we see in Figure 2-2, this is a one-week schedule. On Monday, all of the scheduled activities are prioritized as A or B or both. Because no activities are prioritized as C or D, Monday is a productive day.

Tuesday is not as good. Tuesday starts with reading an irrelevant article for an hour—an activity that can be stopped—so it is prioritized as D and should be rescheduled during personal time. Notice that blocks of time are not scheduled on Tuesday. These times are prioritized as D because something productive could be scheduled during these times. Use unscheduled blocks of time productively. Even if the activity is networking, schedule it and prioritize it.

Wednesday is another productive day, with all A and B priorities.

Thursday is also productive, with all A and B priorities.

Friday is fairly productive. Networking (lunch and office) and attending a luncheon for George's birthday are both opportunities to network so these two activities are scheduled and prioritized. Notice that we run into a problem with reviewing Susan's report in the afternoon. Susan's report is a C priority—something that someone else can do which would leave that time slot open for an activity that advances your goals. (Also, how do you prioritize going home an hour early on a Friday? You do not prioritize it, you just do it.)

Monday			Tuesday	
PRI	**Task**	**Time**	**Task**	**PRI**
A	Staff meeting	8	Read article on snorkeling	D
A	Return calls, emails	9	Draft RFP 2	B
B	Draft RFP 1	10	Return calls, emails	A
B	Draft RFP 1	11		D
B	Lunch	12	Lunch	B
A	IBP 1 meeting, our conference room	1	Meeting with boss	A
B	Draft minutes, action list; send out	2		D
B & A	Break for 15 min; return calls	3		D
A & B	Return emails; make to-do list for tomorrow; create agenda for IBP 3 kick-off meeting Thursday; send out	4	Return calls, emails; make to-do list for tomorrow	A
Wednesday			**Thursday**	
PRI	**Task**	**Time**	**Task**	**PRI**
A	Meeting with IBP 2	8	Return calls, emails	A
A	Return calls, emails; draft minutes, action list; send out	9	Meet with new IBP (IBP 3)	A
B	Revise RFP 1	10	Meet with new IBP (IBP 3)	A
B	Revise RFP 1	11	Draft minutes, action list; send out	B
A	Lunch	12	Lunch	A
B	Revise RFP 2	1	Return calls, emails	A
B	Revise RFP 2	2	Create schedule for IBP 3 procurement	B
A	Break for 15 min	3	Break for 15 min	A&B
A	Return calls, emails; make to-do list for tomorrow	4	Return calls, emails; make to-do list for tomorrow	A
Friday			**Saturday/Sunday**	
PRI	**Task**	**Time**	**Task**	**PRI**
A	Return calls, emails	8		
B	Online course in contract law	9		
B	Online course	10		
B	Online course	11		
A	Lunch; attend George's birthday lunch	12		
B	Networking (lunch/office)	1		
C	Review report for Susan	2		
A	Return calls, emails; make to-do list for tomorrow	3		
???	Go home early	4		

Figure 2-2. Prioritized schedule. PRI, priority.

Just like the prioritizing of personal work, a company has to prioritize its work. Usually a company prioritizes the work that brings in the most profit. The next highest priority is legal requirements, which include regulatory requirements. Then every company prioritizes the rest of the work. Your department needs to be aware of the company's priority list. This list may not be written down anywhere—but be aware that not every executive's priorities line up with the company's list.

Your best bet is to get information from your boss about the priority level of every procurement. For example, executives at the company may not be talking about the training budget for employees. Hopefully your boss is aware that training is no longer a high priority within the company. The only importance placed on training right now is as a cost saver. At some point, you might be tasked with ending the contract with the training supplier as a higher priority than one of your other procurement tasks.

In order to prioritize and schedule your work, you need to know exactly what you will be doing. The next section discusses how to obtain the required information and what to do next.

WHAT KIND OF PROCUREMENT DO YOU HAVE?

Now, you need to know the type of procurement to be done. What is it for? Is it an existing contract renewal with savings to be negotiated? Is it a contract for new services/products/materials? Will it be a competitive contract or a single-source contract? Will you use traditional methods such as an RFP or new methods such as electronic bidding?

When you have the answers to these questions, the answers will lead to more questions. Capturing the answers to all of the questions gives you the information you need for the procurement (project) plan. Let's start at the beginning.

What Is It For?

When you are assigned a new procurement, the first question to ask is "What is it for?" Will you be procuring goods or services?

If the answer is *goods*, then you need to know exactly what goods, all the required technical specifications, and any alterations (options) that are required by your company. You also need to specify the invoice requirements and payment terms.

If the answer is *services*, then you need a well-written description of the work to be done (the scope of work). This description might include personnel qualifications, where and when the work will be done, how the work will be done, any quality requirements, all safety requirements, any security requirements, reporting requirements, billing requirements, etc.

Then you need to know what type of contract needs to be done.

New or Existing Contract?

What type of contract will you be executing: existing or new? Depending on the type of procurement, the starting tasks will differ.

For an *existing* contract, find the procurement file. The procurement file should have the existing, complete, executed contract. The file might be either paper or electronic. In either case, the file should also contain all procurement documents, along with the negotiation notes.

Completely read and understand the contract. The first step is to completely read and understand the existing contract, meaning you read the *entire* contract and *all* of the exhibits and amendments. Jot down questions as you read the contract. Questions that arise often range from specific terms to the exact payment structure. You might also wonder why this vendor was chosen instead of another one. Ask these types of questions to the procurement professional who led the most-recent effort if you do not find the answers when you review the procurement file. (***Note***: The procurement file often contains the original Request for Procurement Services (RFPS) that started the procurement to begin with. The original RFPS should show who led the procurement, who was responsible for signing the contract, who was responsible for approving the final deal, the expectation of annual spend under the contract, etc. If the RFPS does not show that information, you will need to gather it as quickly as possible.)

Review and understand the entire procurement file. The second step is to review and understand the *entire* procurement file. Every document in the file has information that you need to know. In the best case, it has the Request for Proposal (RFP), all questions about the RFP, all answers to those questions, and the scorecard for determining the supplier who was chosen for this contract. If the contract was a sole-source contract, the justification for that decision should be included in the file. Even after you read and understand everything in the entire procurement file, you may have questions.

Interview the company SME or the active contract manager. The third step is to talk with your company's SME or the person who is actively managing this contract now. Using an interview technique, find out what is right with this contract and/or supplier and what is not. Is the supplier doing the work completely? Is the supplier responsive to concerns from your company? Does the supplier invoice too early or too late? What can the supplier do better? Is the supplier providing value for the money your company spends? When you have a good idea of the contract administrator's opinion, talk with other people.

Interview the end user. The fourth step is to talk with the end user of the service/product/material. Again, your sole reason for this interview is to gather information. Find out if the service/product/material works well or not. If it does, find out if it can be improved. For example, if the product is a software program that was written two years ago, maybe there is an update for it. You will need to find out how much an update costs or if the supplier is required to provide the update for free as part of the existing contract. If the service/product/material does not work well, what needs to happen to improve it?

Talk with the final approval authority. The fifth step is to talk with the person who has final approval authority for your procurement. Find out the bottom line for pricing, delivery schedule, payment schedule, etc. Even though this information should be on the RFPS, you will often find that there is a range for contract spend (in dollars) that you will need for your negotiations. During this conversation, other items of interest to you may arise that could also be important for negotiations. (We will discuss negotiations in detail in Chapter 8, *Negotiations.*)

Talk with the supplier's contract manager. The sixth step is to talk with the supplier's contract manager for this contract. You want to discover what is good about the contract and what needs to be improved from the supplier's perspective. Be careful that you do not imply or promise that this supplier will get the new contract. Even if the procurement is a sole-source procurement, this conversation is for fact finding, not negotiations.

Conduct industry research. The seventh step is to do industry research to find out which companies provide the same service/product/material. Along with this information, gather data on each prospective company's financial status. If you work in a small company, you will need to do this research yourself. Start with Hoover's, Inc., a company that compiles information on most United States companies (http://www.hoovers.com). Hoover's is a paid service, with different levels of cost, depending on the amount of information needed. The cost of this service is justified by the risk mitigation it provides (risk mitigation will be discussed Chapter 7, *Risk*). In a larger company, members of your team will be responsible for these information-gathering activities: you will describe the industry and the team members will do the research and provide the information to you.

For a *new* contract, the process is similar, but no existing contract or procurement file will be available to use as a resource. For a new contract, start with the third step described above and interview your company's SME to get the big picture about what exactly is needed in this contract. Then proceed with steps four through seven.

In a new-contract procurement, you will have to figure out a way to show savings. If the new contract will be for services that your company does in-house now, you will need to gather the cost data for the in-house work. Consider the labor costs, materials costs, equipment costs, and overhead costs. Overhead costs will include utilities costs such as electricity, gas, and water. Overhead costs will also include costs of security such as personnel, equipment, etc. All of these costs are the basis for your cost savings by outsourcing the service.

Competitive or Sole-Source Contract?

We talked about sole-source justification in the previous sections. Let's take a closer look at the reasons for either *competing* a contract or *sole sourcing* a contract.

Competition is the major technique used to hold costs down. As a procurement professional, your job is to get the best value for the lowest cost to your company. When you completely describe the goods or services that your company needs, you will be able to get accurate proposals from companies who provide the goods or services that you need. If you were to execute a contract with your Uncle Joe's favorite janitorial service without competing it, you would have no way of knowing if your company was paying too much for the services this company provided, and without knowing competitors' questions about the goods or services, you might leave out an important aspect in the contract. Failing to include an important aspect in the contract will require that you amend the contract and increase the cost to your company. Not good.

Under some circumstances, however, sole sourcing the contract is the best thing for your company. Sometimes you will have a contract extension, a scope amendment, or some other contract change. At other times you will have market or cost reasons to sole source a contract, including:

- Lack of market competition
- Unique product base
- Extremely high transition costs

Lack of market competition. Lack of market competition applies to both goods and services. For example, if only one company in your geographic region provides janitorial services, but your company has determined that outsourcing this service is the best way to save money and reduce liability, you can only negotiate as best you can for the services provided by the janitorial company. Knowing the costs your company is currently paying for in-house janitorial services is very important. You need these costs to document the savings (or lack of savings) that you would incur by outsourcing this contract.

Unique product base. When only one company in the country (or the world) makes a specific piece of equipment, you have no leverage for price negotiation, but you might be able to negotiate the delivery date and shipping costs. Often a company that makes specialized equipment will have their own contract and your company will have to agree to it.

Extremely high transition costs. At times the transition costs incurred with changing suppliers will be extremely high. Using janitorial services as an example, if your company currently uses a janitorial service and the cost to put another janitorial service in its place is more than the savings you would get from using the new company, then you might decide to stay with the existing company. In this instance, your job will be to negotiate better value for less money.

Sole-source justifications that are not appropriate include:

- No contract is in place.
- The IBP likes this supplier.
- The IBP directs the use of this supplier. ("Just do it.")
- The supplier did the work in the past.

Justifications such as these do not provide enough information. You will need to talk with the person requesting the procurement to find out more information. Most of the time, it will be your job to educate the requesting person about the advantages of competition. Be prepared to do that by having examples of competitions that saved the company money, including exactly how much money was saved in each example.

A Traditional Request for Proposal or Internet Reverse Auction?

You and your department will need to make a decision about the most efficient way to compete the contract. The traditional method of sending out a Request for Proposals (RFP), evaluating the proposals, and awarding the contract takes time. Often this is time well spent because it adds value for your company. Sometimes it is not valuable. In those cases, you might decide to use another method to compete the contract. One of those methods is referred to as *Internet reverse auctions.*

In an auction, one seller has something to sell and many buyers bid to buy it. Estate auctions, art auctions, cattle auctions, and foreclosure auctions are examples of one seller and many buyers.

A *reverse* auction is the opposite of that: one buyer and many sellers. For example, you may need to have thousands of copies of your company's annual report printed and bound in time for the shareholder's annual meeting. One method to compete this work is to conduct a reverse auction. Conducting a reverse auction via the Internet instead of snail mail makes the auction an Internet reverse auction (also called an online reverse auction or e-Auction).

An Internet reverse auction is conducted live, in real time, over the Internet. Sellers in different locations simultaneously attempt to underbid each other, driving the prices down. Internet reverse auctions have generated billions of dollars in savings since they were introduced in the 1990s.

Your management might have concerns about using an Internet reverse auction. When this method was first introduced, the software was primitive. If the server where the software was installed did not have enough bandwidth, the server would crash and the reverse auction would suddenly stop. No one was happy with that ending.

Software has improved over time, and servers accommodate wider bandwidth. Although small companies probably will not invest in the software and hardware to conduct Internet reverse auctions, medium-to-large companies can save substantial amounts of money using this method to compete their business.

Internet reverse auctions are used mostly for goods, not services, because the specifications for goods are more readily available. If an excellent scope of work were available, however, services could be competed in this way. Before you jump on the Internet reverse auction method to solve all of your company's problems, do your research. Be prepared to defend this type of competition for your specific procurement.

Cost Versus Value Decisions

Early in the procurement, your company needs to decide if lowest cost is the primary result that it wants or if best value is the result it wants.

Lowest cost is used as the primary result of a competition in cases of consumable goods. For example, you care about lowest price when you buy truckloads of paper towels or copy paper. The quality of the paper towels and copy paper is not as important as the price per unit.

Best value is determined when other supplier requirements are met. Some of those requirements include:

- Technical specifications
- Production facilities
- Capability
- Capacity
- Quality process
- On-time delivery of product and/or service
- Supplier management

- Supplier financial stability and dependency
- Product life cycle cost
- Price, including discounts

This is a short list of requirements that are often needed—not all of the possible requirements your company could have. For example, if your company needs to buy sheets of steel in order to manufacture the product, you will need to evaluate technical specifications, production facilities, capability, capacity, quality process, on-time delivery, supplier financial stability and dependency, and pricing in order to determine best value. If the steel sheets are inconsistent in thickness or no process is in place at the factory to check quality, then you do not buy from that supplier. Your company's success depends on the steel sheets that you buy. (*Note*: Price is one element used to determine best value—but only one of the ten elements listed. An example of weighted evaluation criteria is shown in Appendix C, *Request for Proposals for Janitorial Services*. The time to make price either a greater weight or a lower weight in determining best value is when weighting factors are being decided. Ideally that process is completed before the RFP is released.)

REQUEST FOR PROCUREMENT SERVICES

The Request for Procurement Services (RFPS) template in Figure 2-3 shows how one page can be used to gather all the necessary information to start a procurement. Smaller companies and companies lacking procurement processes may not have an RFPS. You can develop your own RFPS based on this simple model and then use an interview to fill it out:

Date. The RFPS starts with the date of the request. This date is important as a historical fact.

Requestor name. Then the RFPS provides the name and title of the requesting person. Often the requesting person is called the IBP and is the procurement sponsor. Unless otherwise indicated, the requesting person is also the person or department responsible for paying the supplier (known as the cost center in many companies). The requesting person may not be the individual who has signature authority, also known as decision authority. You will need to document every person who has decision authority when you start planning this procurement. The person who has authority to approve the entire contract may be different from the person who has authority to approve how much money is spent under that contract. In large companies, you will have several decision authorities. Your contract is not fully executed until you have signatures from each one.

REQUEST FOR PROCUREMENT SERVICES	
DATE OF REQUEST	
REQUESTOR NAME	
SHIP TO ADDRESS OR LOCATION OF WORK BEING PERFORMED	
REQUESTOR PHONE NUMBER	
REQUESTOR FAX NUMBER	

COMPLETE DESCRIPTION OF PROCUREMENT
(Indicate if New Contract, Revised Contract, Purchase Order, or Other type of procurement.)

EXISTING/EXPECTED CONTRACT AMOUNT SPENT PER YEAR in $	

DATE CONTRACT REQUIRED

CONTRACT REQUIRED DATE	

SUGGESTED VENDORS OR SOLE-SOURCE JUSTIFICATION
(Add additional vendors on an attached sheet with all contact information requested below.)

NAME	
ADDRESS	
CONTACT NAME	
PHONE NUMBER	
FAX NUMBER	

SOLE-SOURCE JUSTIFICATION
(Must include market data if only supplier of goods or services.)

SCOPE OF SERVICE
(Include detailed and complete description of services required, personnel qualifications, etc.; continue on additional sheet if necessary and attach.)

REQUESTOR APPROVAL

NAME (Type or Print)	SIGNATURE	DATE

Figure 2-3. Elements of an RFPS template (a complete template is exhibited in Appendix B).

Address. Next the RFPS provides the address where the goods are to be shipped or the service work is to be performed.

Contact information. The RFPS then provides contact information for the person making this request.

Description of procurement. The next section is for an exact description of the procurement. If you are completing this form, before filling out this area, wait until you know exactly what will be purchased and how it will be purchased: the procurement type, i.e., new contract, existing contract extension, existing contract amendment, purchase order, etc. This section also includes either the amount spent per year if the contract is an existing one or the estimated amount that will be spent per year if this is a new contract. Also include any savings goals for contract extensions or amendments in this area. How much money will the IBP spend on the services or goods? This amount may be only an estimate from the IBP. It needs to be tested by you and/or your financial analyst. Do your research by identifying several companies in your area that provide these goods or services and call them. Ask for pricing information. Be sure to let these companies know that this inquiry is for research purposes only. Keep this list of suppliers as the baseline for sending out your Request for Proposals in the near future.

Date required. You must include the date that the contract is required. This information is essential to build your schedule (timeline) for completing the procurement. You will need to go through the procurement process steps to determine if the date is workable. If it is not, educate the IBP on Procurement's processes and the timelines for them (discussed in detail in Chapter 4, *Scheduling*.) The date that the contract is required is so important that you should not accept the procurement until you have the date.

Suggested vendors. The next section is for listing suggested vendors for the procurement competition or for sole sourcing the procurement. The person making the procurement request is often the best source of knowledge about this particular area of work. This person probably knows all of the vendors who can supply the goods or services and knows which ones are the most reliable. *A word of caution:* Do your own research to find other vendors who supply what this procurement needs. The requestor and the department may be biased toward one company over another without ever having learned more about any other companies. (You will do this in step seven as described earlier in *New or Existing Contract*?) If this is a sole-source (or directed) procurement, this section is where the sole vendor will be listed, along with all the necessary contact information.

Sole-source justification. The next section is where the requestor will justify the sole-source procurement. If the justification is that there is only one supplier, the market data used to make this determination must be included with the RFPS. (This is for historical documentation, and it covers your behind, too. Refer to appropriate and inappropriate sole-source justifications previously in *Competitive or Sole-Source Contract.*)

Scope of service. Now we get to the good stuff, the Scope of Work (SOW). You must have a detailed, specific, complete description of the goods or services you are procuring. The more detailed and specific this SOW is, the better your RFX—a term used to refer to Request for Information (RFI), Request for Proposal (RFP), Request for Quote (RFQ), or Request for Bid (RFB)—will be and the higher value your company will receive from your work. Most of the time, this space is not nearly enough for the complete SOW. Make sure additional pages are attached and identified for use in the future. If you have questions as you read the SOW, jot them down so that you can include them when you interview the SME for this product or service. (We will go into more detail later in the *Statement of Work* section of this chapter.)

Requestor approval. Last is the area for the requestor's signature and date. This area serves as both the authority for you to get started with the procurement and the documentation of who asked for it. If you are filling out the RFPS while you speak with the requestor, be sure to remember to get the requestor to sign and date the RFPS.

In Appendix B, Exhibit 2-3 shows a completed RFPS.

PROCUREMENT TEAM

To get started with the procurement, you need to know who the members of your procurement team will be. In a small company, you may be the only person from Procurement (Purchasing) on the team. If you work in a large company, your team will include other people. Let's look at possible needs for your procurement team. Some questions that are important to ask in helping to make certain that you have a good team include:

- Who makes final decisions on contract terms and/or contract spend, i.e., who has decision authority?
- What skills are required to be a team member?
- Is a financial analyst needed?
- Is more than one procurement professional needed?
- Is a lawyer needed?
- Is a specific SME from the business unit needed?
- Do I pick my team members? Or are they assigned to me?
- Have these people worked together before? If so, were they successful?
- Is there any person who is a weaker performer than the others?

Your team will also include all stakeholders. A stakeholder is anyone who is touched by the procurement, including the employee responsible to oversee delivery if the procurement is for goods or the employee responsible for overseeing the work if this is a procurement for services. All employees who will be end users of the product (e.g., a new software package) are stakeholders. The person having final authority for signing the contract is a stakeholder. The person responsible for paying the supplier is a stakeholder. You are a stakeholder. Your boss is a stakeholder.

In the government, stakeholders range from those listed in the paragraph above to all taxpayers. Those of us who pay for government are stakeholders.

You need to know who all of the stakeholders are in order to include them in all decisions. Some stakeholders will have more involvement in the procurement process than others. You will need to know exactly who these stakeholders are and what they need to do for this procurement. Decision authorities have the power to bring your procurement to a complete halt, so be very sure all decision authorities are included in all phases of decision making.

Everyone on your team also needs to know who the stakeholders are. Communicating with stakeholders is every team member's job. Questions that require answers will arise during the procurement. If your team members know who to ask, they will save time and get better answers.

Stakeholders are valuable members of your team. Each one has specialized knowledge and experience. You usually are not the expert in the industry, but one of your stakeholders is. You might not have done this type of procurement before, but one of your stakeholders has. Stakeholders bring a wealth of knowledge to your team, as well as a different perspective. Utilize them. Table 2-1 gives some titles that medium and large companies use.

Table 2-1. Examples of Stakeholder Titles

Examples of Stakeholder Titles
Chief Financial Officer
Executive Vice President of Procurement
Vice President of Procurement
Director of Procurement
Strategic Sourcing Manager
Strategic Sourcing Team Leader
Purchasing Manager
Financial Analyst – Procurement
Procurement Analyst
Attorney – Procurement

STATEMENT OF WORK

As described earlier, the Statement of Work (SOW) is the complete, detailed, and specific description of the goods or services that this procurement will obtain. The SOW will be referred to in the contract as the definition of the work to be done. So the SOW becomes part of the contract by reference. A good SOW includes several components:

- Purpose statement: states why this procurement is being done (Do not include a business case for the procurement here. It should remain a separate document for internal distribution only.)
- Scope statement: clearly defines exactly what the procurement will do (The priority of this procurement relative to all other procurements for your company, or business unit, can be included here.)
- Procurement deliverables: describes exactly what needs to be purchased (This area is where to list the technical specifications for goods or the exact requirements for services—the written, detailed information about what the contract is for. Just listing the type of services or goods is not detailed enough. You need to know when and where services will be performed and who supplies equipment and materials. Will the supplier insure and bond each of their employees? Will the supplier perform background checks on each employee, including criminal and sexual predator checks? Will the supplier's employees be responsible for any security measures? Will the employees wear uniforms or some other type of identification? In the case of purchasing goods, you need to include the technical specifications here. What are the exterior dimensions? What are the interior dimensions? What materials are required, at a minimum and at a maximum? What is the lead time for shipping? What is the earliest possible delivery date? These are just a few of the many questions that you need to make certain are answered in the scope of work.)
- Assumptions and agreements: lists all assumptions and agreements about the product and the procurement (Any assumption that can limit the procurement must be listed here. Any "side" or "off-line" agreement that impacts this procurement must be listed here. The rule of thumb is to document everything here. Everything.)
- Constraints: provides restrictions to the performance of the procurement (A common constraint is the amount of money available to spend on this contract, for example $1.5 million for next year. You will not be able to negotiate more than this amount of money for the goods or services that you purchase with this procurement.

Constraints can also impact your schedule and will be discussed in detail in Chapter 4, *Scheduling*.)

SUMMARY

In this chapter, we have discussed prioritizing, including the Priority Matrix. Prioritizing is important in order to successfully complete tasks and activities that can make you more successful. In your work, directing your attention to the company's highest priorities will lead directly to your success.

Then we discussed what kind of procurement you have. What is it for? Is it an existing or new contract? Is the procurement competitive or sole sourced? Will a traditional RFP or Internet reverse auction be used?

After that we discussed cost versus value, a topic that continues to be a big debate among procurement professionals and senior management. The type of procurement is essential when deciding if lowest price is the determining factor for awarding the contract or if best value is better for your company's bottom line.

The Request for Procurement Services (RFPS) form was presented and the information that it must contain was described. The information described here is the minimum required. You and your company will decide how much more information is necessary for successful procurements.

We discussed the procurement team. What skills do the members of your team need? Who determines the members of your team? Have these people worked together before and were they successful as a team? We also talked about stakeholders and how they are members of your procurement team.

Finally, we described a Statement of Work (SOW). Minimally, the SOW has a purpose statement, scope statement, procurement deliverables, assumptions and agreements, and constraints to the procurement.

In the Chapter 3, we will discuss planning a procurement.

CHAPTER 3

PLANNING

Planning is the most important aspect of getting your procurement completed. Your plan is the map that gets you from where you are now to a successfully executed contract. (Think about taking a car trip: you need directions, road numbers, and town names to make sure you are on the correct route.) Let's look at the plans that are required to maximize your chances of having a successful procurement. We will start with a case example about procuring janitorial services for your company's building.

CASE EXAMPLE 2: JANITORIAL SERVICES

XYZ Company has 50,000 square feet of mixed-use property. Some of the area is used for offices, some is used for a warehouse, and some is used as a small retail store. The company has decided to outsource its janitorial services to save money and decrease liability concerns.

YOUR ASSIGNMENT

You have been assigned as the procurement professional who will do the strategic sourcing for the new janitorial service. What do you do?

Using the RFPS in Appendix B, Exhibit 2-3, you see that the contract is required by October 31, 2013. The date the request is made is May 3, 2013, which allows almost six months to do this procurement. To determine if this is enough time, you need to come up with a plan, which we will call the *procurement plan*. (In project management, the *project plan* is the basis for all actions and decisions made about the project. In procurement, the procurement plan is also the basis for all actions and decisions.)

PROCUREMENT PROCESS

To develop a procurement plan, you need to know what is involved in a procurement. A procurement is divided into seven basic steps:

- Business need identified (RFPS)
- Procurement plan (also called the procurement strategy)
- Solicitation (sends out a Request for X (RFX), e.g., for proposals, information, quotes, etc.)
- Response analyses (compares and rates responses to the RFX)
- Negotiations
- Finalization of contract
- Contract administration

These seven basic steps are the largest divisions of a procurement. Each one breaks down into multiple tasks and activities. These steps, except for the final three, will be addressed in this chapter. The final three steps will be addressed later: negotiations in Chapter 8 (*Negotiations*), finalization of contract in Chapter 9 (*Signing the Contract and Closing the Procurement*), and contract administration in Chapter 10 (*Contract Administration*).

PROCUREMENT PLAN

Planning an original procurement is a major process. You will be doing a procurement that no one in your company (or department) has ever done before. While this procurement might be similar to other company procurements, it is *unique* in some way. Even a contract extension to pick up an option year is unique. In a contract extension, you will negotiate for better pricing than originally agreed to, or a different schedule, or different terms in the contract. In any case, your procurement plan will be an original document for an original procurement.

This procurement plan will be used for several purposes:

- As the baseline for your procurement: Although the procurement plan can be changed during the procurement, every change must be documented (change order control) so that the changed item in the plan can be compared to the original item to see how it changed. The original item is the baseline against which all future changes are compared (measured).

- To guide the procurement execution: The procurement plan will show what activities or tasks need to be done, by whom, and when.
- To document all assumptions: You and your team will make assumptions about this procurement.
- To document decisions: The reasons for making these decisions can be as important as the decisions themselves.
- To facilitate communication among stakeholders: Every stakeholder will review the procurement plan before the procurement can proceed.
- To define management reviews: when they happen, who does them, and what exactly will be reviewed.

When finished, this procurement plan will be a formal, approved document. *Caution*: Although there will be pressure for you to start working on the procurement without having a procurement plan in place, be sure to only do minimal work until the plan is approved.

The steps for procurement planning are usually done in exactly the same order for every procurement—that is what makes planning a process, not a project in itself. Any of the steps may be iterated (repeated) during the planning process.

Priority

The first step in creating a procurement plan is to determine where your procurement is in the company's (or department's) priority list. If the procurement is the number one priority, you will always be told that. You will be promised all kinds of cooperation because the procurement is such a high priority. Be sure to document this fact in the beginning of the procurement plan. You may need it later during the procurement.

If your procurement is not the number one priority, find out exactly where it is on the priority list. This priority will determine everything from the personnel available for assignment to your procurement team to the level of support from management. Most executives allot their time based on the priority of the work. If your procurement is at the bottom of the list, the executives will not want to deal with it any more than absolutely necessary. By documenting the procurement's priority, you have the basis for asking for more help or changing the schedule as necessary to accommodate higher priorities within the company or department.

Most often, you will need to check with your boss about the priority of each procurement. Then you will need to double check that priority with the procurement requestor and/or signature authority. *Remember*: One person's highest priority may be the next person's lowest. Your boss may not be aware of the issues involved or the politics between departments. If that is the case, make yourself aware of issues, politics, and the actual priority of the procurement so that you can correctly prioritize all of your work. Then you will be ready to begin your procurement plan.

The following sections will describe the elements that are part of a procurement plan. At a minimum, a procurement plan has the Statement of Work (SOW), the Work Breakdown Structure (WBS), the schedule (timeline), the budget for the procurement, the communications plan, and the risk plan. We will describe the purpose for each one below.

Statement of Work (Procurement Charter)

The Statement of Work (SOW) is also known as the procurement charter. As stated in Chapter 2, this is where the procurement is defined in detail. Often the SOW is written by the IBP requesting procurement services. This SOW is usually incomplete and needs more detail in order to be used in the procurement plan.

The SOW has several major components:

- Purpose statement
- Scope statement
- Procurement deliverables
- Goals and objectives
- Cost and schedule estimates
- List of stakeholders
- Chain of command
- Assumptions
- Constraints

You may need to add other components to your procurement SOW, depending on the procurement and your organization. For example, a federal agency may need to add a section on agency-specific regulations and requirements of the FAR.

Let's now discuss the nine major components of the SOW:

Purpose statement. This section gives the reasons for doing the procurement. The business case (cost-benefit analysis) can be referenced here, but is not usually provided in its entirety. Often a summary of decisions from the business case is stated here. Most of the time, this purpose statement is not included in the RFX SOW.

Scope statement. State exactly what is to be procured. In our case example for janitorial services, just listing "janitorial services" is not detailed enough. List the priority of this procurement in this section. Add exact details of the work to be done. You will need to know what types of services will be performed in each area of the property. You will also need to know when those services will be performed and who supplies equipment and materials. Will the supplier insure and bond each of their employees? Will the supplier perform background checks on each employee, including criminal and sexual predator checks? When? Will the supplier's employees be responsible for any security measures? Will the employees wear uniforms or some other type of identification? These are just a few of the many questions that you will need to make certain are answered in the scope of work. *Except for the company's priority for this procurement*, this scope statement will be the SOW for the RFX also.

Procurement deliverables. This section is where the procurement deliverables are defined. The executed agreement, of course, will be listed here. All of the milestones for the procurement will be listed here, too. Include status reports and all other reports that will be required for the procurement, as well as the frequency of each report and its audience. Including this information ensures that methods of communication are known and clearly understood by all the stakeholders.

Goals and objectives. Defining the criteria for success, this section lists all of the goals for the procurement. This section will include on-time criteria, on-budget criteria (if a budget is necessary), desired savings percentage (or dollar amount), and performance measurements for the procurement. For example, one such measurement could be the beginning and ending dates of the hand-off if the procurement is for changing suppliers for this service or product.

Cost and schedule estimates. This section provides high level estimates for both the schedule and the budget for the procurement (if a budget is necessary). Because the SOW sets expectations for all stakeholders, the estimates given here must be realistic. You might have general time and cost estimates for each stage of procurement based on your department's history, or you might have to develop the detailed schedule and budget before you can complete this section of the SOW. *Important*: Be sure to allow some amount of time and money as a contingency to use when things change in the procurement.

List of stakeholders. List the names and roles of key team members and other influencers and decision makers for the procurement in this section. Also include a list of contact information for every person.

Chain of command. A procurement organizational chart can be included in this section. Most procurements, however, do not require this type of chart—a table can be used to show who reports to whom and who makes what decisions. For example, the Strategic Sourcing Manager reports to the Director of

Procurement. Although the Strategic Sourcing Manager makes all decisions regarding the procurement, the Owner of the procurement makes all decisions concerning changes during the procurement. So the Strategic Sourcing Manager reports directly to the Director of Procurement and indirectly to the Owner.

Assumptions and agreements. The list of assumptions shows all assumptions and agreements in detail. Assumptions *limit* the procurement, and agreements *form the basis for interactions* for the procurement. One assumption might be that there will be ten responders to the RFP. An agreement might be that the attorney will review only the legal aspects of the drafted agreement and not the details of the negotiated deal. This becomes documentation in case things go wrong. It also becomes an important historical document for the files. Future procurement professionals can use it as an example for similar procurements.

It is just as important to document in the SOW what your procurement ***will not do*** as it is to document what it ***will do.*** The ***will not do*** information is usually provided as an assumption or a constraint. Assumptions and constraints are used as a basis for negotiating the procurement schedule and the budget, as well as personnel assignments; therefore, including what the procurement ***will not do*** brings this information to the attention of every stakeholder. The assumptions list will then become the basis for negotiating everything that was assumed would be done, but was not listed in the SOW.

Constraints. The list of constraints shows all constraints in detail. A constraint is a major factor that places a *boundary* on the procurement. Examples of constraints include schedule, personnel availability, real world problems that develop while the procurement is underway, budget, and facility and equipment availability. Think about the following situations:

- A higher-priority procurement schedules the conference rooms when you need them for oral presentations.
- Executives go on retreat the week that you need the contract reviewed and signed.
- A collective bargaining agreement that is already in place with your company limits certain aspects of the procurement.

The following is an example of a SOW for *Case Example 2: Janitorial Services:*

Statement of Work for Janitorial Services for XYZ Company

XYZ Company is the importer, distributor, and retailer for an international brand of tea. The company has 50,000 square feet of mixed-use property: 10,000 square feet is used for offices, 25,000 square feet is a warehouse, and 15,000 square feet is a small retail store. The company has decided to outsource its janitorial services in order to save money and improve liability concerns by lowering business insurance levels and premiums. The company will also lower its worker compensation insurance premiums by having fewer employees.

The procurement for janitorial services is a high priority for the company. Although it is not the number one priority overall, it is the first priority for the facilities group. This group will manage and monitor the services provided by the supplier, as well as pay the fees that are agreed upon in the services agreement.

The type of contract will be a firm fixed-price contract. It will include option years with appropriate pricing discounts per year to increase savings to the company.

The janitorial services required are:

Offices—Monday through Friday evening services consisting of cleaning, sanitizing, and stocking restrooms as needed, emptying trash cans, cleaning trash cans as needed, removing trash to designated disposal area, vacuuming common areas, vacuuming cubicles and offices, spot treating carpet stains, spot dusting horizontal surfaces without moving papers or other items on desks, sweeping and/or mopping floors in common areas, cleaning and disinfecting break room surfaces, cleaning and disinfecting drinking fountains, cleaning and disinfecting lobby furniture. Reporting maintenance problems to XYZ Company facilities manager. Quarterly services consisting of deep cleaning of all surfaces in common areas including shelves, fire extinguishers and/or cabinets for them, signs, clocks, etc., stripping and waxing all floors, deep cleaning/disinfecting all surfaces in restrooms. Semi-annual services consisting of carpet cleaning in all common areas and cubicles/offices.

Retail store—Monday through Saturday evening services consisting of cleaning, sanitizing, and stocking restrooms as needed, emptying trash cans, cleaning trash cans as needed, removing trash to designated disposal area, sweeping and/or mopping floors, cleaning and disinfecting drinking fountains, spot dusting horizontal surfaces without moving papers or other items. Reporting maintenance problems to XYZ Company facilities manager. Quarterly services consisting of deep cleaning all surfaces such as shelves, fire extinguishers and/or cabinets for them, signs, clocks, etc., stripping and waxing all floors, deep cleaning/disinfecting all surfaces in restrooms.

Warehouse—Monday through Saturday evening services consisting of cleaning, sanitizing, and stocking restrooms as needed, emptying trash cans, cleaning trash cans as needed, removing trash to designated disposal area, sweeping and/or mopping floors. Reporting maintenance problems to XYZ Company facilities manager. Quarterly services consisting of deep cleaning fire extinguishers and/or cabinets for them, signs, clocks, etc., stripping and waxing floors, deep cleaning/disinfecting all surfaces in restrooms.

Quality cleaning is required, including full performance of all specified daily services on the first official working day of the contract period.

All cleaning personnel are prohibited from disturbing papers on desks or shelves, opening desk drawers or cabinets, or using telephone or office equipment located within XYZ Company property. Emergency situations are exempted from the ban on using XYZ Company telephones.

All contract personnel are required to sign in and out upon arrival/departure of XYZ Company property. A form is located in the janitorial closet located in the offices, warehouse, and retail store areas of the property.

Contractor personnel assigned to this contract will be furnished identification badges by XYZ Company.

Facility master key will be provided to the contractor supervisor only. Contractor will be liable for all costs associated with re-keying, re-issuance, or programming of keys, access cards, and security codes which result from the loss or compromising of keys, access cards, or security codes by contractor's personnel.

Supervisors will be trained on the use of alarm systems. Supervisors will be responsible for training cleaning personnel on the use of alarm systems.

Contractor's employees will be responsible for securing all offices, gates, and exterior entrances/exits upon completion of contracted services unless otherwise directed by the designated XYZ Company representative. Failure to secure all exterior entrances/exits and/or gates will result in a $50.00 charge per occurrence. Repeated failure to maintain a secure facility when providing janitorial services will be cause for termination of the contract.

The contractor will furnish all supplies and materials necessary for the performance of the contract. Any changes to the items on the XYZ Company list of approved supplies and materials must be submitted in writing to the XYZ Company representative and approved prior to use in the XYZ Company property. Contractor must maintain within each janitorial closet a list of Material Safety Data Sheets (MSDS) for each product used by the contractor. The contractor will not use any material that XYZ Company determines unsuitable for the purpose intended or that is harmful to any part of the building, contents, or equipment.

Electricity and hot/cold water will be available, at no charge, to the contractor from existing outlets for use with contractor's equipment.

Contractor will provide all necessary cleaning equipment, including power-driven floor-scrubbing machines, waxing and polishing machines, industrial-type vacuum cleaners, etc. to successfully perform the work agreed to in the contract. XYZ Company representative will approve all equipment before it is used in the property. Equipment deemed to be of improper type or design, or inadequate for the purpose intended, will be replaced by the contractor.

Contractor personnel may use the break rooms within the property.

No one is to accompany contractor's employees to XYZ Company property who is not employed by the contractor and assigned to work in the property.

XYZ Company may require the removal of a contractor employee from the XYZ Company property without cause at XYZ Company's discretion. This includes immediate removal.

Contractor will pay for criminal background investigations for all personnel assigned to work at XYZ Company property for the term of the contract.

All people employed by the contractor will be US citizens or possess papers showing that they are legal aliens. All personnel assigned to the XYZ Company property must be able to understand the English language and be able to read all labels, descriptions, and instructions for all materials used under the contract.

Contract personnel responsible for project management and/or supervision of contractor's employees assigned to this contract are required to understand and speak English fluently.

Failure of contractor to resolve performance issues shall serve as cause for termination of contract.

Contractor is required to maintain at its sole cost and expense Commercial General Liability insurance, Workers' Compensation insurance, Employers' Liability insurance (if applicable), and automobile insurance. The amounts and limits of each type of insurance will be listed in the contract.

The procurement milestones are:

- Kick-Off Meeting
- Procurement Plan
- Solicitation
- RFP Process
- Proposal Analysis
- Negotiations
- Contract Finalization
- Notification of Unsuccessful Suppliers
- Contract Administration

Status meetings will be held weekly. Meeting minutes/action items will be distributed to all team members within 24 business hours after each meeting.

One financial analysis report will be distributed to all team members prior to the RFP being sent out.

The draft contract will be sent for review to all signatories after negotiations are completed.

The procurement file will be completed and reviewed within 21 business days after contract is executed.

The goal of this procurement is to save the company money. This will be accomplished by decreasing the annual spend for janitorial services for the term of the contract. The savings will be measured by using the average amount spent per year for the past three years and using that amount to divide the contractual spend. The equation used is: (1 – (NEW SPEND ÷ AVG SPEND)) × 100 = savings percentage.

The success metrics of this procurement will be the date the contract is executed, the savings percentage, and customer satisfaction. IBP satisfaction will be measured by a survey to be completed before procurement begins and again after contract is completed.

The cost estimate for the procurement is: $40,000

The estimated completion date for the executed contract is: October 31, 2013

The procurement team is listed in Table 3-1:

Table 3-1. Procurement Team for Case Example 2: Janitorial Services

Name	Role	Responsibility
Donna Smith (DS)	Strategic Sourcing Manager (SSM)	Makes all procurement decisions Signs review sheets Signs contract Reports to DP Answers to Owner
Robert Golden (RG)	Director of Procurement (DP)	Approves procurement plan Signs review sheets Signs contract
James Brown (JB)	Financial Analyst (FA)	Signs review sheets Reports to DP Answers to SSM
Bill Green (BG)	Facilities Manager Subject Matter Expert (SME)	Signs review sheets Reports to COO
John Q. Public (JQP)	Chief Operations Officer (COO) Owner	Makes all final decisions on contract terms other than legal requirements Signs review sheets Signs contract
Samantha Grey (SG)	Attorney	Makes all legal decisions on contract Signs review sheets

Assumptions

- Outsourced janitorial services will save the company money.
- Team personnel will be available when they are needed.
- Priority of procurement will not change.
- The actual costs for janitorial services for the past three years are available.
- The amount for contract spend for the first year of the contract will be $500,000.

Constraints

- Contract execution date no later than October 31, 2013.
- Budget for procurement is $40,000.
- Contract spend for the first year as high as $500,000.

Task List and Work Breakdown Structure

The task list and Work Breakdown Structure (WBS) are used as the foundation for your procurement plan. The task list is an essential part of the WBS and identifies tasks that are required to be completed in order for the procurement to reach a successful conclusion—an executed agreement. Figure 3-1 shows the list of tasks necessary to hold the kick-off meeting for the janitorial services assignment. The indents show the relationship of each task to the one above it. (We will discuss task lists in greater detail in Chapter 4, *Scheduling*. As we continue our discussions in this book, we will combine the task list into the WBS, so when the term WBS is used, it includes the task list.)

Task Description
Kick-Off Meeting
Decide on date for meeting
Reserve meeting room
Create agenda
Send out agenda
Receive comments/additons to agenda
Resend amended agenda
Hold meeting
Develop action list and/or meeting minutes
Send out action list/minutes
Receive comments/additions to action list/minutes
Resend action list/minutes

Figure 3-1. Example of a task description list for a kick-off meeting for Case Example 2: Janitorial Services.

The WBS is the "dissected" procurement. After you have completed the task list, you will assign a level to each task. The WBS allows you to then schedule the tasks and budget for each one (if you need to prepare a budget for the procurement). The WBS also gives you the basis for personnel selection.

The WBS uses a top-down planning methodology. Looking at the overall procurement objective (an executed contract), you will clarify goals and milestones for your procurement. Then you will plan activities, resources, and assignments.

We have been using some terminology in this section that needs to be defined:

Tasks. From Chapter 1, Table 1-2, a task is defined as "a cohesive unit of work" required to complete the procurement. Defining the level of a task to list is important. Each task must be easy to assign, easy to estimate, and easy to track. If it is not, then the work is not a task and needs to be broken down further. A task may include several steps (subtasks) that are conceptually related.

Goals. A goal is something that needs to be achieved in the procurement. Each of the seven steps of a procurement listed in an earlier section of this chapter (Procurement Process) is a goal for the procurement. Some procurements have additional goals. One of those is often the goal of savings.

Milestones. From Chapter 1, Table 1-2, a milestone is defined as "a clearly identifiable point in a project that summarizes the completion of an important set of tasks." Milestones are commonly used to summarize the important events in a procurement for managers and stakeholders who do not want or need to see the details in a procurement plan. (We will discuss this concept further in Chapter 5, *Communications.*)

Activities. From Chapter 1, Table 1-2, an activity is defined as "a specific project task" that requires resources and time to complete. The term *activity* can be used interchangeably with the term *task*. Activity is often used to describe tasks that involve more than one person, e.g., meetings. Be certain that you understand how the term *activity* is used in your department/company.

Figure 3-2 shows how to assign levels to the activities for the janitorial services example. The levels identified are all milestones and do not show the tasks involved to reach each one. (We will discuss in detail how exactly to develop a WBS in Chapter 4, *Scheduling.*)

Schedule (Timeline)

The schedule is the *timeline* for your procurement. Some people will list only the date that the contract needs to be executed. Unfortunately, the date needed for contract execution is not enough information for you or your stakeholders.

The schedule has two parts: the WBS and the timeline. We just discussed that the WBS consists of activities and tasks. The schedule is developed when the activities and tasks are assigned time frames. For example, the weekly team meeting will

WBS	Task Description
0.0	Procurement for Janitorial Services
1.0	Receive RFPS
2.0	Kick-Off Meeting
3.0	Procurement Plan
4.0	Solicitation
5.0	RFP Process
6.0	Proposal Analysis
7.0	Negotiations
8.0	Contract Finalization
9.0	Notification of Unsuccessful Suppliers
10.0	Contract Administration

Figure 3-2. Example of a high-level WBS with task descriptions.

last one hour. This time will be reflected as one hour for every member of the team, another hour for you to prepare for the meeting (e.g., to put together an agenda, distribute it, contact individual team members for updates, etc.), and another hour for you to prepare and distribute the meeting minutes/action list. So your schedule will include three hours for the meeting while most of the team will show only one hour for the same meeting.

Remember two very important things about the schedule. First, break down the WBS into very small tasks/activities—the smaller the better. Breaking the WBS down into very small tasks/activities is how to make sure that you do not forget any big components of the work that need to be done. Second, allow enough time for each task/activity. Think about how much time it actually takes you to do the task. Then double it. Yes, double it. Doubling the time will allow for interruptions and "fire fighting." Remember the Priority A tasks, the unexpected things that must be done or addressed immediately, from Chapter 2? This need to double the time for each task is what they do to your schedule!

Figure 3-3 is a high-level schedule that assigns dates to the milestones that need to be accomplished for the janitorial services assignment. (We will discuss schedules and how to create them in great detail in Chapter 4, *Scheduling*.)

Budget

Depending on your company and the type of procurement you will be doing, you may not need to develop a budget. You will not need a budget if you and all of the other members of your team are paid out of an overhead account. If you

WBS	Task Description	Start Date	Finish Date
0.0	Procurement for Janitorial Services	05/03/13	10/31/13
1.0	Receive RFPS	05/03/13	05/10/13
2.0	Kick-Off Meeting	05/13/13	05/17/13
3.0	Procurement Plan	05/20/13	05/24/13
4.0	Solicitation	05/28/13	06/10/13
5.0	RFP Process	06/10/13	06/28/13
6.0	Proposal Analysis	06/28/13	08/02/13
7.0	Negotiations	07/19/13	09/06/13
8.0	Contract Finalization	07/19/13	10/11/13
9.0	Notification of Unsuccessful Suppliers	10/15/13	10/31/13
10.0	Contract Administration	10/31/13	End of contract term

Figure 3-3. Example of a high-level WBS with schedule.

do not charge your work time to specific project numbers, then you are on an overhead account.

On the other hand, if you are assigned to a specific project as the procurement SME, you will need to develop a budget for the procurement. The project manager, as part of her/his overall project budget, will use your estimate. You will need to know the direct costs (salary) and indirect costs (benefits) for each member of your team. It is possible that you will also be required to budget for equipment and materials costs. The project manager will ask you to estimate the cost of the product or service of the procurement. This estimate should include all associated costs of the product or service, including shipping and handling, taxes, disposal costs, etc.

To develop the budget for the procurement itself, use the WBS. Assign costs to every activity. Then add up the costs. This total is your procurement budget. Developing a budget, however, is not as easy as it sounds. Figure 3-4 shows the budget for the janitorial services assignment. This budget only shows the amount associated with each milestone. (We will discuss the exact steps in Chapter 5, *Budget*.)

Communications Plan

A communications plan is developed primarily to document who is assigned to the procurement, each person's role and responsibility, the types and frequency of meetings, who should attend meetings, change control, and the methods of communication (face-to-face, telephone, email, text, instant messaging, hard-copy reports, etc.)

Procurement Team					
ID	**Name/Initials**	**Role**	**Direct Labor Cost ($)**	**Indirect Labor Cost ($)**	**Total/Hour ($)**
DS	Donna Smith (DS)	SSM	39.22	12.94	52.16
RG	Robert Golden (RG)	DP	47.89	15.80	63.69
JB	James Brown (JB)	FA	20.64	6.81	27.45
BG	Bill Green (BG)	SME	31.39	10.36	41.75
JQP	John Q. Public (JQP)	Owner	88.97	29.36	118.33
SG	Samantha Grey (SG)	Attorney	74.84	24.70	99.54

WBS	Task Description	Owner	Role	Effort Hours	Labor Costs
0.0	**Procurement for Janitorial Services**	**DS**	**SSM**	**321.75**	**$40,000.00**
1.0	**Receive RFPS**	**DS**	**SSM, DP**	**7.50**	**$1,357.39**
2.0	**Kick-Off Meeting**	**DS**	**SSM**	**6.00**	**$1,138.40**
3.0	**Procurement Plan**	**DS**	**SSM**	**27.75**	**$7,841.06**
4.0	**Solicitation**	**DS**	**SSM**	**73.75**	**$6,911.54**
5.0	**RFP Process**	**DS**	**SSM**	**12.25**	**$1,183.08**
6.0	**Proposal Analysis**	**DS**	**SSM**	**72.00**	**$7,976.79**
6.11	**Oral Presentations**	**DS**	**SSM**	**20.50**	**$3,394.90**
7.0	**Negotiations**	**DS**	**SSM**	**34.00**	**$4,047.45**
8.0	**Contract Finalization**	**DS**	**SSM**	**62.00**	**$5,292.34**
8.3	**Execute Contract**	**DS**	**SSM**	**Rolled up**	**Rolled up**
9.0	**Notification of Unsuccessful Suppliers**	**DS**	**SSM**	**6.00**	**$857.05**
10.0	**Contract Administration**	**DS**	**SSM**	**N/A**	

Figure 3-4. Example of a high-level WBS with budget for Case Example 2: Janitorial Services. DP, Director of Procurement; FA, Financial Analyst; SME, Subject Matter Expert; SSM, Strategic Sourcing Manager.

Change control is the process used to document when and how changes are accepted into the procurement. Change control ensures that:

- Changes are beneficial.
- A change has occurred.
- The change is managed as it occurs.

Change control requires that performance measurement baselines are maintained, the SOW is updated to adequately reflect the change, and that the change is coordinated with all of the appropriate stakeholders.

Table 3-2 is the beginning of a communications plan for the janitorial services example. (We will discuss communications plans in detail in Chapter 6, *Communications.*)

Table 3-2. Example of a Partial Communications Plan for Case Example 2: Janitorial Services

Procurement Team			
Name	**ID**	**Role**	**Responsibilities**
Donna Smith	DS	SSM	Team leader
Robert Golden	RG	DP	Manager
James Brown	JB	FA	Financial research
Bill Green	BG	Facilities Manager SME	Specialized knowledge
John Q. Public	JQP	Owner	Final approvals
Samantha Grey	SG	Attorney	Legal opinions

Meetings	Timing
Informal discussions with team	Daily
Team meetings	Weekly
Procurement review	Weekly
Status update	Weekly
Contract audit	Once, after agreement reached and before contract execution

Reports	Timing
Status reports to management	Monthly
Update reports to team leader	Weekly (before team meetings)
Progress reports to team	Weekly (at team meetings)

Risk Plan

Let's look at two definitions of risk. According to Harold Kerzner, Ph. D. (*Project Management: A Systems Approach to Planning, Scheduling, and Controlling, 6th Edition,* p. 869, Van Nostrand Reinhold (1997), risk is "... a measure of the probability and consequence of not achieving a defined project goal." Kerzner goes on to say that risk has three primary components:

- An event
- A probability of occurrence of that event
- The impact of that event (the consequence)

The PMBOK® Guide (2003) defines a project risk as "… any uncertain event or condition that, if it occurs, has a positive or a negative effect on a project objective." *Uncertainty* is key to defining risk.

Every one of us has personal risk in our lives. Think about every time that you get in a car or on a bus or airplane to travel. Do you know how your trip will end with 100% certainty? No. Think of another scenario. Do you know if you will be sick tomorrow? No. This is the type of *uncertainty* that is part of the definition of risk. (Your personal risk management plan might include what you, or your family, would do if you were in a car accident or became sick.)

As we know from earlier discussions, if we know *for certain* that something will happen, then we include it in specific sections of the procurement plan. For example, we know for certain that the RFP will be drafted and sent to prospective suppliers. We know for certain that the per-year spend is limited to $500,000 for the janitorial services case example. But what about the things that we *do not know for certain*? We make a risk plan.

The risk plan is the roadmap for risk management. The *PMBOK® Guide* defines project risk management as "the systematic process of identifying, analyzing, and responding to project risk." Procurement risk management is *exactly* the same as project risk management.

Why do you need to do risk management planning for your procurement? The answer is that you need to plan for the *possibility* that something will go wrong. To plan for the possibilities, you identify the potential problems, estimate the probability that each problem will actually happen, evaluate how damaging each problem could be, and prepare for what to do (the responses) in advance. Simply put, you want good stuff to happen, but not bad stuff (*avoidance*). And if bad stuff does happen, you want to make it not as bad as it could have been (*mitigation*).

During every procurement, something unexpected will happen. More serious issues might be that the company you are negotiating a contract with goes out of business, or your management might decide not to proceed with the procurement at all, or the budget for the new contract spend might be reduced significantly. Other less serious issues can arise such as changes to personnel in your procurement team or in a potential vendor's negotiating team. Managing risks that have not been identified by your procurement team is very difficult.

Procurement has two different sets of risks. The first set is the risk to the procurement itself—procurement risk. Procurement risk includes the types of risks identified earlier: a vendor going out of business during negotiations, management decisions, budget changes, personnel changes, etc. The second set is the risk to the executed contract—contract risk. Contract risk includes the supplier going out of business after contract execution, independent contractor status, warranties, indemnity, terms for delivery, terms for payment, etc. In addition to your expertise, rely on lawyers and accountants to help you identify risks to the contract. (Contract risks will not be covered in this book. The focus will be on the risks to the procurement and creating a risk management plan for them.)

Creating a risk management plan takes into account all of the imaginable events that can occur during your procurement and provides you with a roadmap for dealing with each one. There could be risks that you do not need to be concerned with—because of their low impact on your procurement. Other risks could stop your procurement cold. Wouldn't it be a good idea to know what those risks are?

Developing a risk management plan has four basic steps. These steps are identifying risks, analyzing risks, prioritizing risks, and risk response planning:

Identifying risks. The first step is to identify the risks. In a procurement, the types of risk are known, predictable, and unpredictable:

- *Known risks* are identified risks. You and your procurement team have already identified the known risks during the risk management process. You identified these risks using your own experience and knowledge, as well as the knowledge of your procurement team, subject matter experts, the procurement plan, and several other sources.
- *Predictable risks* are based on historical data, lessons learned, the experience of other procurement managers who lead similar procurements in your company, SME experience, etc. Predictable risks can often be identified from "gut" feelings about what might go wrong for your procurement. For example, if your manager usually takes two weeks to even read something that needs his signature, then his usually slow response time will be a risk to your procurement schedule. Will it happen? Probably. So it is a predictable risk.
- *Unpredictable risks* are those things that happen that no one even considered. For example, a region-wide power failure could last for more than a few hours. No one knows when a power failure will happen, if it ever does. A power failure is not a *force majeure.* You cannot reasonably anticipate or control a power failure, but the disruption might impact all aspects of your procurement. Identifying unpredictable risks takes life experience, business experience, and common sense.

Identifying risks is the most important step in a risk management plan. If a risk is not identified, then you have no way to plan how to respond to it. Unknown risks cannot be managed. Risk identification is an iterative process. When anything changes in your procurement, you need to identify the new risks. Sometimes a previously identified risk will have a higher priority after the change. (We will discuss identifying risks in greater detail Chapter 7, *Risk*.)

Analyzing risks. After the risks have been identified, it is time to analyze each risk. You will determine the probability that a risk will occur and the impact it will have on your procurement. Most often, the impact of each risk is discussed at the same time as its probability. These two concepts go hand in hand.

Prioritizing risks. The next step is to prioritize the risks. To prioritize the risks, you need to determine the risks that are the most important for further action. You do that by establishing a risk threshold, which is a measure of the risk acceptance for your procurement. Quite often the risk threshold depends on the risk tolerance of your company, department, and procurement sponsor—and even on your own risk tolerance. (We discuss probability, impact, and the risk threshold in detail in Chapter 7, *Risk*.)

Response planning. The final step in the risk plan is response planning. Response is the action(s) required to avoid the risk, mitigate the risk, or accept the risk. The risk plan includes developing options for responding to risks and assigning individuals or teams to be responsible for each response. (We discuss response planning in detail in Chapter 7, *Risk*.)

Figure 3-5 shows a partial risk plan for the janitorial services example.

After you have your risk plan developed, manage risk to your procurement by monitoring and controlling risks. You need to:

- Keep track of the identified risks
- Identify new risks as changes take place
- Monitor residual risks
- Ensure timely execution of the risk response
- Record risk metrics associated with implementing contingency plans

Regular reviews of the risk log (the product of the risk plan) are vital to monitoring and controlling risks. Review the risk log *every time* you look at the procurement plan for any reason. Reviewing the risk log keeps you ahead of the risk and able to successfully manage your procurement. (We will discuss monitoring and controlling risks in Chapter 7, *Risk*.)

Risk	Probability	Impact	Action	Response
Requested completion date not workable	Low	Very high	Negotiate workable completion date	SSM
Necessary personnel not available to meet schedule	Moderate	Very high	Negotiate personnel schedules with managers	SSM
Team meetings not attended	Moderate	High	Determine best meeting time and place	SSM
No competitors in market	Low	Very high	Find and research competitors in this industry and market	FA
IBP insists on sole-sourced process	Low	Very high	Make sure RFPS is completely filled out and signed; advise management	SSM
Scope of work not detailed enough	Moderate	Very high	Face-to-face (or telephone) interview with SME to complete SOW	SSM
Contract funding not adequate to provide requested services	Low	Very high	Negotiate funding levels	SSM
Contract funding level does not provide savings	Moderate	Low	Get complete 3-year records on in-house costs including insurance premiums	SSM
RFP not delivered on time	Moderate	Very high	Allow enough time in schedule for drafting and reviewing RFP	SSM
RFP responses late	Moderate	High	Allow enough time for questions, responses, and finalizing responses	SSM
RFP responses inadequate	Moderate	Very high	Include extremely detailed scope of work, specifications, draft contract, responses to all RFP questions from suppliers; amend RFP as needed	SSM
Evaluation of RFP responses delayed	High	Very high	Evaluation scorecard drafted, reviewed, and approved per schedule; allow enough time for every person to complete evaluation; negotiate work assignments of team members as necessary	SSM
Top three competitors' oral presentations caused schedule delay	Moderate	High	Allow enough time for competitors to schedule personnel, travel, and create presentation	SSM
Weather adversely impacted oral presentation schedule	Low	High	Allow enough time for competitors to schedule travel; allow float time for oral presentation schedule	SSM

Figure 3-5. Example of a partial risk plan for Case Example 2: Janitorial Services. FA, Financial Analyst; SSM, Strategic Sourcing Manager.

SUMMARY

In this chapter we have discussed the procurement plan using a case example about procuring janitorial services for XYZ Company. We discussed how important planning is to the success of any procurement. The plan is the roadmap for achieving the procurement goal. The basic components of the procurement plan include:

- Procurement priority
- Statement of Work
- Task List and Work Breakdown Structure
- Schedule
- Budget (if necessary)
- Communications plan
- Risk plan

Although a simple procurement can be completed without this level of planning, successfully completing an even slightly more complex procurement without a plan is nearly impossible. The procurement plan also serves to educate the rest of your company about the goals of your department and the activities required to execute legal, ethical, and fair procurements. The perception that procurement is an added burden slowing down the work of the business unit will be replaced—over time—with the knowledge that procurement adds value to the process by creating savings and best value for the business unit.

In Chapter 4, we will discuss developing a procurement schedule.

This book has free material available for download from the Web Added Value™ resource center at *www.jrosspub.com.*

CHAPTER 4

SCHEDULING

Graham's law: If they know nothing of what you are doing, they suspect you are doing nothing.
—Robert J. Graham

The schedule is the foundation of a procurement plan. The schedule is used to communicate who does what—and when it has to be completed. The schedule communicates the resources required to complete the work on time. It also includes how much time each person, piece of equipment, or other resource is required for the procurement. Additionally, the schedule is used to educate others on the requirements for a fair, ethical, and legal procurement.

In this chapter we will discuss how to develop a schedule for a procurement. In learning how to create a schedule, you will also learn how to review contractors' schedules—existing contractor schedules and RFP respondents' schedules. When you have some experience under your belt, you will be able to look at the duration estimated for a task and know if it is realistic or not—for your own schedules as well as for others' schedules.

A part of developing a schedule results from the 80/20 rule, which is also known as the Pareto principle or Pareto's rule. An Italian, Vilfredo Pareto was an engineer, sociologist, economist, political scientist, and philosopher. He developed the 80/20 ratio in 1906. Pareto's principle said that 80% of the land in Italy was owned by 20% of the population of Italy. Thinking about this principle in a broader way, it has been extrapolated to describe the observation that the vital few (20%) are responsible for the trivial many (80%).

There are several examples of the Pareto principle, although the exact ratio may be different. Some examples are that 20% of sales people make 80% of the total sales for a company, 80% of customer complaints come from 20% of the customers, 80% of your profits come from 20% of your customers, etc. This concept of *uneven distribution*, or inversely disproportionate cause and effect, is widely used across many industries and applications.

The reason to think about the 80/20 rule when developing a schedule is that you can identify approximately 20% of the work in your procurement that will give you approximately 80% of what is required to be completed successfully. In other words, you can identify the parts of the schedule where having more time or resources leads to a better overall procurement. This idea is discussed later in this chapter when we create a schedule step-by-step. Keep the 80/20 rule in mind always. It works in your professional life as well as in your personal life.

Let's look at schedules.

MAJOR CONSIDERATIONS FOR SCHEDULES

Interrelationships

The schedule is interrelated with the task list and the budget. Although the task list comes first, the schedule and budget are essentially worked on at the same time. *Remember*: Any change to one of these three components of a procurement plan requires a corresponding change to the other two. For example, if you need to break down one task on the task list into two or more separate tasks, then you need to estimate time for the new tasks (a schedule change) and costs for all of them (a budget change). When you think about the entwining of the task list, schedule, and budget, remember that "time is money." The more time something takes, the more it costs. Changing the task list, schedule, or budget requires a corresponding change to the others.

Float Time

Float time is the difference between the *time available for a task* (duration) and the *time required to complete it* (effort). Float is also known as *slack*. Not all tasks can have float time. Float time is used for tasks with flexible start and finish dates.

As an example, think about drafting an RFP for your procurement. The RFP will need to be reviewed. You know that each member of your team needs 40 hours to do the review. Your schedule allows for the reviews to be started and completed between the dates of July 1 and July 31 (22 working days). The float is 136 hours—the difference between 40 hours and 176 hours:

$$176 - 40 = 136$$

Remember to account for weekends and holidays. That is why you use 22 working days (176 hours) instead of 31 calendar days. In our example, float time is 340% of task effort:

$$(136 \div 40) \times 100 = 340\%$$

Do you need to allow that much time (176 hours) for your team to finish their reviews? Maybe. Who will be taking vacation during July? Who will be attending a conference in July? You will need to consider all of these factors as you develop the schedule.

Having realistic float times in your schedule is important. It is unlikely that any person on your team will be assigned to your procurement full time. All of your team members will have other work to do, other meetings to attend, telephone calls, emails, etc. Plus, it is unrealistic, even with modern slimmed-down workforces, to expect 100% effort every working day from every employee. In many workplaces, expect about 80% effort every working day. In some workplaces, that percentage slips to 40% per work day (workplaces known as "hurry up and wait" because of issues such as security requirements).

Estimating 80% effort for each work day means that an employee will get about 6 hours of work accomplished in an 8-hour day. That means if a task requires 20 hours of effort, you need to allow at least 4 days (32 hours) to complete it. So the float time (or slack) is 12 hours:

$$32 - 20 = 12$$

which translates to float time being 60% of effort:

$$(12 \div 20) \times 100 = 60\%$$

This float time is very reasonable. You might have to allow for more float time if the person doing the work for this task will be working on something else for one or two of those days.

Allowing for float time in your schedule is one method used to develop a realistic schedule. Another method is allowing time for a contingency.

Contingency

A contingency is a *possibility* that is *conditional* on *something uncertain happening*. Even if a particular contingency (an event) is unlikely, the event is still a possibility that you must prepare for and schedule. When we talk about the need for having a contingency plan, we also talk about the thing (or things) that might happen that could change our original plan. A contingency plan is also called *Plan B*.

Developing a schedule includes adding time to the schedule just in case something important is delayed unexpectedly. Sometimes called *padding*, this added time allows the schedule to be adjusted without adversely affecting the final completion date for the procurement. The way to determine contingency time is to add 2% to 7% of the total duration of your procurement to the overall schedule. The actual percentage that you add is dependent on the type and complexity of your procurement. (*Note*: Adding more than a 10% contingency to a schedule may create questions about the accuracy or veracity of the schedule. Questions about accuracy or veracity can harm your credibility. *Remember*: You are adding value to the business unit you are working with—you need good credibility to do that.)

Some people add contingency time to every task, but most add a block of time at the end of the project. If you add contingency time to every task, people on your team may lose focus on the real (or actual) amount of time they have been allotted to complete tasks. Better is to add a small block of time (2% to 7%) as a task at the end of the schedule and call it "Schedule contingency." When questions about this added block of time arise, just explain that it accounts for the unexpected without having to change the date that the contract goes into effect. Table 4-1 shows how to determine contingency time in various situations.

Level of Detail Provided

Not everyone in the company needs the same level of detail. Weigh the value of providing details against the need to know those details. The reason we write an executive summary at the beginning of every business report is to allow busy managers and executives to have the choice of either understanding the important points of the report or digging into the details of the report.

A procurement schedule is organized in the same way. The "big picture" or executive summary schedule lists only the milestones of the procurement. Listing the milestones gives a good overall picture of the procurement and provides a good platform for reporting the completion of milestones. The executive summary schedule lists milestone start and finish dates, along with who is responsible for each milestone. Too much detail can bring your procurement to a halt as you answer question after question about why you are doing this and why you are doing that. *Remember*: Executives are busy people who do not need information overload.

The actual schedule is much more detailed. It documents when tasks start and finish, along with who is responsible for each task. The actual schedule is also the baseline for changes that occur in the schedule as the procurement progresses. You will use this detailed schedule with your team. Any manager or executive who is part of your team will receive the detailed schedule because they

Table 4-1. Example of Calculations for Contingency

1. The project schedule is estimated to take 589 hours (total estimated effort). How much contingency time will be added to it?

   589 × 0.02 = 11.78 hours (round up to an even hour: 12 hours)

   589 + 12 = 601 hours

   Is an additional 12 hours enough to cover most common problems?

   589 × 0.07 = 41.23 hours (round down to even hour: 41 hours)

   589 + 41 = 630 hours

   Is an additional 41 hours enough to cover most common problems?

   Looking at the situation differently, 589 hours = 14.725 working weeks (40 hours per week)

   601 hours = 15.025 working weeks

   630 hours = 15.75 working weeks

   Taking into account the complexity of the project, choose 7% contingency, which gives you an additional 40 hours (1 week) to complete the procurement.

2. The project schedule is estimated to take 2080 hours. How much contingency time will be added to it?

   2080 × 0.02 = 41.6 hours (round up to 42 hours)

   2080 + 42 = 2122 hours (adds about 1 week)

   On the higher side for contingency:

   2080 × 0.07 = 145.6 hours (round up to 146 hours)

   2080 + 146 = 2226 hours (adds a little more than 3.5 weeks)

   In this situation, the estimated time is much higher than in the first situation, which indicates a more complex procurement. Is it reasonable to allow for almost 4 extra weeks just in case something goes wrong during the year of the procurement schedule? Yes. So choose 7% contingency for this case also.

often have to approve it and must know what happens and when it happens. Each team member will use the detailed schedule to know what to do and when to do it. Team members will also know what tasks must be completed before they can start their own tasks.

If you use a project management software program, or spreadsheet, to do your schedule, you just roll up the detailed schedule into the milestone schedule to Print or Send. You can do this with a spreadsheet if it is set up correctly. If you keep the schedule manually (not recommended), you will keep two schedules. Later in this chapter, we will develop a schedule using Microsoft Excel and show how to set it up so that it is easy to roll up the detailed schedule into a milestone schedule.

Stakeholder Agreement

The single most important resource you have for developing an accurate schedule is your team. Have each individual on your team list the tasks involved in their work, estimate the effort required to complete each task, and estimate the duration of time necessary for each task.

Getting the most accurate estimates possible from the members of your team is important. Each member of the team needs to furnish their own estimate for the schedule. This creates buy-in which is so important for a successful procurement. It is also important to know if these estimates are accurate. To do that, you will consult with people who have years of expertise to help you determine that the team members' estimates are accurate. You can find these people inside the company or outside, e.g., procurement professionals in your company or a colleague in another company or an outside consultant. Inside your company, talk with procurement professionals who have more experience at scheduling than you do. Your boss may be a good resource for identifying experienced procurement professionals. To find a consultant or someone in another company who is willing to help, contact the local chapter of your professional association. If you do not belong to one of the procurement associations, Institute of Supply Management local chapters often have a website with contact information for the officers. Contact one of them to find out if they know someone with the experience you need who is also willing to provide their expertise.

Included in the estimates from your team is a risk assessment of each task estimate. Each team member will give you a best-case schedule and a worst-case schedule. The best-case schedule assumes everything goes exactly as planned; the worst-case schedule assumes nothing goes as planned. The final schedule will be your decision. If you go with the worst-case schedule, it may show that too much time is needed. The worst-case schedule will also support the idea that the procurement takes too long and does not add value to the process. If you use the best-case schedule, you are just looking for trouble. Unforeseen circumstances always affect the schedule: people get sick or die, people find new jobs and leave the company, or you might get sick. So you need to come up with a *reasonable* schedule, usually somewhere between the best case and worst case. A reasonable schedule allows for a few problems that cause minor delays. If you use a good contingency amount (see the discussion on *Contingency* earlier in this section), these delays are already accounted for so your schedule deadline remains the same. One way to determine *reasonable* is to use weighting factors with the estimates. Is the likelihood higher that getting the signatures on the contract will take longer than one week? Is it likely that the RFP process will take less than 12 weeks? (We will discuss this idea further in the PERT section.)

Also important is stakeholders agreeing to prioritize their tasks in your procurement. Everyone has more than one thing that they work on at any given time. Juggling work is part of every day of your professional life. Your team will already be more committed to your procurement because you included them in the planning stages. In developing their estimates, the team members considered exactly what they had to do, how long the actual work would take, and how they would schedule the work on their calendars. When your work is on their calendars before anyone else's work, you have priority, but you also need them to agree to make your work a priority just in case something else comes up later. Then when they let you know that some other work needs to be done or something has happened, you need to negotiate a solution—your work needs to be done as much as, or more than, any other work does.

Meeting the Dates

After you have a schedule that is reasonable, understand that this schedule will set the expectations of everyone. People who are on the team, as well as those who are not, will expect that the milestone dates will be met. You will be successful only when you deliver the milestones on, or before, the dates listed in this schedule. Now does your schedule still seem reasonable? If not, do it again.

Everyone who receives a schedule, whether it is the milestone (high-level or big-picture) schedule or the detailed schedule, needs to know about changes. For the high-level schedule, only those changes that affect milestone dates need to be reported to the people who receive it. For the detailed schedule, everyone who receives it must know about every change. Sometimes everyone receiving it knowing about every change will mean that you have to send out information in between status reports/meetings.

As discussed earlier, everyone on the team must prioritize this work. In order to keep work prioritized, each team member must know about changes in the schedule—even if you do not think a particular schedule change will adversely impact their specific work. For example, if you will take a day longer to draft the RFP, all of the reviewers need to know that they will not start reviewing the RFP on the date originally scheduled. They can get some other work done that day or reschedule work already on their calendars for the new due date for the review.

Network Diagrams

A network diagram is a graphic presentation of the task list, the start and completion dates, and the name of the responsible person for each task. Think of a network diagram as a flow diagram of the procurement. It is the logical representation of tasks defining the sequence of work. A network diagram will:

- Show the sequences and relationships among tasks and milestones
- Show the interrelationships of tasks in different parts of the task list and WBS hierarchy
- Reduce uncertainty in the procurement because it is broken down into many small tasks, analyzed and sequenced in advance of starting the work

Do you need a network diagram? Does it just repeat the task list and WBS? Yes and no. For simple procurements, you do not need a network diagram. A simple procurement has fewer than 30 tasks. The other reason for not needing a network diagram is if you are the only person working on the procurement.

For more than 30 tasks, or if more than one person will work on the procurement, the sequence of tasks becomes important. For example, different people can do different, unrelated tasks at the same time. We call that *parallel* work. Also, starting some tasks depends on other tasks being completed and is called *dependency*. The WBS helps with identifying both parallel work and task dependencies, but seeing these relationships and dependencies quickly and clearly can take years of practice. Project management software will take the task list, WBS, and start and completion dates and show them in a Gantt chart. A Gantt chart gives you a visual way of understanding the relationships and dependencies of the tasks by using bars. A Gantt chart is enough for most people. For the other people, a network diagram is a more helpful tool.

Some people need to see blocks and arrows that show the relationships and dependencies of tasks/milestones. A network diagram does that quite well. You can print out the network diagram and put it on a wall for everyone to see. When a task or milestone is completed, mark it off in a bright color. Then the progress of your procurement is "loud and proud" for anyone to see. (You might want to take it down if your team is not meeting the schedule. Why broadcast that?) Three methods are used for constructing network diagrams:

Arrow diagramming. One method, called the Arrow Diagramming Method or ADM, is rarely used. ADM uses arrows to represent tasks and connects them at nodes (boxes or circles) to show dependencies. Very few people can create this diagram, much less read one.

Conditional diagramming. The second method is called the Conditional Diagramming Method. This method allows for non-sequential activities. Loops and conditional branches are used to indicate non-sequential activities. A *loop* is something that is repeated in the procurement, for example, reviews of an RFP or a draft contract. A *conditional branch* is a task that is needed only if something else happens, for example, if a building inspector finds errors, the task of correcting errors is a conditional branch. In procurement you could look at incorporating review comments as a conditional branch *if* you assumed that there would be no comments on your document. Because most of us expect to receive comments on our reviewed documents, receiving comments is usually included as a regular task in the schedule. Conditional diagramming uses techniques such as GERT (Graphical Evaluation and Review Technique) and System Dynamics models. We will not discuss these techniques, but you should be aware of them in case your company, or a company you work for in the future, uses them. You will have at least heard their names.

Precedence diagramming. The third method, called the Precedence Diagramming Method or PDM, is widely used and easy for most people to read. PDM uses nodes (boxes) to represent tasks and connects them with arrows to show dependencies. Figure 4-1 and Figure 4-2 show the fundamental construction elements of a network diagram. (The symbols and elements will be explained when we construct a milestone network diagram later in this chapter.)

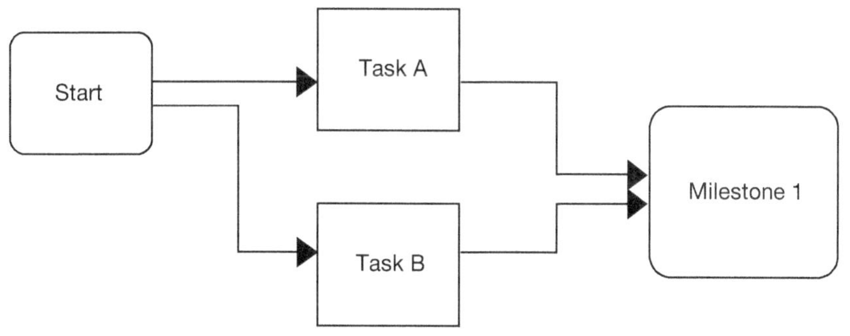

Figure 4-1. Blank network diagram with parallel tasks.

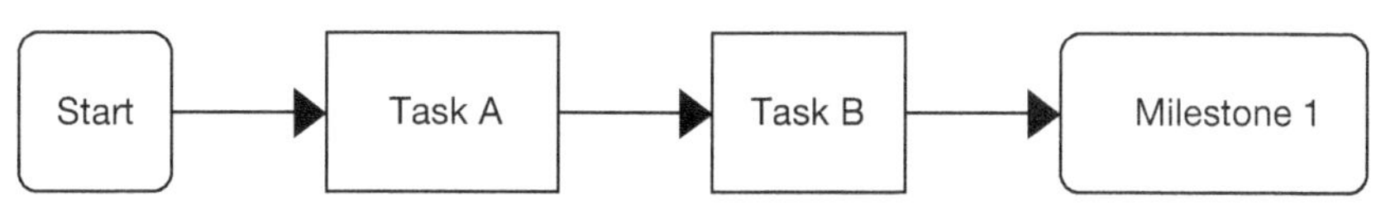

Figure 4-2. Blank network diagram with sequential tasks.

A network diagram is also useful for seeing the critical path on the procurement. The critical path consists of the tasks that, if delayed, will delay the entire procurement. For example, if the RFP is not sent out on time, the entire procurement will be delayed. *Important*: Making sure the estimated effort and duration for the RFP drafting and review are adequate and reasonable is essential. Check it and double-check it. The same is true for all tasks on the critical path.

Now for the contrarian opinion—the critical path is overrated. If you develop a reasonable schedule, do not have imposed deadlines that are unreasonable, and manage the schedule well, identifying the critical path is not needed in most procurements. Many professional project managers have never identified a critical path for any project. We will continue to discuss critical path, however, because people who have only read about project management, and have not actually done it, think the critical path is important. Some professional project managers even believe the critical path is, well, *critical* for project success.

Complexity is associated with critical path. Not all tasks on the critical path are as critical as others. Delays in some tasks on the critical path may cause only slight delays in the procurement. Those delays can be absorbed by the contingency in your schedule that we discussed earlier. Other tasks will delay the procurement beyond the contingency and cause you to need to change the schedule. These tasks are priorities and can be placed on a priority task list. This priority list is a management tool for you to use. By maintaining and reviewing the priority task list, you stay focused on the important 20% and make better decisions when changes occur. *Important*: Regardless of the priority task list or critical path list, when task dependencies, durations, or effort estimates change, you need to reevaluate both the critical path and priority task list.

The Program Evaluation and Review Technique (PERT)

Although many people use the term “a PERT chart,” what they really mean is a network diagram. In reality, PERT, or the Program Evaluation and Review Technique, is a technique used in determining the best estimates for task effort and duration.

Standard PERT methodology (the way of doing it) uses an accepted algorithm (equation) for coming up with a reasonable estimate of a task’s effort and duration. PERT methodology uses three efforts (durations) and three weighting factors—one weighting factor for each duration. The durations (efforts) are:

OD = Optimistic duration	OE = Optimistic effort
MD = Most likely duration	ME = Most likely effort
PD = Pessimistic duration	PE = Pessimistic effort

The weighting factors are:

OWF = Optimistic weighting factor
MWF = Most likely weighting factor
PWF = Pessimistic weighting factor

The weighting factors are traditionally set between 1 and 4:

OWF = 1
MWF = 4
PWF = 1

Weighting the most likely duration (MD) higher than the other two durations (OD and PD) automatically provides a reasonable estimate. Making the pessimistic weighting factor (PWF) higher than the optimistic weighting factor (OWF), for example, 2 and 1, respectively, means that you are not as confident in the MD estimate. Making the OWF higher than the PWF means that you think the MD is too conservative. This explanation applies to effort as well. The algorithm is:

$$\text{Expected Duration} = ((\text{OD} \times \text{OWF}) + (\text{MD} \times \text{MWF}) + (\text{PD} \times \text{PWF})) \div (\text{OWF} + \text{MWF} + \text{PWF})$$

$$\text{Expected Effort} = ((\text{OE} \times \text{OWF}) + (\text{ME} \times \text{MWF}) + (\text{PE} \times \text{PWF})) \div (\text{OWF} + \text{MWF} + \text{PWF})$$

As an example calculation, let's say a task has the following effort estimates.

OE = 2 hours
ME = 6 hours
PE = 12 hours

We assign the following weighting factors, using our experience and the experience of others:

OWF = 1
MWF = 4
PWF = 2

The algorithm is:

$$((2 \times 1) + (6 \times 4) + (12 \times 2)) \div (1 + 4 + 2) = 50 \div 7 = 7.14 \text{ hours}$$

You can round down to 7 hours for this task or round up to 8 hours. Again, rely on your experience or other people's experience to make that decision.

By using a weighting factor of 2 for the pessimistic estimate of effort (PE) and a factor of 1 for the optimistic estimate of effort (OE), you are saying that you think the most likely estimate of effort (ME) is too low. Thus, the math supports the decision.

To get the best estimate for your schedule, do this for every task. If you are using project management software, the software can do this for you. *Caution*: Make sure you understand how the software you are using *calculates everything* before you use it. Some managers have failed to deliver a realistic schedule because they did not adequately understand the software or the theory of project management or both.

Inputs

Your schedule needs to be accurate, realistic, and workable in order for your procurement to synchronize. To be accurate, realistic, and workable, you will use the task list and WBS that you developed for the procurement plan and the network diagram that you will develop next. Working with every one of your team members, come up with realistic durations for each task and a realistic duration for each milestone. These durations will give you the overall duration for the procurement. Several inputs are required to develop a schedule:

Documented schedule assumptions. Even though some people think that documenting assumptions for small or simple procurements is not necessary, it truly is. Not only will documenting assumptions get you in the habit of thinking about the assumptions on every procurement, but it will also provide a documented record of what you were thinking and why you performed the procurement as you did. Documenting assumptions can teach others what to include, or not, in their procurements. And, unfortunate as it is, documenting assumptions helps you make your case if you are called to answer for a failed procurement. Schedule assumptions are primarily found in two areas—resources and dates. Each procurement will start with these assumptions:

- Resources: Are the right people for your team available to work on this procurement when you need them? What about equipment or facilities? Can you add people to the team in order to meet schedule priorities? Can you pay overtime for work on weekends? Are all the people suggested for your team trained for the work that's expected from them?

- Drop-dead date: What is the "drop-dead date" or the date by which the contract must be executed? If necessary, can you add resources to get the contract done by this date? Can you negotiate this date after you have a realistic schedule?

More complex procurements will have more assumptions, but the assumptions do not necessarily become more complex.

Task list. You have developed a high-level task list already that includes the milestones for your procurement. The task list that you will use for the schedule must be very detailed. *Remember*: The smallest breakdown of tasks must still be trackable—assigned a task duration. Some experts say to break tasks down to a time unit smaller than the reporting periods. For example, if you have a status meeting every week, your smallest tasks can be at the minute level, but you would not have a task that covers more than a week. If you have a procurement that will take more than a year, and you have status meetings every month, then you could break down tasks to the daily or weekly level, but not to more than one month in duration. Your team is the single most important source of information in putting together the task list. Each member needs to think about the tasks involved in their piece of the procurement and provide you with the task list for it. You can also use other procurement professionals, either those you work with or professionals outside of your company, to get better task lists. Experience is the real way to learn what works best, and procurement professionals have that experience.

Calendar. You will need to use a calendar to assign dates to the beginning and ending of each task. The calendar will help you avoid scheduling work on weekends and holidays. The calendar will help you know when team members will take time off during the procurement. It will also help your team to know when to schedule time off without adversely impacting your procurement. You can maintain a procurement calendar in addition to the schedule. It can be handy for a quick reference for managing the procurement.

Figure 4-3 shows all of the tasks required to complete the procurement for *Case Study 2: Janitorial Services*. Please note that each of the subtasks listed under "Brainstorm" are of very short duration. Tasks at this level do not need to be listed in any schedule—they are listed here as a *prompt* so you will know tasks that will be covered in the initial brainstorming session. The same is true for the subtasks under "Establish the procurement team."

Task Description
Procurement for Janitorial Services
Receive RFPS
Brainstorm
Strategy
Mutual non-disclosure agreement
Contract type
Length of agreement
Sourcing approach
Review current and historical supplier contracts
Identify all stakeholders
Establish the procurement team
Decide what skills are required
Find out who has required skills
Find out availability of these people
Get these people assigned to procurement team
Define roles and responsibilities
Silent period with existing supplier
Establish a high-level schedule
Kick-Off Meeting
Decide on date for meeting
Reserve meeting room
Create agenda
Send out agenda
Receive comments/additons to agenda
Resend amended agenda
Hold meeting
Develop action list and/or meeting minutes
Send out action list/minutes
Receive comments/additions to action list/minutes
Resend action list/minutes

Figure 4-3. Complete task list for Case Example 2: Janitorial Services.

Task Description
Procurement Plan
Finalize procurement strategy
Review strategy with team members
Develop procurement WBS
Review WBS with team members
Develop procurement schedule
Review schedule with team members
Develop procurement budget
Review budget with team members
Develop procurement communications plan
Review communications plan with team members
Develop procurement risk plan
Review risk plan with team members
Review procurement plan with entire team
Finalize procurement plan
Distribute procurement plan
Solicitation
Silent period with potential suppliers and existing supplier
Draft RFP
Memorial Day holiday
RFP Schedule
Review with team
Statement of Work (Scope of Work)
Review with team
Determine type of agreement document
Sample terms and conditions
Develop pricing model
RFP general instructions
Mutual non-disclosure agreement
Proposal signature page
Develop weighted evaluation criteria
Review with evaluation team

Figure 4-3. Complete task list for Case Example 2: Janitorial Services (continued).

Task Description
MWDBE certification
HUB certification
Form W-9
Review entire RFP with team
Make changes as required
Distribute to team for final review
Commodity strategy
Industry/commodity profile analysis
Purchasing profile
Supplier financial analysis
Total cost of ownership
Determine qualified supplier bid list
Contact names and information
Send all information to SSM
Finalize RFP
Send RFP out
RFP Process
RFP silent period with potential suppliers an existing supplier
Receive questions on RFP
Assemble questions and answers
Send out assembled questions and answers to all participants
Proposal Analysis
Receive proposals
Reject all proposals that are not signed
Reject all proposals submitted after the deadline
Distribute all acceptable proposals to evaluation team
Team evaluates all proposals independently
4th of July holiday
Team returns all evaluations
Review and collate all evaluations
Distribute collated evaluations to team
Evaluation team meets to decide on top proposals

Figure 4-3. Complete task list for Case Example 2: Janitorial Services (continued).

Task Description
Collect questions on proposals for short-listed potential suppliers
Notify short list
Schedule oral presentations
Verify date and time with each company
Reserve meeting room
Notify evaluation team
Oral presentations
Make sure someone greets presenters
Make sure equipment is ready and working
Make sure refreshments are ready
Questions
Prepared and who will ask each one
As presentation is given
Thank yous and walking presenters out
Meeting to decide on contract awardee
Negotiations
Develop negotiation strategy
Where negotiation takes place
Win-win or hard ball
Identify negotiation team
Fully identify and communicate roles
Conduct Negotiations
Finalize deal including terms and conditions
Contract Finalization
Draft contract
Review contract
Obtain approval signatures
Labor Day holiday
Execute contract
Notification of Unsuccessful Suppliers
Preliminary notification
Formal debriefing
Contract Administration

Figure 4-3. Complete task list for Case Example 2: Janitorial Services (continued).

Before leaving this section on scheduling, let's review the definitions of some of the terms we have been using in this chapter (also refer to Table 1-2 in Chapter 1):

Activity: same as task (in this book)
Buy-in: agreement to concept or specifics
Contingency: time available in case things go wrong
Critical path: sequence of tasks that determine the minimum schedule for a procurement (if even one task on the critical path is delayed, the schedule will be late)
Duration: span of time over which the effort takes place
Effort: amount of work or labor required to complete a task
Float: amount of time for a task to be scheduled without affecting other tasks; the difference between the duration available for a task and the effort required to complete it; also known as slack
Lag: amount of time after one task is started before the next task can be started *or* the amount of time after one task is completed before the next task can be completed
Loading: amount of time each person (resource) has committed to the procurement
Milestone: a clearly identifiable point that summarizes the completion of a related or important set of tasks; commonly used to summarize the important events in a procurement for those who do not need to see the details
Padding: adding extra time to estimates
Precedence: one task must be finished before another task can be started; the first task has precedence over the second
Resource leveling: distributing the work among different resources, e.g., one person may have too much work to do in a 40-hour week so divide the work between two people
Slack: same as float
Subtask: a step required to complete a task; can be tracked
Task: a cohesive unit of work requiring resources and time; can be tracked

DEVELOPING A SCHEDULE

Nine major steps are required in developing a schedule (timeline). When you have gained sufficient experience, these steps will become so simple that they will feel like you are doing only one step. Until then, do all nine steps every time.

Step 1. List Tasks

Use your team and other experts to compile the task list (discussed in Chapter 3).

Step 2. Create the WBS

The WBS is the assignment of a level to each task. These levels determine task sequence and identify milestones (discussed in Chapter 3).

Step 3. Identify Milestones

In developing the task list, WBS, and network diagram, you identified milestones. Take another look at the procurement to make sure all milestones have been identified and sequenced.

Step 4. Assign Responsible People

To assign the responsible people, you have to know who is available and has the skill sets and knowledge that you need. When these people have been assigned to your team, you can assign responsibility for each task to the person (or people) who will actually do the work. Milestones are assigned to the responsible person—the person who makes sure the work is completed well and on time.

Step 5. Develop Network Diagrams

Network diagrams were discussed in a previous section (*Network Diagrams*), so in this step, we will only discuss the symbols used and how precedence works. The symbols used for network diagrams are simple and easy to understand:

A task is shown in a square-cornered box:

A milestone is shown in a round-cornered box:

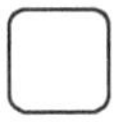

Lines with arrowheads are used to show which task(s) needs to be done before another task(s):

Precedence for sequential tasks is shown in this way:

Precedence for parallel milestones is shown in this way:

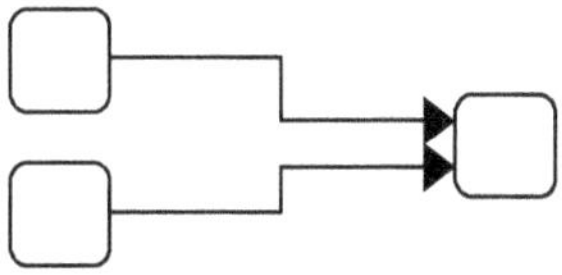

Concurrent tasks or milestones are shown as boxes on different lines with no lines or arrows showing precedence. No precedence is necessary for concurrent tasks. Concurrent tasks occur infrequently in most procurement schedules.

Step 6. Estimate Task Effort

Using your team and other experts, estimate the amount of time required to actually perform each task. It is wise to come up with three estimates: optimistic, most likely, and pessimistic. As discussed earlier in the PERT section, the optimistic estimate assumes everything will go exactly as planned. This never happens! (Have you heard of Murphy's law? See Chapter 7, *Risk*, if you have not.) Something always goes wrong.

The most likely effort estimate includes time for other things that might happen. These things are not unexpected, but are usually things that interrupt the flow of work. Some examples are telephone calls, emails, impromptu meetings, etc. This is the time to think about the average productivity of each day. Remember that in an eight-hour day, an employee might only get six hours of actual work completed. Allow for that productivity level here.

The pessimistic effort estimate includes many things going wrong. Include other risks to the effort in the pessimistic effort estimate. Talk to your team members. Each one of them knows the risks that they deal with every day. Maybe it is a manager who calls daylong meetings without notice, or a vice president who likes to drop in and chat for a while, or any one of hundreds of other threats to getting the work done in the amount of time that it *should* take.

When you have all of the effort estimates, you and your team need to do PERT. After the PERT is complete, you have the estimated task effort for your procurement schedule.

Step 7. Estimate Task Duration and Assign Dates

Using a similar method as in Step 6 (*Estimate Task Effort*), estimating task duration includes the use of a calendar. The difference is that you need to put this estimate together by yourself and then have your team review it. To do this step, you must have each team member's:

- Regular work schedule
- Time off schedule
- Time out of the office schedule
- Overtime permission from management (if necessary)
- Company's holiday schedule

Assigning dates for each task can be daunting at first. It is best to start at the beginning and work each task in sequence order. This process is an iterative one—you will repeat parts of this process as you work on each task. Looking at the calendar, assign a start and finish date for a particular task. Then look at the responsible employee's time off schedule—you might need to add a week to the finish date for that task. Next look at the company's holiday schedule to see dates that you need to change. *Important*: Every duration is subject to change until all of the variables have been considered. Even after the procurement plan has been approved and the schedule becomes the baseline, changes can occur. If your contingency is enough, these changes might not adversely impact the overall schedule.

Step 7 will let you know if the expected deadline for the procurement is reasonable—or not. If you are dealing with an imposed deadline, you can use this information to show that the estimated schedule is reasonable and that the imposed deadline is not.

The first time you estimate task durations and assign dates may take a while. Be patient. Have your team review your task durations and date assignments against their work calendars. The team members will let you know of any conflicts that you might have overlooked. Remember that these estimates and dates are not complete until the entire procurement plan has been approved.

Step 8. Review the Schedule

The final step in developing your schedule is to have your team review the entire schedule. Any managers or executives who are responsible for approving the procurement plan should review the schedule, too. They can provide valuable insight about unpublished activities that can adversely impact the estimated schedule. These managers and executives may also have experience that indicates some of the effort or duration is not reasonable. Some questions to ask when the schedule is under review include:

- Are tasks properly sequenced?
- Are milestones identified?
- Is all precedence identified and necessary?
- Are any tasks/milestones missing?

Step 9. Control the Schedule

After the procurement plan is approved, your schedule changes from an estimate to the baseline schedule for your procurement. As the procurement lead, you need to:

- Influence factors that create changes (make sure they are either beneficial or mitigated).
- Know about the changes (change requests).
- Manage the schedule when changes occur.

Everything that changes the schedule must be managed in order to meet the deadlines within the schedule. Remember that changes in resources, budget, and risk also need to be reflected in the schedule. Some tasks will be completed ahead of schedule (before the finish date assigned) and some will take longer than scheduled. Change requests can take different forms: oral or written, direct or indirect, external or internal, legally mandated, or entirely optional. Your job is to make sure each change is well documented and that the updated schedule reflects the baseline as well as the change (the new date).

Schedule updates need to be issued as soon as possible to the team members who are directly affected. The rest of the team can be notified during regular status meetings. Also report the task completion levels on the schedule. A Gantt chart is a great way to do this because it shows in graphic form exactly how much duration was scheduled and how much is complete as of now.

Now it is time to do a step-by-step schedule, including a task list, WBS, network diagram, and Gantt chart.

STEP-BY-STEP SCHEDULE DEVELOPMENT

We will develop a schedule using a spreadsheet in this section. If you are unfamiliar with spreadsheets, you can develop a schedule by hand. Using a spreadsheet, however, is easier because software facilitates changes. Sorting information is also easier with a spreadsheet. Project management software will do some of the work for you, but you need to know what needs to be done and how to do it. Remember that this scheduling technique has been used since people carved in stone, so no choice of preparation method is incorrect. Now open that spreadsheet or pull out that paper. Here we go.

Step 1. List Tasks

You and your team put together the task list by thinking about the work that needs to be done and by listing the tasks necessary to get the work done. Using *Case Example 2: Janitorial Services* from Chapter 3 as an example, the task list could start with these milestones:

Receive RFPS
Kick-Off Meeting

Procurement Plan
Solicitation
Negotiations
Contract Execution
Contract Administration

You will then decompose each of these milestones into tasks—meaning you will list all of the tasks that have to be done for each milestone to be completed. The decomposition of Receive RFPS could look like this:

Receive RFPS
  Brainstorm
  Review current and historical supplier contracts
  Identify all stakeholders
  Establish the procurement team
  Communicate silent period with current supplier
  Develop a high-level schedule

Then, along with your team, you will decompose these activities further. The time to stop decomposing is when a task cannot be measured. In other words, the task is too small to assign time to it. The next level of tasks could be:

Receive RFPS
  Brainstorm
  Strategy
  Review current and historical supplier contracts
  Identify all stakeholders
  Establish the procurement team
  Skills required
  Who has the skills?
  Availability of these people
  Seek their assignment to this procurement
  Define roles and responsibilities
  Communicate silent period with current supplier
  Develop a high-level schedule

Can these tasks be decomposed even further? Yes. This is the time to list everything and make choices about what to actually include on the task list later. Your task list could now look like this:

Receive RFPS
  Brainstorm
  Strategy

Use a mutual non-disclosure agreement?
Contract type
Length of agreement
Sourcing approach to use
Review current and historical supplier contracts
Find files on intranet or in file room
Talk with other procurement professionals who have done this type of procurement before
Talk with financial analysts who have experience in this industry
Identify all stakeholders
Who has to sign in order to get approvals?
Who can make final decisions?
What areas of responsibility does each person have?
Who needs to be included for political reasons?
Who will be assigned for political reasons?
Establish the procurement team
Skills required
Who has the skills?
Availability of these people
Seek their assignment to this procurement
Define roles and responsibilities
Communicate silent period with current supplier
Write a formal letter
Mail it with return receipt required
Develop a high-level schedule
All major milestones

Continue the task list in this way. Each member of your team will do this type of listing for his or her part(s) of the work. Integrating all of the team members' tasks into one task list is a good idea. It is better for one person to do the integration (instead of asking two or more people to do it). Involving more than one person creates too much confusion and opportunity to drop important tasks. After the entire list is put together, review each task with this question in mind: *how do I assign a time to this task?* If the answer is *it can be done,* then keep that task in the list. If the answer is *it cannot be done,* then take that task out of the list. During the team review of the task list, if any member of your team wants to keep a task in the list that you think should be removed, ask that team member exactly how much time they would assign to it. If the person has a quick answer, consider leaving the task in the list. If not, remove the task from the list and move on.

When you first put a task list together, you need to indent the tasks that are required to complete the task above them. For example, the list below is indented to show the relationships between tasks. The indents are not an indicator of dependency or priority:

Receive RFPS
- Brainstorm
  - Strategy
- Review current and historical supplier contracts
- Identify all stakeholders
- Establish the procurement team
  - Skills required
  - Who has the skills?
  - Availability of these people
  - Seek their assignment to this procurement
  - Define roles and responsibilities
- Communicate silent period with current supplier
- Develop a high-level schedule

Figure 4-3 shows all of the tasks that are important for completing your procurement. Your task list may vary from this one. That is okay. As long as all of the work is accounted for, your schedule will be accurate.

The next step is to assign the WBS to the task list. Assigning the WBS to the task list provides you with an opportunity to refine the task list further.

Step 2. Create the WBS

You will assign levels to every task in the task list, creating the WBS. The method for assigning levels of the WBS has become standardized, thanks to computer software that does this for you. In this discussion, however, we will do the assigning ourselves so that you will understand the reasoning and methodology behind it. It is difficult to know if the results that a program spits out are reasonable if you have no knowledge of what the program is supposed to do.

Usually the overall procurement is given a WBS level. Some people start with 1.0, while other people start with 0.0. The argument for starting with 0.0 is that the overall procurement is not a task or milestone. Conversely, the argument for starting with 1.0 is that the overall procurement is the most important milestone. If the people you work with already use a WBS, find out what they do. It is important for this tool to communicate information to the people who read it—this happens more easily when they see a format that they are familiar with.

The convention for a WBS is to use X.0 for milestones and to bold the entire row of information for each milestone. For Case Example 2, the milestones would look like this:

0.0 Procurement for Janitorial Services
1.0 Receive RFPS
2.0 Kick-Off Meeting
3.0 Procurement Plan
4.0 Solicitation
5.0 Negotiations
6.0 Contract Execution
7.0 Contract Administration

The next level of tasks in the task list will be assigned X.1 (and more digits), which allows each task to be identified independently while showing where in the task list the task belongs. We are also beginning the setting up of precedence—the dependencies of tasks. This level of tasks now looks like this:

0.0 Procurement for Janitorial Services
1.0 Receive RFPS
1.1 Brainstorm
1.1.2 Strategy
1.1.2.1 Mutual non-disclosure agreement
1.1.2.2 Contract type
1.1.2.3 Length of agreement
1.1.2.4 Sourcing approach
1.2 Review current and historical supplier contracts
1.3 Identify all stakeholders
1.4 Establish the procurement team
1.4.1 Decide what skills are required
1.4.2 Find out who has these skills
1.4.3 Find out availability of these people
1.4.4 Get these people assigned to the procurement team
1.4.5 Define roles and responsibilities
1.5 Silent period with existing supplier
1.6 Establish a high-level schedule

Continue with this numbering system throughout the task list. Complex procurements will have many more levels than simple procurements.

As noted earlier in this section, using a spreadsheet makes assigning the levels much easier. With a spreadsheet, you can see all of the levels at once, insert a row to add a task, delete a row to remove a task, etc. The WBS should be located in the far left column of the spreadsheet. Figure 4-4 shows how the WBS looks on a spreadsheet.

Now you will identify milestones in your procurement.

WBS	Task Description
0.0	**Procurement for Janitorial Services**
1.0	**Receive RFPS**
1.1	Brainstorm
1.1.2	Strategy
1.1.2.1	Mutual non-disclosure agreement
1.1.2.2	Contract type
1.1.2.3	Length of agreement
1.1.2.4	Sourcing approach
1.2	Review current and historical supplier contracts
1.3	Identify all stakeholders
1.4	Establish the procurement team
1.4.1	Decide what skills are required
1.4.2	Find out who has required skills
1.4.3	Find out availability of these people
1.4.4	Get these people assigned to procurement team
1.4.5	Define roles and responsibilities
1.5	Silent period with existing supplier
1.6	Establish a high-level schedule
2.0	**Kick-Off Meeting**
2.1	Decide on date for meeting
2.2	Reserve meeting room
2.3	Create agenda
2.4	Send out agenda
2.4.1	Receive comments/additons to agenda
2.4.2	Resend amended agenda
2.5	**Hold meeting**
2.6	Develop action list and/or meeting minutes
2.7	Send out action list/minutes
2.7.1	Receive comments/additions to action list/minutes
2.7.2	Resend action list/minutes

Figure 4-4. Complete WBS for Case Example 2: Janitorial Services.

WBS	Task Description
3.0	**Procurement Plan**
3.1	Finalize procurement strategy
3.1.1	Review strategy with team members
3.2	Develop procurement WBS
3.2.1	Review WBS with team members
3.3	Develop procurement schedule
3.3.1	Review schedule with team members
3.4	Develop procurement budget
3.4.1	Review budget with team members
3.5	Develop procurement communications plan
3.5.1	Review communications plan with team members
3.6	Develop procurement risk plan
3.6.1	Review risk plan with team members
3.7	Review procurement plan with entire team
3.8	Finalize procurement plan
3.9	Distribute procurement plan
4.0	**Solicitation**
4.1	Silent period with potential suppliers and existing supplier
4.2	Draft RFP
	Memorial Day holiday
4.2.1	RFP Schedule
4.2.1.1	Review with team
4.2.2	Statement of Work (Scope of Work)
4.2.2.1	Review with team
4.2.3	Determine type of agreement document
4.2.3.1	Sample terms and conditions
4.2.4	Develop pricing model
4.2.5	RFP general instructions
4.2.6	Mutual non-disclosure agreement
4.2.7	Proposal signature page
4.2.8	Develop weighted evaluation criteria
4.2.8.1	Review with evaluation team

Figure 4-4. Complete WBS for Case Example 2: Janitorial Services (continued).

WBS	Task Description
4.2.9	MWDBE Certification
4.2.10	HUB Certification
4.2.11	Form W-9
4.3	Review entire RFP with team
4.3.1	Make changes as required
4.3.2	Distribute to team for final review
4.4	Commodity strategy
4.4.1	Industry/commodity profile analysis
4.4.2	Purchasing profile
4.4.3	Supplier financial analysis
4.4.4	Total cost of ownership
4.4.5	Determine qualified supplier bid list
4.4.5.1	Contact names and information
4.4.5.2	Send all information to SSM
4.5	Finalize RFP
4.6	**Send RFP out**
5.0	**RFP Process**
5.1	RFP silent period with potential suppliers and existing supplier
5.2	Receive questions on RFP
5.2.1	Assemble questions and answers
5.2.2	Send out assembled questions and answers to all participants
6.0	**Proposal Analysis**
6.1	**Receive proposals**
6.1.1	Reject all proposals that are not signed
6.1.2	Reject all proposals submitted after the deadline
6.2	Distribute all acceptable proposals to evaluation team
6.3	Team evaluates all proposals independently
	4th of July holiday
6.4	Team returns all evaluations
6.5	Review and collate all evaluations
6.6	Distribute collated evaluations to team
6.7	Evaluation team meets to decide on top proposals

Figure 4-4. Complete WBS for Case Example 2: Janitorial Services (continued).

WBS	Task Description
6.8	Collect questions on proposals for short-listed potential suppliers
6.9	Notify short list
6.10	Schedule oral presentations
6.10.1	Verify date and time with each company
6.10.2	Reserve meeting room
6.10.3	Notify evaluation team
6.11	**Oral presentations**
6.11.1	Make sure someone greets presenters
6.11.2	Make sure equipment is ready and working
6.11.3	Make sure refreshments are ready
6.11.4	Questions
6.11.4.1	Prepared and who will ask each one
6.11.5.1	As presentation is given
6.12	Thank yous and walking presenters out
6.13	**Meeting to decide on contract awardee**
7.0	**Negotiations**
7.1	Develop negotiation strategy
7.1.1	Where negotiation takes place
7.1.2	Win-win or hard ball
7.2	Identify negotiation team
7.2.1	Fully identify and communicate roles
7.3	**Conduct negotiations**
7.3.1	Finalize deal including terms and conditions
8.0	**Contract Finalization**
8.1	Draft contract
8.1.1	Review contract
8.2	Obtain approval signatures
	Labor Day holiday
8.3	**Execute contract**
9.0	**Notification of Unsuccessful Suppliers**
9.1	Preliminary notification
9.2	Formal debriefing
10.0	**Contract Administration**

Figure 4-4. Complete WBS for Case Example 2: Janitorial Services (continued).

Step 3. Identify Milestones

We have already discussed milestones. We know that a milestone is a clearly identifiable point that summarizes the completion of an important set of tasks. Keep in mind that *important* is in the eye of the beholder. Tasks that are important to the procurement professional, for example, may not even matter to the SME or owner. (The most important things to the SME or the owner will be the dates of meetings and the contract execution date.) To accommodate all of the important sets of tasks, find out what is most important to each member of your team. Also find out what dates the executives in your company want to know. The rolled-up schedule (milestone schedule) needs to include the important events for those who do not need to see task-level details.

Identifying milestones allows you to manage the procurement. When you know that something has to happen no later than a specific date, you can juggle tasks to make that happen. You remind members of your team that certain work must be completed by a specific date. Also, you report the procurement status using the identified milestones.

Figure 4-5 shows a milestone list with the WBS. Procurement steps are listed as milestones. Some important meetings are shown as milestones.

WBS	Task Description
0.0	Procurement for Janitorial Services
1.0	Receive RFPS
2.0	Kick-Off Meeting
2.5	Hold meeting
3.0	Procurement Plan
4.0	Solicitation
4.6	Send RFP out
5.0	RFP Process
6.0	Proposal Analysis
6.1	Receive proposals
6.11	Oral presentations
6.13	Meeting to decide on contract awardee
7.0	Negotiations
7.3	Conduct negotiations
8.0	Contract Finalization
8.3	Execute contract
9.0	Notification of Unsuccessful Suppliers
10.0	Contract Administration

Figure 4-5. Milestone list for Case Example 2: Janitorial Services.

One milestone listed, "Notification of Unsuccessful Suppliers," might not be considered important enough to include as a milestone in your company, but notifying unsuccessful suppliers is a good practice. To make sure this happens, including it in the milestones list is completely acceptable.

If you use a spreadsheet to develop your schedule, as we are doing, you can simply Filter or Sort on the WBS column to get the milestone list (refer to your software user guide to learn how). We call this *rolling up tasks.* Using project management software makes this is very simple.

Next you will assign responsible people to the tasks/milestones.

Step 4. Assign Responsible People

Fundamental to management is assigning responsibilities to employees. No one can do a job unless they know what the job is. Expectations are set when responsibilities are defined. As the manager of this procurement, it is your job to assign responsibilities to your team members.

In order to assign people to be responsible for each task/milestone, you first need to know exactly who is on your team. When you have the task list completed, look at the skills, knowledge, and experience that you need to successfully complete your procurement. Decide which person on your team is the best fit in each skill area. Then list who they are and their role on this procurement.

Unfortunately, many companies assign your team without consulting you. If that happens to you, take the time before you start the schedule to analyze the skills that this procurement needs, compare the required skills against the skills of the people assigned to the team, and if necessary either argue your case to change the assigned personnel or document this difference in skills as a constraint to the procurement plan. A difference in skills can also be a risk to the plan (discussed in Chapter 7, *Risk*).

Table 4-2 shows the fictitious team for the example procurement we are using. Notice that initials follow each team member's name and that either initials

Table 4-2. Procurement Team for Case Example 2: Janitorial Services

Procurement Team	
Name	**Role**
Donna Smith (DS)	Strategic Sourcing Manager (SSM)
Robert Golden (RG)	Director of Procurement (DP)
James Brown (JB)	Financial Analyst (FA)
Bill Green (BG)	Subject Matter Expert (SME)
John Q. Public (JQP)	Owner
Samantha Grey (SG)	Attorney

or a short title follows each role on the team. Using initials for both the name and role in the spreadsheet schedule is simpler and takes up less space. You will use this table when you develop the communications plan within the procurement plan (discussed in Chapter 6, *Communications*). Project management software will insert the full name and role from a pivot table after you enter this information (when requested by the software).

Next is the network diagram.

Step 5. Develop Network Diagrams

We discussed network diagrams and their symbols and conventions earlier in this chapter. The network diagram is a graphic representation of the task list, WBS, and responsibility assignments. The network diagram is another chance to review the task list to make sure it is complete. Figure 4-6 shows a network diagram for the milestones of the Case Example 2 procurement. When you are

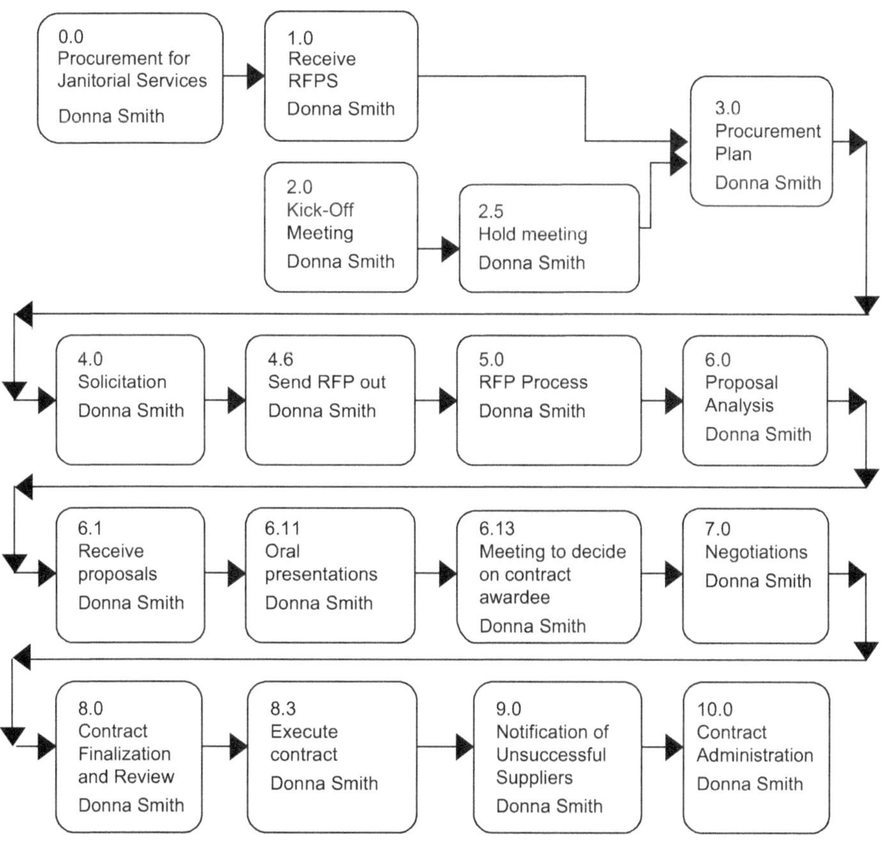

Figure 4-6. Milestone network diagram for Case Example 2: Janitorial Services.

managing a procurement, you will develop the network diagram for every task in that procurement.

Next is estimating task effort.

Step 6. Estimate Task Effort

Task effort is the amount of time that a task actually takes. Developing a schedule can take several hours, or several days, depending on the complexity of the procurement. Now, however, is not the time to consider the start and finish dates—that comes next.

We have already discussed how to get effort estimates from your team members, using three different estimates:

Optimistic
Most likely
Pessimistic

We have also discussed using PERT to get a weighted average of these estimates to come up with the expected effort.

Figure 4-7 shows the expected effort for each task. Note that the milestone effort is the sum of all the task efforts necessary to complete the milestone. For example, the Kick-Off Meeting duration is 6.00 hours, which may seem to be a very long meeting, but look at all of the tasks required to complete the kick-off meeting and you can see why 6.00 hours may be necessary.

If you are developing your own schedule for our example procurement, your durations may differ significantly from these. That is okay. Your assumptions will probably differ from those used here. Our assumptions are:

- Every member of the team has at least 10 years of experience in their role.
- The procurement lead, Donna Smith, has 20 years of experience.

Looking at WBS 3.3 (Develop procurement schedule), you see that the expected effort to develop this schedule is 4.00 hours. That is the time for Donna Smith, who is assumed to be very experienced developing schedules, to draft enough of the schedule that the rest of her team can review it and make changes. The effort required for those tasks, reviewing and making changes, is included separately.

Next is task duration estimates and assigning dates.

WBS	Task Description	Effort (Hours)
0.0	**Procurement for Janitorial Services**	**321.75**
1.0	**Receive RFPS**	**7.50**
1.1	Brainstorm	1.25
1.1.2	Strategy	0.25
1.1.2.1	Mutual non-disclosure agreement	0.25
1.1.2.2	Contract type	0.25
1.1.2.3	Length of agreement	0.25
1.1.2.4	Sourcing approach	0.25
1.2	Review current and historical supplier contracts	2.00
1.3	Identify all stakeholders	1.00
1.4	Establish the procurement team	1.00
1.4.1	Decide what skills are required	0.20
1.4.2	Find out who has these skills	0.20
1.4.3	Find out availability of these people	0.20
1.4.4	Get these people assigned to procurement team	0.20
1.4.5	Define roles and responsibilities	0.20
1.5	Silent period with existing supplier	0.25
1.6	Establish a high-level schedule	2.00
2.0	**Kick-Off Meeting**	**6.00**
2.1	Decide on date for meeting	0.25
2.2	Reserve meeting room	0.25
2.3	Create agenda	0.50
2.4	Send out agenda	0.50
2.4.1	Receive comments/additons to agenda	0.50
2.4.2	Resend amended agenda	0.50
2.5	**Hold meeting**	**1.50**
2.6	Develop action list and/or meeting minutes	0.50
2.7	Send out action list/minutes	0.50
2.7.1	Receive comments/additions to action list/minutes	0.50
2.7.2	Resend action list/minutes	0.50
3.0	**Procurement Plan**	**27.75**
3.1	Finalize procurement strategy	0.50
3.1.1	Review strategy with team members	1.00
3.2	Develop procurement WBS	6.00
3.2.1	Review WBS with team members	1.00

Figure 4-7. Complete task effort for Case Example 2: Janitorial Services.

WBS	Task Description	Effort (Hours)
3.3	Develop procurement schedule	4.00
3.3.1	Review schedule with team members	1.00
3.4	Develop procurement budget	
3.4.1	Review budget with team members	
3.5	Develop procurement communications plan	2.00
3.5.1	Review communications plan with team members	1.00
3.6	Develop procurement risk plan	2.00
3.6.1	Review risk plan with team members	1.00
3.7	Review procurement plan with entire team	4.00
3.8	Finalize procurement plan	4.00
3.9	Distribute procurement plan	0.25
4.0	**Solicitation**	**73.75**
4.1	Silent period with potential suppliers and existing supplier	0.25
4.2	Draft RFP	73.50
	Memorial Day holiday	
4.2.1	RFP Schedule	4.00
4.2.1.1	Review with team	2.00
4.2.2	Statement of Work (Scope of Work)	8.00
4.2.2.1	Review with team	2.00
4.2.3	Determine type of agreement document	1.00
4.2.3.1	Sample terms and conditions	2.00
4.2.4	Develop pricing model	1.00
4.2.5	RFP general instructions	4.00
4.2.6	Mutual non-disclosure agreement	2.00
4.2.7	Proposal signature page	0.50
4.2.8	Develop weighted evaluation criteria	8.00
4.2.8.1	Review with evaluation team	2.00
4.2.9	MWDBE Certification	0.50
4.2.10	HUB Certification	0.50
4.2.11	Form W-9	0.50
4.3	Review entire RFP with team	1.00
4.3.1	Make changes as required	2.00
4.3.2	Distribute to team for final review	0.25
4.4	Commodity Strategy	22.25

Figure 4-7. Complete task effort for Case Example 2: Janitorial Services (continued).

WBS	Task Description	Effort (Hours)
4.4.1	Industry/Commodity Profile Analysis	4.00
4.4.2	Purchasing Profile	2.00
4.4.3	Supplier Financial Analysis	8.00
4.4.4	Total Cost of Ownership	4.00
4.4.5	Determine Qualified Supplier Bid List	2.00
4.4.5.1	Contact names and information	2.00
4.4.5.2	Send all information to SSM	0.25
4.5	Finalize RFP	8.00
4.6	**Send RFP out**	**2.00**
5.0	**RFP Process**	**12.25**
5.1	RFP silent period with potential suppliers and existing supplier	0.25
5.2	Receive questions on RFP	2.00
5.2.1	Assemble questions and answers	8.00
5.2.2	Send out assembled questions and answers to all participants	2.00
6.0	**Proposal Analysis**	**92.50**
6.1	**Receive proposals**	**8.00**
6.1.1	Reject all proposals that are not signed	4.00
6.1.2	Reject all proposals submitted after the deadline	4.00
6.2	Distribute all acceptable proposals to evaluation team	4.00
6.3	Team evaluates all proposals independently	20.00
	4th of July holiday	
6.4	Team returns all evaluations	2.00
6.5	Review and collate all evaluations	8.00
6.6	Distribute collated evaluations to team	2.00
6.7	Evaluation team meets to decide on top proposals	6.00
6.8	Collect questions on proposals for short listed potential suppliers	2.00
6.9	Notify short list	2.00
6.10	Schedule oral presentations	5.00
6.10.1	Verify date and time with each company	4.00
6.10.2	Reserve meeting room	0.50
6.10.3	Notify evaluation team	0.50
6.11	**Oral presentations**	**16.50**
6.11.1	Make sure someone greets presenters	1.00
6.11.2	Make sure equipment is ready and working	1.00

Figure 4-7. Complete task effort for Case Example 2: Janitorial Services (continued).

WBS	Task Description	Effort (Hours)
6.11.3	Make sure refreshments are ready	0.50
6.11.4	Questions	7.00
6.11.4.1	Prepared and who will ask each one	4.00
6.11.5.1	As presentation is given	1.50
6.12	Thank yous and walking presenters out	1.50
6.13	**Meeting to decide on contract awardee**	**4.00**
7.0	**Negotiations**	**34.00**
7.1	Develop negotiation strategy	8.00
7.1.1	Where negotiation takes place	4.00
7.1.2	Win-win or hard ball	4.00
7.2	Identify negotiation team	1.00
7.2.1	Fully identify and communicate roles	1.00
7.3	**Conduct Negotiations**	**8.00**
7.3.1	Finalize deal including terms and conditions	8.00
8.0	**Contract Finalization**	**62.00**
8.1	Draft contract	12.00
8.1.1	Review contract	8.00
8.2	Obtain approval signatures	40.00
	Labor Day holiday	
8.3	**Execute contract**	**2.00**
9.0	**Notification of Unsuccessful Suppliers**	**6.00**
9.1	Preliminary notification	4.00
9.2	Formal debriefing	2.00
10.0	**Contract Administration**	**N/A**

Figure 4-7. Complete task effort for Case Example 2: Janitorial Services (continued).

Step 7. Estimate Task Duration and Assign Dates

Estimating task duration and assigning dates go hand in hand. You use calendars for this step—individual calendars for your team members, holiday calendars, and company calendars. For every team member, and stakeholder, some dates are already scheduled for important meetings, vacations, conferences, etc. You must take this into account during this step. Your goal now is to complete the schedule.

Some experienced procurement managers put every holiday that the company observes into the schedule. Some put scheduled time off and time out of the office for each team member into the schedule. Using the technique of including scheduled time off and time out of the office for all team members allows each member of the team to see what is scheduled for every other team member. Including these times can make it easier for the procurement lead to manage the schedule. As you gain experience creating schedules, you will learn if this is a good method for you.

As we discussed earlier in this chapter, duration differs from effort. Duration is how many days, weeks, or months within which a task must be completed. Looking at a task that has an estimated effort of 24 hours, the first instinct we have is to give the task a duration of 3 days. But take a step back and look at the task differently. We know from an earlier discussion in this chapter that the most optimistic level of efficiency is 6 hours of work per working day, which translates to 80% efficiency, so we should assign the task a duration of 4 days:

$$(24 \div 6 = 4)$$

Did you notice the word *optimistic*? A wise manager avoids the optimistic estimate and moves to 5 days. When you look at the calendars, however, you see that the particular employee assigned to this task is scheduled for 2 weeks of vacation when the task needs to be done. So you come up with an effort of 24 hours and a duration of 3 weeks (15 working days). The duration of 3 weeks gives the employee 1 extra day to get back into working mode (and catch up on emails, calls, etc.).

Using calendars (individual calendars for the team members, holiday calendars, company calendars, and stakeholder calendars) is required to determine durations and start and finish dates. When you know the duration for each task, you then look at all of the calendars that affect your procurement and decide on an exact date when the task will start and an exact date when the task must be completed.

We have also discussed float (slack) time and padding. Duration is one area where many managers add padding. Padding is not necessary if you use a contingency task at the end of your schedule.

Figure 4-8 shows how the finished schedule will look. Notice that no WBS is assigned to holidays. You can choose to do that differently in your schedule.

WBS	Task Description	Predecessor	Owner	Role	Start Date	Finish Date	Effort (Hours)
0.0	**Procurement for Janitorial Services**		**DS**	**SSM**	**05/03/13**	**10/31/13**	**321.75**
1.0	**Receive RFPS**		**DS**	**SSM, DP**	**05/03/13**	**05/10/13**	**7.50**
1.1	Brainstorm	1.0	DS, RG	SSM, DP	05/07/13	05/07/13	1.25
1.1.2	Strategy	1.0	DS, RG	SSM, DP	05/07/13	05/07/13	0.25
1.1.2.1	Mutual non-disclosure agreement	1.0	DS, RG	SSM, DP	05/07/13	05/07/13	0.25
1.1.2.2	Contract type	1.0	DS, RG	SSM, DP	05/07/13	05/07/13	0.25
1.1.2.3	Length of agreement	1.0	DS, RG	SSM, DP	05/07/13	05/07/13	0.25
1.1.2.4	Sourcing approach	1.0	DS, RG	SSM, DP	05/07/13	05/07/13	0.25
1.2	Review current and historical supplier contracts	1.0	DS, RG	SSM, DP	05/06/13	05/06/13	2.00
1.3	Identify all stakeholders	1.0	DS, RG	SSM, DP	05/06/13	05/06/13	1.00
1.4	Establish the procurement team	1.0	DS, RG	SSM, DP	05/07/13	05/10/13	1.00
1.4.1	Decide what skills are required	1.0	DS, RG	SSM, DP	05/07/13	05/07/13	0.20
1.4.2	Find out who has these skills	1.4.1	DS, RG	SSM, DP	05/07/13	05/07/13	0.20
1.4.3	Find out availability of these people	1.4.2	DS, RG	SSM, DP	05/07/13	05/07/13	0.20
1.4.4	Get these people assigned to procurement team	1.4.3	DS, RG, JB, BG, JQP, SG	SSM, DP, FA, SME, Owner, Attorney	05/07/13	05/10/13	0.20
1.4.5	Define roles and responsibilities	1.0	DS	SSM	05/07/13	05/07/13	0.20

WBS	Task Description	Predecessor	Owner	Role	Start Date	Finish Date	Effort (Hours)
1.5	Silent period with existing supplier	1.0	DS, RG, JB, BG, JQP, SG	SSM, DP, FA, SME, Owner, Attorney	05/03/13	10/31/13	0.25
1.6	Establish a high-level schedule	1.1.2	DS	SSM	05/07/13	05/10/13	2.00
2.0	**Kick-Off Meeting**	**1.6**	**DS**	**SSM**	**05/13/13**	**05/17/13**	**6.00**
2.1	Decide on date for meeting	2.0	DS	SSM	05/13/13	05/13/13	0.25
2.2	Reserve meeting room	2.0	DS	SSM	05/13/13	05/13/13	0.25
2.3	Create agenda	2.0	DS	SSM	05/13/13	05/13/13	0.50
2.4	Send out agenda	2.0	DS	SSM	05/13/13	05/13/13	0.50
2.4.1	Receive comments/additons to agenda	2.4	DS	SSM	05/14/13	05/14/13	0.50
2.4.2	Resend amended agenda	2.4.1	DS	SSM	05/15/13	05/15/13	0.50
2.5	**Hold meeting**	**2.4**	**DS, JB, BG, JQP**	**SSM, FA, SME, Owner**	**05/17/13**	**05/17/13**	**1.50**
2.6	Develop action list and/or meeting minutes	2.5	DS	SSM	05/17/13	05/17/13	0.50
2.7	Send out action list/minutes	2.6	DS	SSM	05/17/13	05/17/13	0.50
2.7.1	Receive comments/additions to action list/minutes	2.7	DS	SSM	05/17/13	05/17/13	0.50
2.7.2	Resend action list/minutes	2 7.1	DS	SSM	05/20/13	05/20/13	0.50

Figure 4-8. Partial schedule for Case Example 2: Janitorial Services.

The full schedule for Case Example 2 is in Appendix B, Exhibit 4-8, *Schedule for Case Example 2: Janitorial Services*. The full schedule shows the holidays that fall within the procurement schedule.

Looking at the full schedule in Appendix B, Exhibit 4-8, *Schedule for Case Example 2: Janitorial Services*, you will see the contract execution (**8.3, Execute contract**) date is 9-9-13, a date that allows much less time than the requested date of 10-31-13. This is the time when you put a contingency into the schedule. The technique used to determine this contingency is much simpler than using a percentage of the overall schedule—it uses all of the time allotted for the procurement, 5-3-13 through 10-31-13. This technique for putting contingency into the schedule is not meant for people outside of your team to see. It should not be included in a milestone schedule, although a milestone schedule can have the contingency called out as a separate task at the end of the schedule if your management requires it. In this case, the "Contingency" task would start on 9-9-13 and finish on 10-31-13 or about 4 weeks (20 days) for contingency in a 6-month procurement. All assumptions for the full schedule are that:

- All team members have at least 10 years of experience
- No one works weekends
- No overtime is approved
- Team members will be taking time off during the procurement
- Ten submitted proposals for the RFP
- Three oral presentations (allow 4 hours for each, including questions from the team)

The final step in schedule development is reviewing the schedule.

Step 8. Review the Schedule

Before you turn in the procurement plan for approval, take some time to review the entire schedule in one sitting. Have your calendars handy and look closely at every task, effort, duration, start and finish dates, and responsibility assignments. Does it all make sense?

When your procurement plan is approved, this schedule becomes the baseline against which your procurement success is measured. Take a little extra time now to review it so that you have every opportunity to be successful.

Step 9. Control the Schedule

Figure 4-9 is the most common way to present a schedule. This Gantt chart is the major product of most project management software programs. By using a Gantt chart, everyone can easily see the tasks, start and finish dates, effort estimates, and

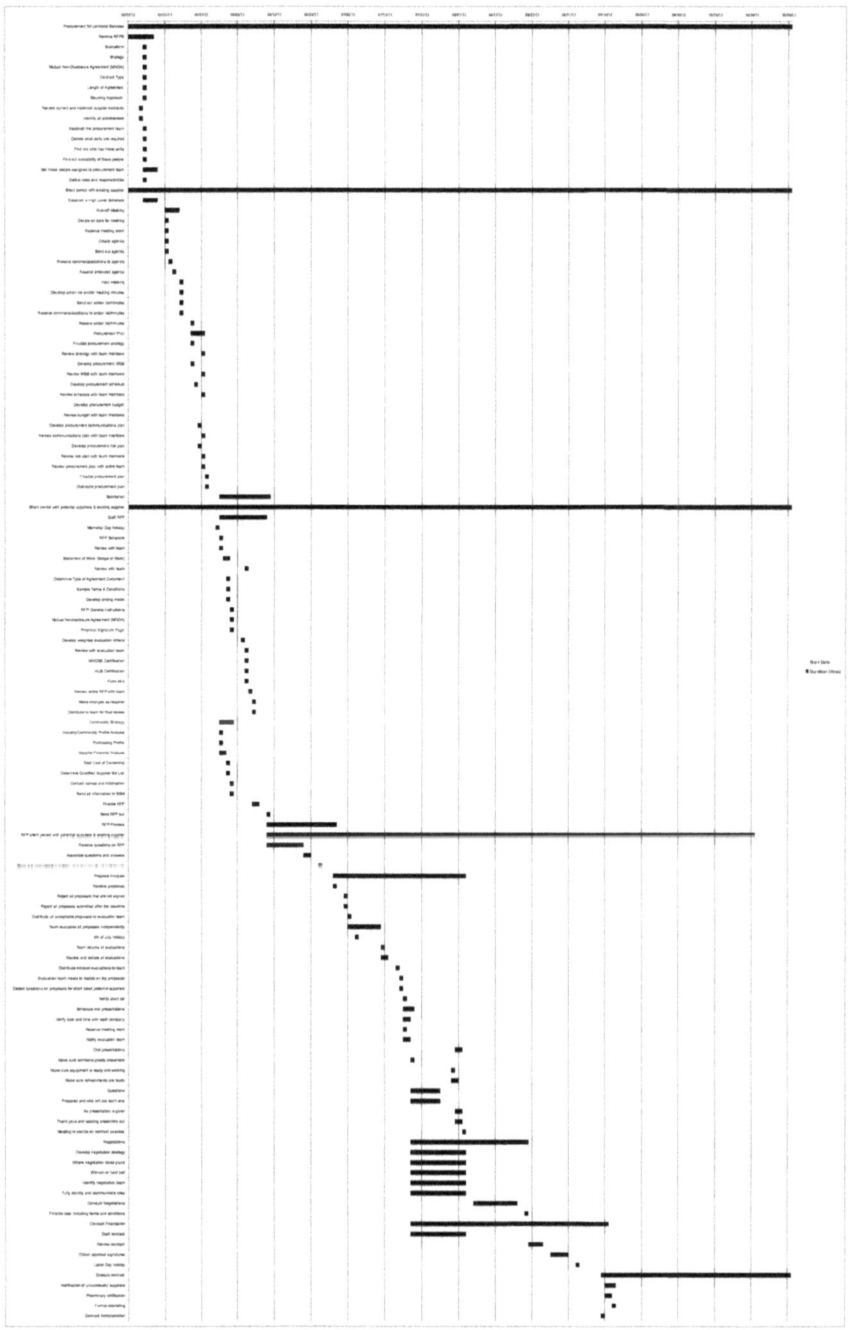

Figure 4-9. Gantt chart for Case Example 2: Janitorial Services.

duration estimates. All of the other information that is needed to understand the procurement schedule is available in the spreadsheet. If a project management program is used, all of the information will be available as a table to the left of the Gantt chart.

As the procurement progresses, you will update the schedule with completion percentages. Those will be reflected on the Gantt chart that the project management program produces when you enter the completion percentage into the program. Whether you do the schedule and the Gantt chart with a spreadsheet or by hand, you will be required to do the completion updates manually. Entering the completion updates manually takes a little more time than using project management software for a simple procurement, but doing them is necessary to monitor and control the schedule. For a complex procurement, you will want to use a project management program.

SUMMARY

This chapter has covered the schedule. The schedule is the single most important part of the procurement plan for ensuring success. The schedule is a communications tool to show:

- What is required for a procurement
- How long it takes to complete a procurement
- Who is involved and what each person does in the procurement
- When tasks/milestones will be started—and completed

One last thought about schedules. People who watch the TV series, *Star Trek*, and the movies it spawned, are familiar with the chief engineer, Scotty. When asked why he was able to pull off miracles, Scotty said that he tells the captain it will take much more time that it actually does. That is why Scotty is always the hero. Some people call this the "Scotty method" of reporting schedule. Make it your method and you will be successful more often than not.

We will talk about developing a budget in the next chapter.

This book has free material available for download from the Web Added Value™ resource center at *www.jrosspub.com.*

CHAPTER 5

BUDGET

The definition of *budget* as used in this book is:

A plan for allocating resources, especially money, during a particular period

Money for a particular purpose or period of time

DO YOU NEED A BUDGET?

Some procurements need a budget and some do not. If your company pays all of the procurement team out of an overhead (administrative) account, then you do not need a budget for your procurement. If, however, your company uses a project management organization model, you will probably need to develop a budget for your procurement. In a project management organization business model, all work is organized by project and all funds are allocated based on project. If you are the procurement SME for a specific project in your company (or agency), then you will definitely have to develop a budget for the procurement part of the project. Working closely with the project manager, your procurement budget will likely include all purchases made for the project, plus the costs for you and your team to do the work.

If you do not need to develop budgets where you work right now, this chapter should be of interest anyway. We will discuss a simple, straightforward way to develop budgets. This technique can be applied to any budget development—a personal budget, volunteer organization budget, etc. You never know what you will be doing next or where you might work in the future. By having the knowledge in this chapter, you could get a promotion or find a better paying job in another company where you will need to develop budgets.

WORDS OF CAUTION ABOUT ATTITUDES TOWARD PROCUREMENT

Whether your department is called Procurement, Purchasing, Supply Chain, Buying, Strategic Sourcing or something similar, people in many companies and agencies have entrenched attitudes about the department. Some of the comments that are made openly include:

"Purchasing doesn't save me money—they cost me more than doing it myself."

"Strategic Sourcing stands in the way of getting a contractor and getting the work done."

"We have our own attorney and we know the work that needs to be done. Why would we involve people who don't know anything about it?"

"Supply Chain is only for equipment purchases. We don't need them for services. We've always done it ourselves and the company's doing just fine."

Some project management books actively discourage using the procurement department "... unless they have proved helpful in a timely manner in the past." They also say things like "... get permission from senior executives to avoid working with them." And simply, "... avoid working with them." With attitudes like that, it is a wonder there are any jobs in procurement.

To offset negative opinions about the procurement department, one personal goal to aim for is to be the "go to" person for all purchasing in your company or for the business units you work with. To do that, developing a schedule and completing the work within it on time goes a long way—it may even be your most important tool for creating trust. Successfully completing the procurement within budget also cements your relationship and encourages using the procurement department.

Even if you do not need to submit a budget for a procurement, it helps to develop one. A budget can be used, along with the schedule, to educate people in the business units about the procurement department's value to them. If you add the estimate for your procurement to the estimated cost of the contract, you can show a business unit the total cost. For example, if the estimated value of the contract is $270,400 and the cost for the procurement is $34,560, then the business unit sees $304,960 as the *actual cost* of the contract for the first year. The business unit can then make a better decision about the financial feasibility of this effort. You added value just by developing a budget (that aided decision-making)—and it is only one more step than the schedule, which you will be doing anyway.

BUDGETING METHODS

The ultimate goal of any procurement is to get the best value for the money. That is your job as a procurement professional. Getting the best value for the money is also what adds value to your company—costs decrease, profits increase, legalities are observed, ethics are displayed, and your company stays in business. Several budgeting methods are used in business today.

Bottom-up budgeting. The most common budgeting method is bottom-up budgeting. In this method, employees estimate the budget at the task level. By doing it this way, the people with the most experience are estimating the costs of what they do. As in schedule development, the employees who actually do the work understand it more completely than managers or executives. The bottom-up budgeting method encourages discussion that is frank and direct. It also allows for team members to give each other ideas for better ways to get the work done. *Better* usually translates directly into lower costs.

Top-down budgeting. Less often used is top-down budgeting. A top-down budget is handed down from upper management. In the case of a top-down budget, a manager or executive uses his/her experience to estimate the costs of doing the procurement. Unless the manager or executive is highly experienced in doing procurements, many tasks will be left out and the budget will be inadequate.

Phased budgeting. The phased budgeting method is used for very long or complex procurements. The budget is developed for one phase of the procurement at a time. Although this method is frequently used in construction and software development, it is not found often in procurement.

The best method for budgeting is a combination of the bottom-up and top-down budgeting methods. This combination uses the experience of both workers and management. Top-down numbers establish general expectations and bottom-up numbers are the reality. This combined method ensures that budget expectations are grounded in reality.

Now let's look at creating a budget.

HOW TO CREATE A BUDGET

Creating a budget seems very simple and straightforward, and for many procurements it is. The more complex the procurement, however, the more complex the budgeting process will become. No matter how complex the budget is, you will follow a process. Again, this is an iterative process. The more complex the procurement, the more iterations you will need to do. Several steps are used to create a budget.

Step 1. Get Estimates

Get estimates for every task in the task list. Some ways to get the estimates include:

- Have your team give you estimates of their costs for the tasks for which they are responsible. This estimate includes any materials and equipment costs associated with the work. Just as with the schedule estimates, each team member will give you costs associated with the optimistic, most likely, and pessimistic time estimates. Using the PERT technique from Chapter 4, you will come up with an estimate for costs. It makes sense for you and your team to do both the cost estimates and the time estimates at the same time. This is when you see how closely related schedule and budget estimating are. Then you apply the PERT technique once and get a good estimate for both time and cost.
- When the product of a project is equipment or software, you must also get estimates from outside sources. Examples of outside sources are equipment vendors, materials distributors, software developers, etc. Although the product of the project is the purpose of the procurement, and will follow a typical procurement process, you need to supply a rough estimate to the project manager before the procurement starts in order for the project to get approval.
- Utilize the expertise of other managers and executives within your company.
- Consult SMEs inside your company or outside your company. (If you use outside experts, they add cost to the procurement.)
- Use standard pricing guides provided by government-regulated organizations. (The construction industry depends on these guides for estimating all costs.) Some companies also provide standard pricing. Even with pricing found on the Internet, you need to call to confirm that the pricing is accurate.

Step 2. Combine Estimates

Step 2 seems simple, but often it is not. If all it takes is doing the math, Step 2 *is* simple, but you will also be thinking about how realistic each estimate is after combining direct costs with indirect costs.

Direct costs include:

- Labor: actual cost of each person's time while they work on the procurement (salary)
- Supplies: actual cost of materials consumed by the procurement (paper, staples, etc.)

- Raw materials: usually part of the project product (not the actual procurement process)
- Equipment: usually part of the overall project (not the procurement process); exceptions include copiers, projectors, etc. used for procurement documents and presentations
- Travel: usually part of the overall project; applies to the procurement for attending project meetings, supplier location walk-throughs, etc.
- Legal fees: services provided by outside counsel for either the project or the procurement; for in-house counsel, use the actual salary
- Training: as required for the procurement team; possibly you will provide estimates for training of other project team members, project end users, or customers (project managers usually provide this estimate)
- Marketing/advertising: costs of product introduction, announcements, promotions, advertising, and public relations (project managers usually provide this estimate)

Indirect costs include:

- Employee benefits: some companies include employee benefits as a direct cost; more companies supply a percentage of all overhead costs for housing the employee (includes benefits, administrative overhead, facility costs, equipment costs, Internet and telephone service, etc.)
- Fees or licensing: state or county charges for business operations; most often included in administrative overhead
- Administrative overhead: costs for managers and support staff even though they do not work on the project/procurement; often referred to as "overheads" or "overhead costs" (many procurement professionals fall into this category)

Step 3. Add All Task Estimates

When you have completed the estimates for every task in the procurement, add them all up. The total gives you the beginning of an overall budget for this procurement effort.

Now you start the iteration process. The numbers that you have now are preliminary. The next step is to fine-tune each estimate. Use your entire procurement team to go over all the task estimates that you have. Review the documentation that exists. Check and double check that the numbers are the best estimation of actual costs. Make sure every task has been included.

Note: Using a spreadsheet for developing a budget is very common. The example schedule used in this book, Exhibit 4-8 in Appendix B, is already on a spreadsheet. You will add another column on this spreadsheet in order to input task estimates. Then you will have the spreadsheet calculate the total budget. Caution: Do calculations manually (with a calculator) in addition to setting up the spreadsheet to do the calculations for you. Equations in the cells could contain errors that would significantly change the final budget number.

Step 4. Determine Contingency

Just as in scheduling, budgeting is not exact. Use some contingency (also called *padding*) to allow for the unexpected. Many people will include a line item called "Contingency" at the end of their budget. Contingency uses the same line (row) as the schedule item for Contingency for the entire procurement. Each company has a preferred percentage of the budget to add for contingency, which can range from 10% to 100%. Ideally the percentage used should reflect your confidence in the estimates, but your company may dictate the percentage to use.

A contingency can get you into trouble if it is too much. Most of the time, a 100% contingency will get raised eyebrows—it confirms the belief that procurement adds costs, but not value.

Step 5. Present Budget

Presenting the budget is the final step before your budget is approved. When you are the procurement SME on a project, your budget will be presented to the project manager. The project manager may ask you to go back and reduce your number. If that happens, ask lots of questions. Find out how much—exactly—the project manager needs you to trim.

Negotiate with the project manager if the reduction requested is not realistic. Show the project manager your entire budget and explain the work that is required for the procurement. Get the reduction to an amount that can be absorbed by the contingency included in your budget. Then you still have a realistic chance at meeting the budget.

When the project manager has accepted your budget, and the project budget has been approved, this is the budget number you will be stuck with for the entirety of the procurement. Do everything you can to make sure your number is a realistic number.

If you are doing a procurement that is not specific to a project, for example, a service for a business unit, then you will present the budget to the owner of the procurement. Usually the owner is a manager or executive who is in charge of the business unit. The same concerns as above about obtaining a realistic budget number apply, so make sure you find out exactly what the owner needs as a final number.

Let's look at how to develop a realistic number.

STEP-BY-STEP BUDGET CREATION

The best way to learn is by doing. We will now create a budget for *Case Example 2: Janitorial Services*, the example that we have been using in previous chapters. There are two assumptions for this budget:

- Indirect costs are included in labor costs at 33% added to the employee's hourly salary.
- The procurement budget includes only the procurement process (this is a services procurement, not equipment or software).

Start with the procurement team. Using the first two columns of Table 3-1 from Chapter 3 (*Procurement Team*), add three columns for labor costs. Figure 5-1 is an example of the new table.

Name	Role	Direct Labor Cost ($)	Indirect Labor Cost ($)	Total per Hour ($)
Donna Smith (DS)	Strategic Sourcing Manager (SSM)	39.22	12.94	52.16
Robert Golden (RG)	Director of Procurement (DP)	47.89	15.80	63.69
James Brown (JB)	Financial Analyst (FA)	20.64	6.81	27.45
Bill Green (BG)	SME	31.39	10.36	41.75
John Q. Public (JQP)	Owner	88.97	29.36	118.33
Samantha Grey (SG)	Attorney	74.84	24.70	99.54

Figure 5-1. Procurement team direct/indirect costs for Case Example 2: Janitorial Services.

The salaries needed to produce Figure 5-1 are the actual amounts paid for each employee. (If your company will not give you that information, then you must obtain the salary + overhead amounts on an hourly basis.) For this example, the direct and indirect costs are determined this way:

Donna Smith	Annual salary $80,000	Overhead 33%
Robert Golden	Annual salary $97,688	Overhead 33%
James Brown	Annual salary $42,104	Overhead 33%
Bill Green	Annual salary $64,035	Overhead 33%
John Q. Public	Annual salary $181,500	Overhead 33%
Samantha Grey	Annual salary $152,678	Overhead 33%

Take each annual salary and divide by 2040 hours—the number of working hours in a year, assuming 40 hours per week. Using Donna Smith, a procurement professional with 20 years of experience, that gives us:

$$\$80{,}000 \div 2040 = \$39.22 \text{ per hour}$$

Adding in the overhead costs (indirect costs, $39.22 \times 0.33 = \$12.94$), we get total labor costs:

$$(\$39.22 + 12.94) = \$52.16 \text{ per hour}$$

To present this table to others, we use separate columns for Direct Labor Cost, Indirect Labor Cost, and Total per Hour. It is easier to explain the costs to busy executives, or project managers, if every component is listed separately.

Using the schedule that was developed in Chapter 4 (*Scheduling*), add a column to the right of Duration. This column is called Labor Costs. In the spreadsheet, you will enter equations in the cells in this column that will calculate the estimated amount of money for each task using the dollar amount from Total per Hour in Figure 5-1.

Now we have Figure 5-2 (the first 40 rows of the full budget). (*Note*: The full budget is found in Exhibit 5-2 in Appendix B.) In Figure 5-2 the total costs for the entire procurement ($34,558.46) will roll up into the task called **Procurement for Janitorial Services**, WBS **0.0.** Each milestone will consist of the costs of the tasks specific to it. For example, the first milestone is **Receive RFPS (1.0).** Then we have "Brainstorm" as a task under it. "Strategy" is under Brainstorm and consists of four tasks. Strategy and its four tasks will roll up to Brainstorm ($115.85), while Brainstorm is one task under **Receive RFPS**. Note that durations (in the Effort column) are indented. This is to indicate quickly which costs roll up and the milestones that they roll up into. (You may choose not to use this technique if you find it easier not to do so.)

Notice in the full budget in Exhibit 5-2 in Appendix B that no duration is indicated for holidays. Because no one is working, salaries and overheads are usually charged to a different account, not the project. (Some companies may charge holiday time to a project, however, so check with the project manager.) Now let's look at calculations for the budget.

The equation in each cell will differ, depending on if it is a milestone or not. Using Microsoft Excel, the equation for the milestone **Receive RFPS (1.0)** is:

=sum (J13,J19,J20,J21,J27,J28)

which adds the amounts in the cells corresponding to:

Brainstorm (J13)
Review current and historical supplier contracts (J19)
Identify all stakeholders (J20)
Establish the procurement team (J21)
Silent period with existing supplier (J27)
Establish a high-level schedule (J28)

	A	B	C	D	E	F
1	**Procurement Team**					
2		**Name**	**Role**	**Direct Labor Cost ($)**	**Indirect Labor Cost ($)**	**Total per Hour ($)**
3		Donna Smith (DS)	SSM	39.22	12.94	52.16
4		Robert Golden (RG)	DP	47.89	15.80	63.69
5		James Brown (JB)	FA	20.64	6.81	27.45
6		Bill Green (BG)	SME	31.39	10.36	41.75
7		John Q. Public (JQP)	Owner	88.97	29.36	118.33
8		Samantha Grey (SG)	Attorney	74.84	24.70	99.54
9						
10	**WBS**	**Task Description**	**Owner**	**Role**	**Effort (Hours)**	**Labor Costs**
11	**0.0**	**Procurement for Janitorial Services**	**DS**	**SSM**	**321.75**	**$34,558.46**
12	**1.0**	**Receive RFPS**	**DS**	**SSM, DP**	**7.50**	**$813.23**
13	1.1	Brainstorm	DS, RG	SSM, DP	1.25	$115.85
14	1.1.2	Strategy	DS, RG	SSM, DP	0.25	$28.96
15	1.1.2.1	Mutual non-disclosure agreement	DS, RG	SSM, DP	0.25	$28.96
16	1.1.2.2	Contract type	DS, RG	SSM, DP	0.25	$28.96
17	1.1.2.3	Length of agreement	DS, RG	SSM, DP	0.25	$28.96
18	1.1.2.4	Sourcing Approach	DS, RG	SSM, DP	0.25	$28.96
19	1.2	Review current and historical supplier contracts	DS, RG	SSM, DP	2.00	$231.69
20	1.3	Identify all stakeholders	DS, RG	SSM, DP	1.00	$115.85
21	1.4	Establish the procurement team	DS, RG	SSM, DP	1.00	$115.85
22	1.4.1	Decide what skills are required	DS, RG	SSM, DP	0.20	$23.17
23	1.4.2	Find out who has these skills	DS, RG	SSM, DP	0.20	$23.17
24	1.4.3	Find out availability of these people	DS, RG	SSM, DP	0.20	$23.17

Figure 5-2. Partial budget for Case Example 2: Janitorial Services.

	A	B	C	D	E	F
10	**WBS**	**Task Description**	**Owner**	**Role**	**Effort (Hours)**	**Labor Costs**
25	1.4.4	Get these people assigned to procurement team	DS, RG, JB, BG, JQP, SG	SSM, DP, FA, SME, Owner, Attorney	0.20	$80.58
26	1.4.5	Define roles and responsibilities	DS	SSM	0.20	$10.43
27	1.5	Silent period with existing supplier	DS, RG, JB, BG, JQP, SG	SSM, DP, FA, SME, Owner, Attorney	0.25	$100.73
28	1.6	Establish a high-level achedule	DS	SSM	2.00	$104.31
29	**2.0**	**Kick-Off Meeting**	**DS**	**SSM**	**6.00**	**$594.24**
30	2.1	Decide on date for meeting	DS	SSM	0.25	$13.04
31	2.2	Reserve meeting room	DS	SSM	0.25	$13.04
32	2.3	Create agenda	DS	SSM	0.50	$26.08
33	2.4	Send out agenda	DS	SSM	0.50	$26.08
34	2.4.1	Receive comments/ additons to agenda	DS	SSM	0.50	$26.08
35	2.4.2	Resend amended agenda	DS	SSM	0.50	$26.08
36	**2.5**	**Hold meeting**	**DS, JB, BG, JQP**	**SSM, FA, SME, Owner**	**1.50**	**$359.53**
37	2.6	Develop action list and/or meeting minutes	DS	SSM	0.50	$26.08
38	2.7	Send out action list/ minutes	DS	SSM	0.50	$26.08
39	2.7.1	Receive comments/ additions to action list/minutes	DS	SSM	0.50	$26.08
40	2.7.2	Resend action list/ minutes	DS	SSM	0.50	$26.08

Figure 5-2. Partial budget for Case Example 2: Janitorial Services (continued).

In most spreadsheets, just as in Microsoft Excel, columns are labeled with letters and rows are numbered. Figure 5-2 includes these labels for quick reference. Spreadsheets use a comma in addition (sum) equations to add values from cells that are not adjacent to each other and a colon between the first and last cells to be added when the cells are adjacent.

Let's get back to the calculations.

The cost for each task uses a different equation. To find the **Labor Costs** (column F) for WBS 1.2 (row 19), "Review current and historical supplier contracts," start by finding who is working on the task (**Owner** column, column C). We see that Donna Smith (DS) and Robert Golden (RG) are assigned. Then we look at the **Total per Hour** for these individuals in column F (cells F3 and F4). Next we look at the **Effort** column for the task (column E, row 19) to see how long the task is estimated to take. The equation for the **Labor Costs** for this task is:

=sum(F3:F4)*E19

The total estimate for this task is $231.69.

You will do this for every task in your procurement. Then you will roll up the task numbers into the milestone numbers. The final calculation will be the overall budget number which is the sum of all the milestones. That equation for our example budget is:

=sum(F12,F29,F41,F57,F89,F94,F111,F120,F128,F134)

CAUTIONS

Some cautions about spreadsheets include:

- Be careful if you copy and paste equations from one cell to another. Microsoft Excel automatically changes the reference cells inside the equations. This feature is an attempt to help users create spreadsheets faster, but the feature can easily become a stumbling block that yields bad information. As noted before, check your calculations manually in order to find problems like this in the spreadsheet.
- To correctly roll up values, be sure you use the correct formula in milestone cells. Most spreadsheets use a comma in a sum equation to add values from different cells that are not adjacent to each other. They use a colon between the first and last cells to be added when the cells are adjacent. Manual calculations will reveal incorrect formulas as well.

- When you add up all of the numbers by hand, you may notice a small difference between the numbers you get and the numbers shown by the spreadsheet. This is most common in the overall budget number. The reason for this difference is that most spreadsheets use a floating-point standard, IEEE 754, to do calculations. The Arabic numeral system we use, known as base 10, is not used in floating point calculations. The floating-point standard uses binary representations of our digits, and base 8, which produces a different result than manual calculations. Wise procurement professionals compare the two numbers and use the one that makes the most sense—usually the most conservative (highest number). Check out the difference between manual calculations and the spreadsheet sums in our example in Figure 5-2. The spreadsheet total is $34,558.46, while the manual calculation is $34,558.45. The difference is only one penny. You can submit the more conservative number, $34,558.46, as your budget for approval or you can round up to $34,600 (or more) as your submitted budget. You decide which number is most realistic for your procurement and organization.

SUMMARY

In this chapter we learned the five steps necessary to create a budget for our procurement. Using our schedule as a basis, it is relatively easy to come up with a reasonable budget. We used a spreadsheet to develop a budget, but you can do a budget manually or use project management software. We also discussed the equations needed to calculate the budget.

The biggest nightmare that most procurement professionals, project managers, and executives have is that they forgot to include something very important in a budget—and that does happen sometimes. The way to minimize the chances of it happening to you is to follow the five steps when you develop a budget. Only by having as many eyes as possible review the budget can you rest easy that the big ticket items have been included.

Finally, make an extra copy of the network diagram for your procurement. Note the budget for each task in its box (or above it or next to it) so that it is easy to quickly see where most of the money is being spent.

Next we will discuss the communications plan.

This book has free material available for download from the Web Added Value™ resource center at *www.jrosspub.com.*

CHAPTER 6

COMMUNICATIONS

According to *BusinessDictionary.com*, communication is defined as a "two-way process of reaching mutual understanding, in which participants not only exchange (encode-decode) information, news, ideas and feelings but also create and share meaning. In general, communication is a means of connecting people or places. In business, it is a key function of management—an organization cannot operate without communication between levels, departments and employees."

As you can see from this definition, communication is very important—not only in business, but also in life. The definition makes it clear that communication goes in more than one direction. (This book will refer to the person initiating the communication as the *sender* and the person the communication is aimed at as the *receiver*.)

As a procurement professional, everything that you do involves communication. The RFPS starts the communication process for a procurement, and the execution of the contract and file closeout end the procurement communication process. Or do they? (We will discuss this idea further in Chapter 10, *Contract Administration*.)

COMMUNICATION AS THE FAILURE POINT

How you communicate with everyone associated with your procurement influences its outcome. Procurement professionals can be ambushed in several specific areas. Know about these areas and you will be ahead of the game.

Expectations

Every person that the procurement touches has expectations. The end user expects a product that is usable. The procurement sponsor expects the end user to be satisfied. Each member of the procurement team expects to understand what they have to do to make the procurement successful. Senior executives expect the procurement to reduce costs. Procurement professionals expect success in every aspect of the procurement.

Expectations and scope are not synonymous. Scope is identified and defined very specifically in writing—in the procurement plan, the RFX or purchase order, and the contract. Scope is used to develop schedule, budget, and resources. *Scope creep* is the result of expectations not being clearly communicated. Scope creep is the term used for the subtle, and not so subtle, changes in scope. Left unaddressed, these changes will directly affect the procurement and cause it to fail. Rarely, scope changes can be beneficial to a procurement. An example of a scope change being beneficial is when the business unit decides that the new contract needs to be in place at a later date than originally requested. Their expectation changed and now yours has changed, too.

Looking at expectations from a global perspective, expectations can be identified using the WIIFM model, "What's in it for me?" You, however, need to answer this question from the point of view of every single stakeholder: every expectation—every stakeholder. Only then will you understand what your procurement has to do to be successful.

Stakeholders

Knowing every expectation of every stakeholder brings us to the skill of correctly identifying each and every stakeholder and their stake in the project. Until you know exactly who and what, WIIFM cannot begin to be answered. Let's look at the janitorial services example (*Case Example 2: Janitorial Services* from Chapter 3). Who are the stakeholders? In addition to the team members, other stakeholders include:

Every employee of the company: They are the end users of the janitorial services.

Every employee of the supplier: They rely on the work to support their families.

All executives/managers of the company: They expect cost reduction.

The top boss of the company: The CEO expects cost reduction, quality, security, etc.

The company's facilities manager: Not only as the SME stakeholder, but the company's facilities manager is also the person responsible for managing the janitorial services contractor and reporting the contractor's performance.

This list is actually a small list of stakeholders. Imagine a large highway construction project. The stakeholders for that project range from the taxpayers of the state, to the federal government, to the drivers who use the roadway—now and in the future. That is a lot of stakeholders—every taxpaying citizen in the country!

Stakeholders can be diverse and have different priorities from each other and probably from you. As the sender of communications, different stakeholders will likely receive your message differently. How do you make sure the message you want to send is the one that is received? Now you can see why effective communications can be difficult and take a lot of time. (We will talk about communications processes and systems that successful procurement professionals use later in this chapter.)

Leadership

Procurement professionals are leaders. Procurement professionals lead projects, known as procurements. Procurement professionals also lead teams.

A leader has vision and is able to motivate other people to see the same vision. When many people share the vision, a symbiosis is reached and miraculous things can happen. In a procurement, the procurement professional has the vision. This vision includes many aspects: what the product/service will look like, what the product/service will do, what the quality requirements are, what the timeframe will be, how much the product/service will cost, how much the procurement owner will pay for the product/service, etc. Once that vision is clear, the procurement professional has to be able to communicate it to all of the procurement stakeholders.

A procurement professional does more than only lead a procurement team. A procurement professional also leads the procurement owner, end users, funding team, executive management, sometimes the public, and possibly others. Successful procurement professionals recognize that leadership is based on effective communication. The most effective form of that communication is the procurement plan, which includes the communication plan.

What do the most respected leaders in any profession do? If you answered, "Communicate effectively," you are right.

Tracking and Reporting

Successfully managing a procurement includes the skills of identifying, documenting, tracking, and reporting procurement requirements. Without these skills, a procurement cannot be managed. When a procurement professional is weak in any of these skill areas, the procurement will fail. Let's look at the skills separately.

Identifying and documenting requirements. A successful procurement professional utilizes the knowledge and skills of the procurement team, including the procurement owner. Each of us knows a finite amount of information. Several of us together know much more information. By effectively asking questions, and actively listening to answers, a procurement professional will be able to identify and document requirements—especially requirements that are outside the procurement professional's expertise.

Active listening involves paying close attention to what the speaker (the *sender*) is saying, as well as paraphrasing what the sender said. Active listening also involves the *receiver* (the person who the communication is aimed at) blocking out all other noise (distractions) and listening attentively while the sender speaks. Then the receiver paraphrases the sender's message, including any emotion involved. The sender then knows that either the receiver correctly heard the message or that the receiver did not. If not, the sender will continue to communicate the message, maybe using different words, until the receiver correctly understands.

People very often only half listen when someone else is speaking. Do you ever catch yourself putting together your response, or point, while the other person is speaking? When you do, you are not actively listening. If you are not actively listening, stop what you are thinking about and refocus your attention. You may need to ask questions to completely understand the parts of the message that you missed. Conversely, have you suddenly realized that the person you are talking to has stopped listening to you? When that happens, either stop talking until they realize nothing is being said or ask them a question. Either method requires the receiver to stop what they are thinking about and focus on you again.

Because males and females communicate differently, communication between the genders is often difficult. Many books deal with this specific type of communication. Do research online for books, articles, seminars, workshops, etc. about communication between the genders. One good book is *Men Are From Mars, Women Are From Venus: A Practical Guide for Improving Communication and Getting What You Want in Your Relationships*, HarperCollins (1992), by John Gray, Ph.D. Apply what you learn from this book at work and watch the difference it makes in your communications.

Tracking requirements. Most procurement professionals use software to track and report the status of procurement requirements. Tracking all of the requirements is basic to managing the procurement. Not every stakeholder is interested in the status of every requirement, but that level of interest is inconsequential when you are tracking the requirement. You will track *all* requirements in order to manage a successful procurement. The decision of what information to send to what stakeholder comes later when you report requirements.

Reporting requirements. You decide who sees what information. While transparency inside your company, and with the procurement team, is a good practice, deciding what all of the other stakeholders see can be challenging. If your company does not have protocols for information sharing, your job will be harder. To decide how much information to share, ask stakeholders individually what they want to know about. When someone says that they want to know "everything," ask even more specific questions to rule out information that is not required. If a stakeholder is not available for questions, ask other procurement professionals in your department or company for guidance or ask your boss. If all that fails to answer your questions, just go with your assumptions, but be willing to hear that you were incorrect. Receiving this type of feedback gives you the opportunity to fine-tune what each stakeholder needs to see.

No one likes to hear that they made a mistake, but being willing to hear unpleasant things leads us to conflict resolution.

Conflict-Resolution Skills

Anytime you have more than one person in a room, there is potential for conflict. Not all conflict is bad, however. Disagreements among a procurement team can show involvement and passion. New information can surface during debates. One team member may discover skills that another member has. Sometimes conflict can produce a friendly competitive spirit within the team and things get done better and faster. As the procurement lead, it is up to you to foster an atmosphere of positive conflict rather than negative conflict.

How do you minimize or prevent negative conflict in your procurement? Encourage your team to actively participate in the procurement. Although each team member has specific tasks and area(s) of expertise, valuable ideas and strategies can come from surprising sources. The SME may know much more about the financial situation in a particular industry than the financial analyst does. If so, the SME can work closely with the financial analyst to make sure little-known elements of the industry's costs, profits, material shortages, etc. are considered before the RFP goes out.

Another way to minimize negative conflict is to know when it is happening and to step up to address the conflict directly so that it can be resolved. For example, if a person in your procurement owner's department is making statements that rile up your manager, address the problem directly with the person making the statements. Part of your challenge is to figure out what motivates this person to make these comments and to understand why the comments bother your manager so much. Is there a history of animosity between these two? Is there past conflict between the departments that has not been resolved? You may never get to the real cause of the negative behavior, so your goal is to find a way to get the behavior to change. Minimizing hurtful behaviors is both an art and a skill and it takes excellent communication skills.

Communicating effectively about your procurement with all organizational levels in your company (or organization) also minimizes negative conflict. When all stakeholders know the procurement objectives and the decisions made during procurement planning, you have already minimized the conflict that arises out of confusion or misinformation. Avoiding confusion and misinformation is why regular status meetings are so important. Just as important, regular status reports need to go to all stakeholders. (Determining what information each stakeholder needs, and how often, will be discussed in further detail in this chapter.)

Additionally, you can minimize negative conflicts in your procurement by:

- Developing an effective procurement plan
- Developing effective contingency planning
- Securing commitments in a timely manner
- Involving top management when necessary

Conflict management is a huge subject. This chapter and this book cannot cover all aspects of it, but many books, articles, and courses address the subject of conflict management in detail. You can also search the Internet for information using terms such as "conflict management," "conflict resolution," etc.

COMMUNICATIONS PLAN

From Chapter 3 (*Planning*), we know that a communications plan is developed primarily to document who is assigned to the procurement, each person's role and responsibility, types and frequency of meetings, who should attend those meetings, methods of communications, and change control. Let's now discuss each of these.

Team Communications

For internal team communications include:

- Who: names and titles
- What: roles and responsibilities
- Where: contact information
- When: time zone and work schedule

Figure 6-1 illustrates how this information can be placed in a single document. This document is the first part of a communications plan.

Name	Initials	Role	Responsibilities	Phone	Fax
Donna Smith	DS	Strategic Sourcing Manager	Team Leader	972-555-1345	972-555-1346
Robert Golden	RG	Director of Procurement	Management	972-555-1301	972-555-1346
James Brown	JB	Financial Analyst	Financial research	972-555-1356	972-555-1357
Bill Green	BG	Facilities Manager	Specialized knowledge	972-555-1401	972-555-1402
John Q. Public	JQP	Owner	Final approvals	972-555-1234	972-555-1235
Samantha Grey	SG	Attorney	Legal opinions	972-555-1523	972-555-1501

Name	Email	Time Zone	Work Schedule
Donna Smith	dsmith@xyz.com	CST	0800 – 1700
Robert Golden	rgolden@xyz.com	CST	0800 – 1700
James Brown	jbrown4@xyz.com	CST	0800 – 1700
Bill Green	wgreen@xyz.com	CST	0800 – 1700
John Q. Public	jpublic@xyz.com	CST	0800 – 1700
Samantha Grey	sgrey@xyz.com	CST	0800 – 1700

Mailing Address:
XYZ Company
P. O. Box 1325
Dallas, TX 75032

Shipping Address:
XYZ Company
1325 Texas Blvd.
Dallas, TX 75032

Figure 6-1. Contact list for Case Example 2: Janitorial Services.

Status Reports

Status reports communicate where the procurement is in relationship to where it was estimated to be on a particular date. In other words, the report compares actual dates/costs with the baseline values. Status reports and progress reports can be shown in the same report, but many companies require them to be different reports: progress reports may only report the schedule and budget on a specific date, whereas status reports will indicate the overall condition of the procurement.

As a combined report, a status report will cover:

- Schedule
- Budget (if done)
- Action items (who they are assigned to and when they are due)

- Risks avoided or mitigated
- Change orders
- Assumptions during the reporting period
- Agreements reached during the reporting period
- All other pertinent information

If a task (or tasks) is late, the status report will give that information as well as the steps being taken to catch up. Examples of these steps could include:

- Assigned another employee to help get this work done
- Decided to pay overtime to get this work done on a weekend
- Changed the milestone deadline

You need to create effective status reports by finding out how your company (the audience) views status reports. Do they need to be simple progress reports or do they need to be more complex status reports? As the procurement lead, you will probably need to create both reports and send them out based on the audience. As discussed several times previously in this book, senior executives want information conveyed as quickly as possible, so a simple progress report may suffice for them, but your team needs to know everything about where the procurement is, so the team will get the more complex status report. Know who your audiences are and how much information they need. Tailor your reports accordingly and you will communicate well.

To create reports, you need input. Your procurement team will have the most input. Sometimes managers and executives will have information you need to know. Provide every stakeholder with the opportunity to give input to you. If your status reports are distributed weekly, the input needs to be delivered to you *at least* one day before the report is due. Each week publish the schedule for both the input deadline and the report deadline for the next week. Putting that information at the end of the weekly status report keeps it handy for your stakeholders.

Using a status report ensures that you will review progress in your procurement regularly. You monitor work completed, work in progress, and work still to do. Meeting with your team every week also makes certain that all of you are up to date on the status of the procurement. During weekly meetings, you:

- Report procurement status.
- Listen to each team member's status update.
- Ask for challenges in upcoming tasks.
- Ask for new assumptions about upcoming tasks.
- Review existing assumptions about upcoming tasks.
- Disseminate the Action List.

The Action List is an essential tool for moving procurements forward. This list is essentially a to-do list for the next week. Separate action items by category (you can use one or both):

- Person responsible
- Date due

You can also group actions differently, depending on your specific procurement or your company.

The Action List needs to report both the due dates for tasks and the anticipated dates of completion, meaning you need to get information from the responsible individuals. When the due date and the anticipated date of completion are different, you need to ask questions about the reasons. Often the reasons for a task running behind schedule have to do with workload. To get the task back on schedule, you might be able to negotiate a higher priority for the work for your procurement.

The Action List also needs to include tasks that start this reporting cycle (the week) as well as tasks that start in the near future. For most procurements, one month is long enough for this preview. Complex procurements, however, will require different reporting periods and longer forward-looking Action Lists.

When a person has completed all of their work on the procurement or on an action item, you can drop their name from the Action List. You can also drop completed tasks after reporting their completion once. There is no need to continue carrying completed work on the Action List because no more action is required on this work.

Figure 6-2 shows a two-page, more complex status report. Note that the Gantt chart on the second page of the report now reflects actual schedule accomplishments shown against the baseline schedule.

Potential Suppliers (Vendors)

To be fair and ethical, having effective management of communications with potential suppliers is very important. All communications with potential suppliers should go through the procurement lead. It is also a good idea to have a backup person in the procurement department for potential suppliers, and employees within your company, to contact in case the procurement lead is out of the office or otherwise unavailable.

Let's say that again: all communications with potential suppliers must go through the procurement lead.

In a fair and ethical procurement, all potential suppliers have the right to know what information is being communicated to all of the other potential suppliers to minimize the opportunities for under-the-table deals between any employee of your company and a supplier. Ensuring that all potential suppliers

Status Report for Janitorial Services Procurement		
May 15, 2013		
Overall Status:	On time	
Work Completed Last Week:	RFPS received; reviewed historical supplier contracts; identified stakeholders; established procurement team; drafted schedule; set weekly meeting dates; set kick-off meeting date; sent agenda for review and comments for kick-off meeting	
Work Planned for Next Week:	Kick-off meeting; begin drafting procurement plan to include finalizing strategy, WBS, schedule	
Issues:	No financial analyst available as of now	
Risks:	Having no financial analyst available will increase the time this procurement takes	
Action Items	**Assigned to**	**Date Due**
Description	Donna Smith	5/16/13
Negotiate for a financial analyst	Donna Smith	5/17/13
Kick-off meeting	Donna Smith	5/24/13
Begin drafting procurement plan		
Next Meeting: 5/22/2013		

Figure 6-2. A two-page, more complex status report for Case Example 2: Janitorial Services.

know what is being communicated to all of the other potential suppliers will also stand up in court if a disgruntled potential supplier sues your company for illegal practices.

Note: If a potential supplier can prove that someone in your company made a deal with another supplier that materially harmed the plaintiff, your company is subject to paying actual damages as well as punitive damages. Not all courts will find for the plaintiff, but many will. Make sure you listen well to any attorney who represents your company in lawsuits. This attorney will know what the courts have done in cases like these.

You must educate everyone in your company who might be contacted by potential suppliers about the issues associated with speaking with these suppliers. Impress on them the possible legal implications, the risk of incurring unexpected legal costs, and the potential for damage to supplier relationships that unauthorized communication can cause. Frequently remind these employees to always refer potential suppliers to you with any communication that is needed.

The same rules apply to an existing supplier for the goods or services that are the subject of your procurement (the only exception to this rule is the day-to-day

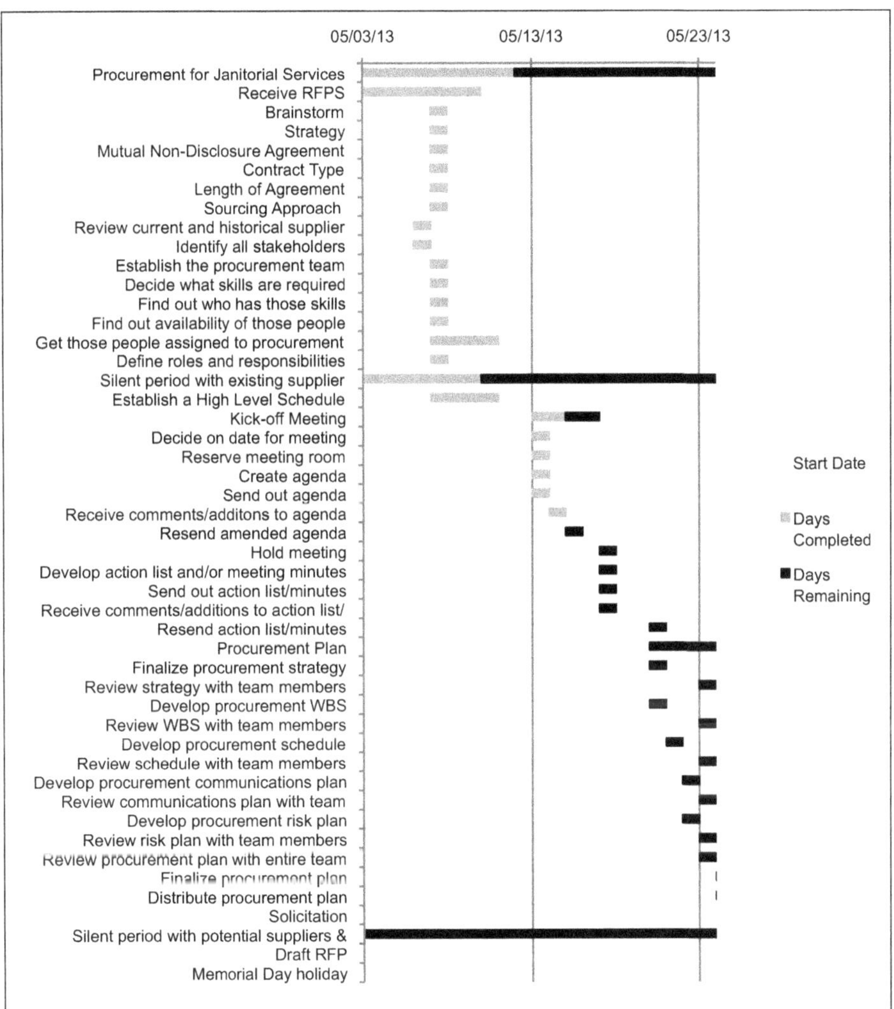

Figure 6-2. A two-page, more complex report for Case Example 2: Janitorial Services (continued).

management of the contract). All employees of your company who deal directly with an existing supplier must understand that any information about the procurement is to be handled through the procurement lead. Often this is a difficult challenge because your company's employee(s) may have a good working relationship with this supplier, but sometimes things are said in passing that are important to the procurement—something that the employee does not understand can adversely impact the procurement. Again, frequently remind these employees that communications about the procurement must go through you.

What about potential suppliers talking with each other? It can be very difficult to request that potential suppliers not speak with each other about your procurement. These days, suppliers often partner together in order to supply the goods or services that you need. As a procurement professional, you already know to watch for estimates that are too similar, just as you watch for estimates that are too disparate.

If you work for a government agency, or a government contractor, you will have regulations in place about communicating with potential and existing suppliers. Federal laws, and many states' laws, have specific punishments for violating the communications regulations. Make sure you know these regulations and follow them.

Frequency of Communication

How often you communicate is also dictated by the person who will receive your communication. Some members of the procurement team need to have informal discussions with you every day. Even if these team members do not initiate a conversation, you need to check in with them frequently to see if they need anything in order to get their work done. In addition to these informal discussions, you will also have weekly meetings so your team can go over the status of the procurement. The weekly meeting is a more formal process in which the procurement status is reported in detail. Distribute an agenda before each weekly meeting and issue a final status report after each meeting.

Other stakeholders can be communicated with informally and formally. How often you need to communicate informally with each stakeholder depends on the role and responsibility of the stakeholder. For formal communications, some stakeholders will only need monthly updates on progress, while others will want to know every time you run into problems. You can find out who needs to know what, and when they need to know it, by asking each stakeholder what they expect. If a stakeholder is unavailable to ask directly, find out from your boss or other procurement professionals about what this stakeholder wanted in the past.

Best Forms of Communication

We have many ways to communicate in today's world. Some examples include:

- Face-to-face
- Hard-copy letters, reports, etc.
- Shared files (on servers)
- Telephone
- Email
- Video conferences

- Online screen-sharing services
- Texting
- Voice Over Internet Protocol (VOIP) services (Skype and other services which make telephone calls over a high-speed Internet connection and incur no expense other than the cost of Internet access)
- Instant messaging (IM)
- Faxing
- Mail (snail mail)

Not all forms of these communication examples are effective in all situations. Your team may be scattered across different geographical areas and time zones. Potential suppliers may be located in different countries. In a perfect world, all stakeholders would be located in the same building. Even if your world is not one in which your stakeholders are conveniently located, you should still take advantage of the opportunities available to you to talk face-to-face with all of them. You and your team will need to decide the most appropriate method to use to communicate with everyone.

The best forms of informal communication include:

- Face-to-face
- Telephone
- Texting
- IM
- Email
- VOIP

The best forms of formal communication include:

- Hard copy and snail mail
- Faxing
- Shared files
- Telephone
- Email
- Video conference
- Online screen-sharing services
- VOIP services

As communications technology changes in the future, some of these forms of communication will become obsolete. One thing that will never become obsolete is speaking directly with people, either face-to-face or by telephone.

Caution: Consider whether you want a communication to go into the "permanent record" or not. Some information is best shared in written form (to be a permanent record). Other information is best shared verbally (to not be a permanent record). *Remember*: Emails, texts, IMs, etc. are written records. Some video conferences and telephone calls are recorded and become permanent records. Be cautious about the form of communication that you use. You want it to be useful, but not detrimental.

Change Control

Change happens. Change even happens to your "perfect" procurement. Change control is how you manage changes when they occur. Change control ensures that:

- Changes are beneficial.
- A change has been approved.
- A change is managed as it occurs, not later.

Note: Change control is also called *configuration management* in project management terminology. We use the term *change control* because it is simpler terminology and conveys the concept completely.

Every proposed change to your procurement may not be beneficial to it. Many changes, in fact, will adversely impact your work, so consider each one carefully before you agree to it. One way to convince another person that a change is unacceptable is to show exactly how the change will affect the procurement. Being able to do this means that you must maintain the baseline schedule, the baseline budget (if used), the risk log, etc. (Risk logs will be discussed in Chapter 7, *Risk.*) Then you have to be able to indicate the progress of the procurement as it has occurred—the weekly status reports.

Before approving a change, contact the affected stakeholders. Ask them for information about how the change will impact their work. The stakeholders need to be specific. "It'll make me late," does not give you enough information. "It'll delay my review of the RFP by 2 weeks," is much better information. This specific information tells you that both the schedule and the budget will be affected—remember that time is money so delays add on cost. If the change will not bring positive impact to the procurement, use the baseline information to argue against the change.

When a change is approved, you need to update the SOW (the procurement charter) and coordinate the change with all appropriate stakeholders. Letting stakeholders know that there is a change, and that it affects them, is key to good communications. Expect feedback from these stakeholders, especially if they did not know about the possibility of the change.

Change control requires that performance measurement baselines are maintained, that the Statement of Work (SOW) is updated to adequately reflect changes, and that the changes are coordinated with all of the appropriate stakeholders. Figure 6-3 shows how a change log can be created. *Remember*: For a change log to be a good tool, you need to keep it updated and review it often.

Change Control Log							
Change Number	**Change Description**	**Priority**	**Date Requested**	**Requested by**	**Date Implemented/ Cancelled**	**Status**	**Comments**
001	Postpone RFP release date	1	6/8/13	John Q. Public		On hold	Need reasons in writing before decision can be made
002	Include companies from Ft. Worth	1	6/9/13	Bill Green	6/9/13	In progress	Financial Analyst implementing company list/research

Figure 6-3. Example change log for Case Example 2: Janitorial Services.

We know from the beginning of this section that the primary reason for having a communications plan is to document several aspects of the procurement: the people who are assigned to the procurement, the roles and responsibilities of each of these people, the types and frequency of status meetings, who should attend the meetings, the methods of communications, and the importance of change control. Building on Figure 6-1, Figure 6-4 shows one way to document a communications plan.

Procurement Team					
Name	**Initials**	**Role**	**Responsibilities**	**Phone**	**Fax**
Donna Smith	DS	Strategic Sourcing Manager	Team Leader	972-555-1345	972-555-1346
Robert Golden	RG	Director of Procurement	Management	972-555-1301	972-555-1346
James Brown	JB	Financial Analyst	Financial research	972-555-1356	972-555-1357
Bill Green	BG	Facilities Manager	Specialized knowledge	972-555-1401	972-555-1402
John Q. Public	JQP	Owner	Final approvals	972-555-1234	972-555-1235
Samantha Grey	SG	Attorney	Legal opinions	972-555-1523	972-555-1501

Name	Email	Time Zone	Work Schedule
Donna Smith	dsmith@xyz.com	CST	0800 – 1700
Robert Golden	rgolden@xyz.com	CST	0800 – 1700
James Brown	jbrown4@xyz.com	CST	0800 – 1700
Bill Green	wgreen@xyz.com	CST	0800 – 1700
John Q. Public	jpublic@xyz.com	CST	0800 – 1700
Samantha Grey	sgrey@xyz.com	CST	0800 – 1700

Mailing Address:
XYZ Company
P. O. Box 1325
Dallas, TX 75032

Shipping Address:
XYZ Company
1325 Texas Blvd.
Dallas, TX 75032

Figure 6-4. Communications plan for Case Example 2: Janitorial Services.

Communications Plan			
Meetings	**Team**	**Management**	**Others**
Informal discussions	Daily	As needed	As needed
Procurement review	Weekly	As needed	As needed
Status update	Weekly	Monthly	As needed
Contract audit			Once, after agreement reached and before contract execution

Reports	Team	Management	Others
Status reports	Weekly	Monthly	As needed
Update reports to team leader	Weekly (before team meetings)	N/A	As needed
Savings report			Once, after agreement reached and before contract execution
Contract audit			Once, after agreement reached and before contract execution

Change Control	Responsible	Reports to
Change log maintenance	DS	N/A
Change reports	JB	DS

Figure 6-1. Communications plan for Case Example 2. Janitorial Services (continued).

SUMMARY

In this chapter we talked about communications. Without good communications, a procurement will struggle and likely fail. A person who does not communicate well will not be as successful as a person who does—both at work and in life.

We talked about how people's expectations influence the outcome of communications and how leadership means communicating well.

We also discussed tracking and reporting a procurement and conflict-resolution skills. Then we described developing a communications plan for your procurement. The primary reason to develop a communications plan is to document who is assigned to the procurement, each person's role and responsibility, types and frequency of meetings, who should attend those meetings, methods of communications, and change control.

Even though communicating well is the one skill that will determine success or failure—at work and in life—this chapter barely skims the subject of communications. Many sources offer extensive information about communications, including college courses, workshops, online training, books, seminars, etc. Communicating well is a skill that takes a lifetime of study and practice.

In the next chapter, we will look at risk and risk management.

This book has free material available for download from the Web Added Value™ resource center at *www.jrosspub.com.*

CHAPTER 7

RISK

*Anything that **can** go wrong **will** go wrong.*
—Murphy's law

When it comes to procurement management, Murphy's law says it all. As with any project, procurements run into unexpected things all the time. In this chapter, we will learn what risk is, how to identify risks, determine their probability, determine their impacts, create responses, and monitor and control those risks.

Why do we care about risks? During all procurements, something unexpected will happen. It could be that the company we are negotiating a contract with goes out of business. It could be that our management decides not to proceed with the procurement at all or the budget for the new contract spend is reduced significantly. Other more common issues can arise such as changes to personnel on your procurement team or the potential vendor's negotiating team. Managing risks that are unknown or have not been identified by your procurement team is very difficult.

As a procurement professional, you need to consider two different sets of risks. The first set is risks to the procurement itself: an important supplier for your procurement goes out of business, your management cancels the procurement, your management reduces the spend for the contract, etc. The second set is risks to the executed contract: independent contractor status, warranties, indemnity, terms for delivery, terms for payment, etc. In addition to your expertise, rely on attorneys and accountants to help you identify risks to the contract. (Contract risks will not be covered in this book. Focus will be on risks to the procurement and creating a risk management plan for them.)

Creating a risk management plan takes into account all of the imaginable events that could occur during your procurement and gives you a roadmap for dealing with each one. There might be risks that you do not need to deal with—they will have low impact to your procurement. Other risks could be fatal. Would it be a good idea to know which risks will have low impact and which risks can stop your procurement from ever happening?

Look at risk in another way. Think about change orders. Change orders are those pesky increases to costs. They usually delay scheduled events, such as delivery dates. As a procurement professional, you already know to minimize change orders to any contract to manage costs. Every risk that is identified and managed well is one fewer change order that will cost your company money.

Let's look at procurement risk in more detail.

PROCUREMENT RISK

Remember the definitions of risk that were first introduced in Chapter 3? According to Harold Kerzner, Ph. D., the definition of risk is "… a measure of the probability and consequence of not achieving a defined project goal" (*Project Management: A Systems Approach to Planning, Scheduling, and Controlling, Sixth Edition*, p. 869, Van Nostrand Reinhold (1997). Kerzner goes on to say that risk has three primary components:

- An event
- A probability of occurrence of that event
- The impact of that event (the consequence)

Also remember from Chapter 3 that the *PMBOK® Guide* adds that a risk can have a *negative* or *positive* impact. We also know from Chapter 3 that *uncertainty* is key to defining risk.

If you know *for sure* that something will happen, then you have already included it as part of the procurement plan. Think about something you know for sure will happen: your knowledge that the sun will rise tomorrow morning. Do you need to do anything to make sure that the sun rises? No. Do you have to think about what you would do if it did not rise? No. There is no risk that the sun will not rise tomorrow morning because you know that it will. There is no need to even make a plan for dealing with the sun rising or not rising. (We are not talking about billions of years in the future when the sun expands and destroys the planets in our solar system. That, of course, is too far in the future to impact our procurement.)

We all have risk in our lives. Think about every time we get in a car or bus or board an airplane. Do we know how the trip will end with 100% certainty? No. Think about tomorrow. Do we know if we will get sick tomorrow? No. This is the type of uncertainty that is part of the definition of risk. (A personal risk management plan could include what we, or our families, would do if we were in a car accident or became ill.)

Kerzner also states that the effect an event has on a project must be *negative* in order to be a risk, but the *PMBOK® Guide* says that the effect on the project can be either positive or negative. This difference is another case of experts disagreeing on something that is fundamental. It is not particularly intuitive that an unexpected event could have a *positive* effect on your procurement. It takes some time to think about the positive effects and the consequences of having them. Kerzner's assertion, that an event must have a negative effect in order to be a risk, comes from the reality that a negative effect must be managed, but a positive effect does not need to be managed. The most you have to do about a positive effect is to communicate it—money was saved, better delivery dates were achieved, payment was sent in 60 days instead of 30 days—and then make sure you get the credit.

Taken from a lesson in the Next Level Purchasing Association's certification training courses (www.nextlevelpurchasing.com), think about an example of one event that could have either negative or positive consequences. The example is about an airplane trip you were scheduled to take in early 2010 from New York City to London. You anticipated the time it would take to get checked in and past security. You knew that your flight would take a specific amount of time in the air. You figured that there would probably be some delay before the plane took off and again when you landed. Did you anticipate that a volcano in Iceland would erupt and cancel your trip for several weeks? Was the volcano a negative effect (consequence) on your trip? Sure it was—the trip did not happen.

Now let's talk about the positive consequence of the unexpected volcanic eruption. Imagine that your trip to London was required so you could inform the British government that your company would no longer be able to supply equipment. Because this contract provided a revenue flow that was keeping your company in business through the contemporaneous recession, no one at the company was looking forward to the discussions in London. During those weeks of flight cancellations between New York and London, you (being the purchasing superstar that you are) found a new materials supplier, thus enabling your company to continue providing equipment to the British government. You saved your company's business and you did not even have to spend money to make that trip to London.

An informative interview about risk analysis is on the Next Level Purchasing Association's website. The interview is in two parts and is between Charles Dominick, President of the Next Level Purchasing Association, and this author. You can listen to it at http://www.nextlevelpurchasing.com/procurement-risk-audio.html.

TYPES OF RISK

From Chapter 3, remember the three types of risk:

- Known
- Predictable
- Unpredictable

These three types of risk are shown in Table 7-1.

Table 7-1. Types of Risk

Known risks	Identified; internal and/or external
Predictable risks	Identified; occur often
Unpredictable risks	Not identified; do not occur often

Known risks. Known risks are risks that can be *identified.* You and your procurement team identify these risks during the risk management process by using your personal experience and knowledge as well as the knowledge of your procurement team, the SMEs, the procurement plan, the WBS, and several other sources (to be discussed in greater detail later in this chapter.) Known risks can also be internal or external. *Internal risks* are the most common risk to procurements. Internal business risks include funding, the schedule, staffing, stakeholder relations, quality requirements, procurement manager experience, and loss of political support. Risks such as these are not the only internal risks you could experience, of course, but they show up in procurement after procurement in every industry. The most common internal risk is the schedule—not having enough time to complete a well-organized and strategic procurement. *External risks* arise from outside your company or organization. Some external risks are new (or changing) government regulations, changes in technology, vendor bankruptcies, labor issues, and civil unrest. Depending on your specific industry, there can be many more external risks, e.g., changing federal or state funding levels are a major external risk in many industries. (*Note*: Although they are external, acts of God, *force majeure*, such as floods, tornadoes, earthquakes, erupting volcanoes, wild fires, shifting magnetic poles, meteor impacts, etc., usually require a disaster recovery plan rather than risk management. As a procurement professional, become familiar with your company's disaster recovery plans so that you can include them in all vendor agreements.)

Predictable risks. Predictable risks are based on historical data, lessons learned, the experience of other procurement managers who have lead similar procurements in your company, SME experience, etc. Predictable risks can also be a result of your "gut feelings" about what might go wrong in the procurement.

For example, if some of your managers usually take extra time to even read a report or a change order request or something else that needs their signatures, then their historically slow response time will be a risk to your procurement schedule. (Will it happen? Probably.)

Unpredictable risks. Unpredictable risks are events that occur that no one even thought about. Examples of unpredictable risks are a train derailment, a coup d'état, a processing plant explosion, a power failure, etc. In the case of a region-wide power failure that will last for some time, no one can possibly know when that will happen, if it ever does, but the disruption could impact all aspects of your procurement. Identifying unpredictable risks takes life experience, business experience, and common sense.

We will discuss risk identification techniques (what you can do to identify risks) and risk response (what you can do to respond to, or mitigate, risks) in the next section, *Procurement Risk Management Processes.*

PROCUREMENT RISK MANAGEMENT PROCESSES

The *PMBOK® Guide* defines the processes needed to completely manage project risk. Some of these processes are combined and make risk management for procurement simpler than it looks. The formal processes involved in risk management are:

- Planning
- Identification
- Qualitative risk analysis
- Quantitative risk analysis
- Risk response planning
- Risk monitoring and control

Although it is good to know that formal processes exist, many procurements just do not require that level of management. The simpler the procurement, the simpler the risk management:

Simple procurement = simple risk management
Complex procurement = complex risk management

We will combine two sets of processes: the planning with identification, and the qualitative with the quantitative risk analysis. So we will be discussing four processes for risk management within a procurement:

- Risk identification
- Risk analysis

- Response planning
- Monitoring and control

In this chapter we will discuss simple risk management techniques. If you want to learn more about risk management, many colleges and organizations teach courses and conduct workshops. ISM hosts an annual risk management conference (information on the next conference may be found at http://www.ism.ws/index.cfm). Look for risk management training online, too. You will find many resources.

Risk Identification

Identifying risks is the most important step in a risk management plan. If a risk is not identified, then you have no way to plan how to respond to it. Unidentified (unknown) risks cannot be managed.

At first you will simply identify the risks. You will decide how to rank and respond to them later. You will often find, however, that a risk response is easy to develop as soon as a risk is identified. A risk response can be implemented as soon as it is developed if the response is simple and effective.

Risk identification is an iterative process. When anything changes in your procurement, you will need to identify the new risks. Sometimes a previously identified risk will have a higher priority after the change. Some things you will need in order to identify risks include:

- Procurement Plan, especially the Assumptions List and Constraints List
- Schedule, including the WBS
- Contract product description or what the final goods or services of the procurement are (e.g., janitorial services in the example procurement we have been using)
- Cost estimates, especially if this is a project-related procurement
- Project-related Procurement Plan, if this is a project-related procurement
- Resource Plan

How to Identify Risks

The simpler the procurement, the fewer the risks and the easier it is to identify them. You might be tempted to use only your own experience as a procurement manager to identify all of the risks to your procurement. Be very careful not to assume that you know all of the risks. (An arrogant procurement manager is an unemployed procurement manager.)

Risks to a procurement can be identified in several ways. Depending on the complexity of the procurement, a good procurement manager will use as many of these as possible. Some of the techniques that can be used to identify risks to your procurement will now be discussed. This is not an exhaustive list. In addition to the techniques described, use all of the other resources that are available to you.

Review the procurement plan. Look at the documents from the total procurement file (the big picture) and the detailed scope levels. Look at as many prior procurement files as you can, especially procurements that are similar to yours. If you have procurement lessons learned files, review them.

Interview subject matter experts. One favored way to identify risks is to interview SMEs face-to-face before a brainstorming meeting. Arrange for each SME to review the procurement information (plan, WBS, list of assumptions, etc.). After each SME has reviewed the information, ask open-ended questions to get as much information as possible. (An open-ended question is one that a "yes" or "no" will not answer.) During the interview, new ideas about risk may come up as the SME warms up and starts talking openly. Do your interviews before scheduling the brainstorming session so that you will know as much as you can before turning the procurement team loose to brainstorm.

Brainstorm. Brainstorming is probably the most frequently used risk identification technique. Include the entire procurement team in the brainstorming session. (Depending on the size of your team and the complexity of the procurement, you might need to have several brainstorming sessions.) It is also a good idea to include SMEs who are not on your team. You can facilitate the session or you can bring in another procurement manager to facilitate it for you. Let your team know that no idea is out of bounds when brainstorming. (You will prioritize the risks after the brainstorming session ends. So anything that seems ridiculous can be put at the very bottom of the priority list then, not during the session itself.) Use the thought "create first, judge later" to stay on track during a brainstorming session. Judging ideas during the brainstorming process makes people less likely to contribute ideas. You want to identify as many risks as possible, knowing that you can always filter them down later.

Analyze the assumptions and constraints. Analyze the assumptions and constraints that have been identified in the procurement plan. Look at each assumption or constraint individually to see if it is inaccurate, inconsistent, or incomplete: if any of your procurement assumptions are problematic, you will find the problems right away. *Remember*: All of your constraints will be risks to your procurement.

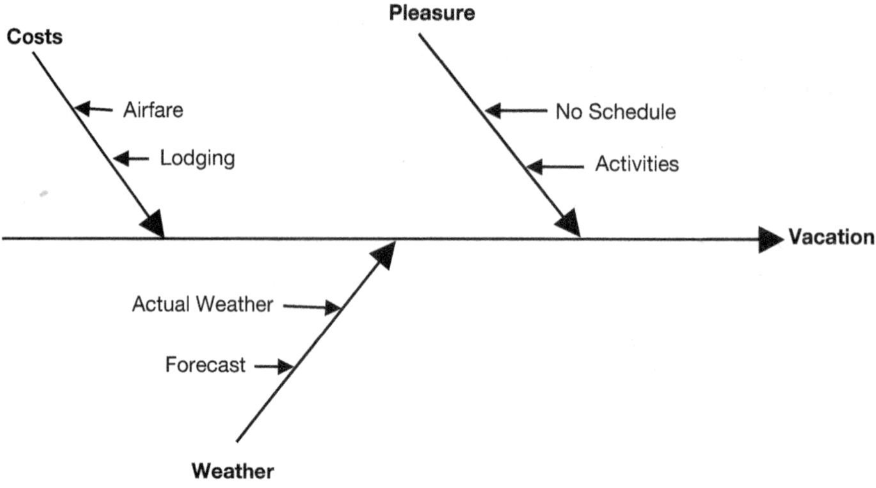

Figure 7-1. Cause and effect diagram.

Use diagramming techniques. Sometimes it is best to create visual risk identification. You can use diagramming techniques to do this. Diagramming techniques include cause-and-effect diagrams, system (or process) flow charts, and influence diagrams:

- Cause-and-effect diagrams: Cause-and-effect diagrams (also known as Ishikawa or fishbone diagrams) are often used by quality control and safety personnel in root cause analysis. These diagrams can also be used to identify risks to procurements and even risks to a company or organization. The basic idea is to start with the largest result of risk—the procurement ends suddenly—and ask *why* and *how*. With every resulting answer, ask *why* and *how* again. This repetition continues until there are no more answers. When there are no more answers, you have identified the major risks to your procurement. Figure 7-1 is an example of a cause-and-effect diagram. Using the simple idea of taking a vacation, this fishbone diagram shows the intended result (effect)—a vacation—at the right of the diagram. Several inputs (causes) to getting to this result are shown: Costs, Weather, and Pleasure. Then the sub-causes of each of these are shown. For Weather, there is the Forecast and the Actual Weather. For Costs, there is Airfare and Lodging. For Pleasure, there is No Schedule and Activities. Both causes and sub-causes are risks in this example. Can you think of more causes? More sub-causes? (One place to learn more about using the fishbone diagram is on this website: http://fishbonediagram.org.)

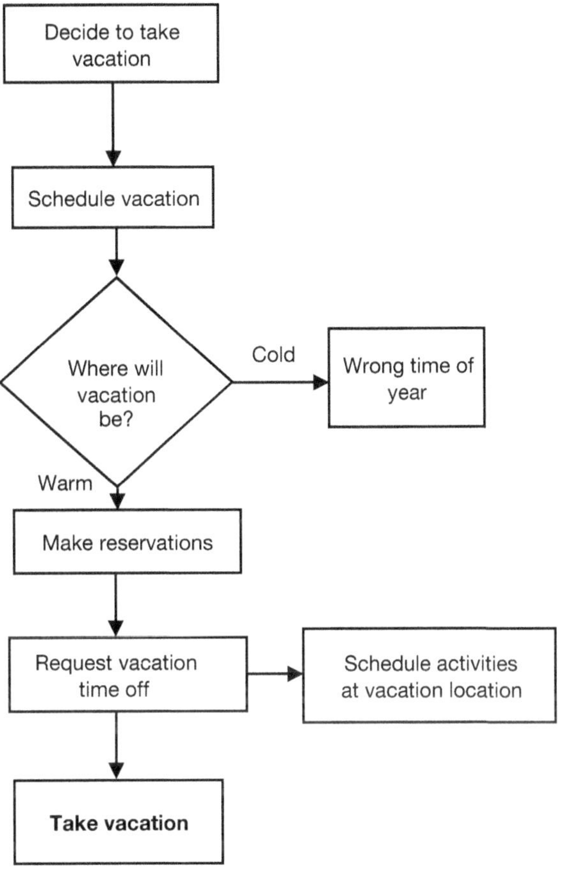

Figure 7-2. Flowchart.

- Process flowcharts: Business process experts use flowcharts to find repetition in processes or to find bottlenecks that stop process completion. Procurement professionals can use flowcharts for the same reasons or to identify risks to the procurement. When you chart the procurement process for your organization, you can help your executives make procurement more efficient and effective (thus showing your initiative and organization skills). To find risks to your procurement, look for repeated steps, places where everything goes to one person and the procurement is slowed down because of it, and places that go nowhere. All of these are risks to your procurement. Figure 7-2 is an example of a flowchart. This visual identification shows exactly what steps are needed to get to the desired end—a vacation. To keep this flowchart simple, only the major steps have been

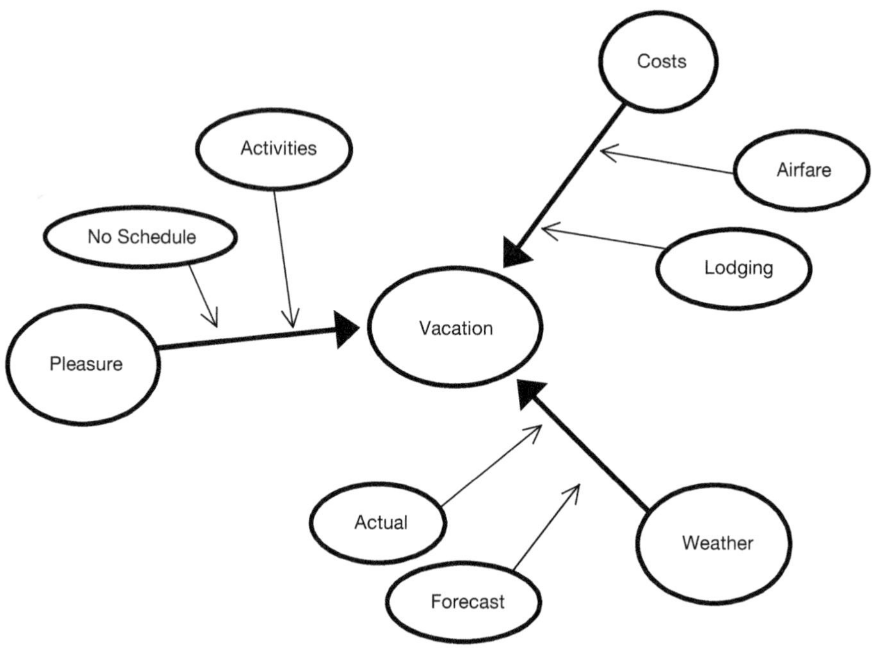

Figure 7-3. Influence diagram.

identified. As you can see, the major risks are the weather, costs, and pleasure. These risks match the cause-and-effect diagram in Figure 7-1. Can you list more steps in this flowchart and identify more risks to the vacation?

- Influence diagrams: An influence diagram is a graphical display of risk factors affecting a decision, how each risk factor influences the other, and how a combination of factors will lead to a decision and ultimately lead to an outcome. An influence diagram is not linear like a flowchart, but is more like a "mind map." In the case of identifying risks to a procurement, the influence diagram starts with the big idea (the largest result of risk) in the center, i.e., the procurement suddenly ends. Then every idea that contributes to that risk is identified and connected to the center by a line (a branch). Then every idea that contributes to that idea is identified and connected to the idea by a line (a twig). Contribution is equivalent to influence in this technique. When an idea is identified several times in the diagram, it is a strong risk to the procurement. Figure 7-3 is an example of a simple influence diagram. You can see the desired thing is in the center of this diagram—a Vacation. Branched to it are the three major risks: Weather, Costs, and Pleasure. The contributing factors to the branches are the twigs. In this case, Weather has the twigs Forecast and Actual. Cost has the twigs Airfare and Lodging. Pleasure has the twigs No Schedule and Activities. Can you brainstorm and find many more risks?

For more information about diagramming techniques, consult text books and search the Internet with the specific type of diagram you want to know more about.

Use a checklist analysis. Checklist analysis can be used to identify risks. Develop checklists by using historical information and knowledge that you find in procurement files. Checklists can also be developed using the knowledge and experience of senior procurement professionals. Risk checklists will never be exhaustive because they can never identify every possible risk to your procurement. When your procurement is complete, add your risk checklists to your procurement file during the closeout process. Including your risk checklists in the procurement file will help you with your next procurement. It may also help your co-workers now and in the future.

Use SWOT analysis. SWOT (Strengths, Weaknesses, Opportunities, and Threats) analysis is one more tool to identify risks to your procurement. The SWOT approach is especially useful to identify internal risks—risks that come from inside your own company/organization/department/team. In SWOT analysis, you will look at the strengths and weaknesses of each level of your organization and identify risks from weaknesses and opportunities from strengths.

Risk Analysis

Your goal for the risk identification process is to create a document that will identify and define specific risks to your procurement. Many project managers use a risk log (or risk register) to document the risk management process and you can, too. Use a simple spreadsheet or document table to develop your risk log, unless the procurement is very complicated.

Figure 7-4 shows an example of a simple risk log using a MS Word table. This risk log has five columns: Risk, Probability, Impact, Response, and Action. The first column, Risk, is where all identified risks are listed. This listing is the first step in creating a risk log. Next you will analyze risk probability and impact.

Risk Probability and Impact

When you have identified the risks in the risk log, you will analyze the probability that each risk will occur along with the possible impact to the procurement of each risk. The *PMBOK® Guide* calls this qualitative and quantitative risk analysis.

Risk Log				
Risk	**Probability**	**Impact**	**Response**	**Action**
Requested completion date not workable				
Necessary personnel not available to meet schedule				
Team meetings not attended				
No competitors in market				
IBP insists on sole-sourced process				
Scope of work not detailed enough				
Funding not adequate to provide requested services				
Funding level does not provide savings				
RFP not delivered on time				
RFP responses late				
RFP responses inadequate				
Response evaluation delayed				
Top three competitors' oral presentations delayed schedule				
Weather adversely impacted oral presentation schedule				

Figure 7-4. Risk log with risk identification.

Qualitative risk analysis is the process of assessing the impact and likelihood of identified risks. Qualitative risk analysis is used to prioritize risks according to their potential effect on the procurement. Quantitative risk analysis assigns a number to the probability of each risk and the impact on the procurement. Qualitative and quantitative analyses are used together for most procurements. Only the most complex procurement would require separating the two analyses.

Step 1. Determine Each Risk's Probability

The first step to determining a risk's probability is to use common sense. Then look at historical data on procurements that have been completed. Also use the combined experience of senior procurement managers and the SMEs assigned to your team. You can assign probabilities in a draft form and then ask your team and major stakeholders to review them and make comments, or you can have a meeting to go over the draft probabilities.

Most often, the impact of each risk is discussed at the same time as the probability. These two concepts go hand in hand.

Timing is important in determining a risk's probability and impact on the procurement. In general, the later in a procurement a risk happens, the greater its impact is. For example, your procurement started out with a funding level of $500,000 per year. After your team has selected the top three suppliers to interview in person, you receive word that the funding authority has changed the funding level to $250,000 per year. You know that you can never secure the services described in the RFP for that amount. So now you have to stop the procurement to find out what can be done about the spend level.

Had the funding authority cut the funding level in half before the RFP went out, you would have:

- Had an opportunity to make some different choices
- Asked why the funding level is so low
- Changed the scope of work to drop the level of services to match the lower spending amount
- Presented facts about pricing in the industry and your market area in order to increase the funding level

In our example, the earlier you receive word about the reduction in funding, the more actions you can take to mitigate the impact of this risk.

While you are analyzing the probability and impact of each risk, remember to evaluate the quality of the available information. Does the risk apply to your procurement? Is each assumption valid? Are the constraints real or can they be negotiated? The old adage of "garbage in, garbage out" applies here, too.

You can describe risk probability either with words or with numbers. The one you use will be determined by your organization's culture. If you work with mostly verbal people, use words. If you work with mostly analytical people, use numbers.

Use the following terms to describe risk probability in words:

Very high
High
Moderate
Low
Very low

To describe risk probability using numbers, use a scale of 1 to 10, with 1 being almost no possibility and 10 being absolute certainty that the risk will happen.

Step 2. Determine Each Risk's Overall Impact

The second step is to determine the overall impact of the risk to your procurement. Do this by using the same terms or same numerical scale as used for risk probability:

Very high
High
Moderate
Low
Very low

Remember that on a scale of 1 to 10, 1 means almost no impact and 10 means the procurement will stop suddenly.

The probability factor does not have to match the impact factor. For example, a risk can have a very high probability of occurring, but have a very low impact—or vice versa, a risk can have a very low probability of happening, but bring your procurement to a complete halt if it does. Quite often a risk will have a moderate probability and a moderate impact. Figure 7-5 is an example of a risk log with probability and impact (PI) in word terms. This risk log has the same identified risks as in Figure 7-4 with probabilities and impacts added to each risk. No matter what probability and impact are assigned to each risk, you need to prioritize the identified risks.

To prioritize the risks, you need to determine which risks are the most important for further action. You do that by establishing a *risk threshold*, which is a measure of risk acceptance for your procurement. Quite often the risk threshold depends on the risk tolerance of your company, department, procurement sponsor, and even on your own risk tolerance.

You can use a matrix to set the risk threshold. Figure 7-6 is a numeric probability and impact matrix (PI Matrix). Using the probability score (the vertical numbers in column 1) and the Impact on Procurement score (the horizontal numbers on the bottom row), find the risk score. For example, a probability that a risk will occur is **8** and the impact of that risk on the procurement is **7**. Notice where **8** and **7** intersect in the PI Matrix: this intersection is the risk score. The risk score is 8×7 or 56. Also notice that **56** is in a shaded box. Shaded boxes indicate risk that is above the company's risk tolerance.

Shaded risk scores require further analysis. In our example, because the score is **56**, you will need to do more analysis to determine if any action needs to take place. In this matrix, the number **40** (in the Risk Score area: column 3, row 2) is completely arbitrary—it represents the threshold for risk tolerance in our example company. You will use the number that reflects the risk tolerance of your organization. If your company's risk tolerance is lower, e.g., **30** instead of **40**, then the risk score **56** will require even more scrutiny because it is even higher than the risk tolerance.

Risk Log				
Risk	**Probability**	**Impact**	**Response**	**Action**
Requested completion date not workable	High	Very high		
Necessary personnel not available to meet schedule	High	Very high		
Team meetings not attended	Moderate	High		
No competitors in market	Moderate	Very high		
IBP insists on sole-sourced process	Moderate	Very high		
Scope of work not detailed enough	High	Very high		
Funding not adequate to provide requested services	Moderate	Very high		
Funding level does not provide savings	Moderate	Low		
RFP not delivered on time	High	Very high		
RFP responses late	Moderate	High		
RFP responses inadequate	Moderate	Very high		
Response evaluation delayed	High	Very high		
Top three competitors' oral presentations delayed schedule	Moderate	High		
Weather adversely impacted oral presentation schedule	Low	High		

Figure 7-5. Risk log with probability and impact.

Probability	Risk Score = P × I					
10	10	30	**50**	**70**	**90**	**100**
8	8	24	**40**	**56**	**72**	**80**
6	6	18	30	**42**	**54**	**60**
4	4	12	20	28	36	**40**
2	2	6	10	14	18	20
Impact on Procurement	1	3	5	7	9	10

Figure 7-6. Probability and impact (PI) matrix using numbers.

Figure 7-7 is a PI Matrix using the descriptive terms of Very high, High, Moderate, Low, and Very low. As in the numerical PI Matrix, shaded scores require further analysis of the risk. Keep in mind that the severity of the risk also depends on the risk tolerance of your organization.

Probability	Risk Score				
Very high	No analysis needed	No analysis needed	Needs more analysis	99% certainty; urgent action required	99% certainty; urgent action required
High	No analysis needed	No analysis needed	Needs more analysis	99% certainty; urgent action required	99% certainty; urgent action required
Moderate	No analysis needed	No analysis needed	No analysis needed	Needs more analysis	99% certainty; urgent action required
Low	No analysis needed	No analysis needed	No analysis needed	No analysis needed	No analysis needed
Very low	No analysis needed	No analysis needed	No analysis needed	No analysis needed	No analysis needed
Impact on Procurement	Very low	Low	Moderate	High	Very high

Figure 7-7. Probability and impact (PI) matrix using words.

Response Planning

Now that you have identified the risks to your procurement and determined their probability and impact, it is time to figure out how you will respond if they actually happen. (Remember Murphy's law—if it ***can*** go wrong, it ***will***.)

Risk response planning allows you to develop options and determine actions needed to reduce threats (risks) to your procurement. You can also enhance any opportunities that your risk identification has yielded. As part of planning, you will create a risk response plan that includes assigning individuals or teams to be responsible for each response, referred to as *action*. In this context, action means *someone specific has been assigned to the response.* Before making an assignment, you must be sure that the specific individual or team has agreed to accept each assignment. Obtaining agreement creates buy-in from your team. To be effective, responses need to be:

- Appropriate to the severity of the risk
- Cost effective in meeting the challenge
- Timely
- Realistic within the procurement context
- Agreed upon by all individuals involved (buy-in)
- Owned by a responsible individual or team

Several types of risk responses are available to you. Depending on the exact risk, your organization, and the individuals involved, you and your team will need to come up with unique responses. We will now discuss some common response types. Most of your responses will fall into at least one of these categories.

Avoidance. This category of response requires changing the procurement plan in some way. Sometimes a risk is identified early in the procurement. When early identification happens, you might be able to avoid the risk by clarifying the scope, improving communication, or acquiring personnel with the best expertise. For example, to clarify the scope, you can talk with the originator of the procurement request and get more details on the scope. To improve communication, you can ask your team for a better way to communicate with them: texting, email, instant messaging, telephone calls, etc. To obtain personnel with better expertise, you can negotiate with a senior executive to assign the best person for your procurement by making sure that individual's work will be done, and done well, by someone else. In each of these examples, the risk goes away. You then move the risk to the bottom of your risk log with a note recording your exact actions. Moving the risk to the bottom of the risk log indicates that it now has lowest priority of all the identified risks.

Transference. This response usually involves payment of a risk premium to the party taking the risk. Transference includes the use of insurance, performance bonds, warranties, guarantees, etc. Think of it as transferring liability as you would in a contract, except this response is to protect your procurement.

Mitigation. Most risk responses fall into the mitigation category. Mitigation reduces the consequences of a risk, but does not make the consequences go away completely. By taking action as soon as a risk is identified, you will lower the probability that the risk will happen. For example, if the SME that you need on your procurement team is not available when you need her, negotiating with her boss as soon as you find out could get you either that SME or the next best qualified SME. The risk does not disappear, but the impact on your procurement has been minimized. Mitigation can involve implementing a new course of action to reduce the risk or to reduce the severity of the consequences. A new course of action might be contracting an outside SME to work on your procurement team. *Caution*: Be careful about responses such as this. If the cost to mitigate a risk is more than the cost to not mitigate it, then the risk response is not appropriate. To reduce the severity of the risk of the SME that you need on your procurement team not being available, your decision to either go with the second best qualified SME or a contracted SME works. You will still get an expert opinion to make this a great procurement. You just need to weigh the cost against the value of each option to make a good decision.

Acceptance. In acceptance, you do not do anything. There are two types of acceptance: passive and active. *Passive* acceptance means that you and your team will deal with problems associated with the risk as they occur. Often called fire fighting, this is not the best way to deal with most risks, but if the consequences are small, so that they do not threaten the procurement in any way, this approach is acceptable. *Active* acceptance means that you and your team will develop a contingency plan. That way, if the risk occurs, you will be ready to take appropriate action to keep your procurement on target. Having a contingency plan involves establishing a contingency allowance (or reserve) that could include amounts of time, money, or personnel. A contingency allowance for time is called *float time* (discussed in Chapter 4, *Scheduling*). A contingency allowance for money (discussed in Chapter 5, *Budget*) is having a separate fund that is set aside "just in case." A contingency allowance for personnel is having back-up personnel assigned to your team.

Figure 7-8 is an example of how risk responses are recorded on the risk log. (At the end of the next section, you will see how actions are recorded.) Now that you have recorded your risk responses, you are ready for the final part of risk management—risk monitoring and control.

Risk Log				
Risk	**Probability**	**Impact**	**Response**	**Action**
Requested completion date not workable	High	Very high	Negotiate	
Necessary personnel not available to meet schedule	High	Very high	Negotiate	
Team meetings not attended	Moderate	High	Determine better meeting time and place	
No competitors in market	Moderate	Very high	Find and research competitors in this industry and market	
IBP insists on sole-sourced process	Moderate	Very high	RFS completely filled out and signed; advise management	
Scope of work not detailed enough	High	Very high	Face-to-face (or telephone) interview with SME	
Funding not adequate to provide requested services	Moderate	Very high	Negotiate funding levels	
Funding level does not provide savings	Moderate	Low	Negotiate lower spend levels	
RFP not delivered on time	High	Very high	Allow enough time for drafting and reviewing RFP	
RFP responses late	Moderate	High	Allow enough time for questions, responses, and finalizing responses	
RFP responses inadequate	Moderate	Very high	Include extremely detailed scope of work, specifications, draft contract, responses to all RFP questions from suppliers; amend RFP as needed	
Response evaluation delayed	High	Very high	Negotiate work assignments of team members as necessary	
Top three competitors' oral presentations delayed schedule	Moderate	High	Allow enough time	
Weather adversely impacted oral presentation schedule	Low	High	Allow float time for oral presentation schedule	

Figure 7-8. Risk log with responses.

Monitoring and Control

The final step in the procurement risk management process is monitoring and controlling risks to your procurement. You will need to keep track of the identified risks, identify new risks, monitor residual risks, ensure the timely execution of the risk plan, and record risk metrics associated with implementing contingency plans (if you have any). Reasons to monitor the risk management plan include ensuring that:

- A risk trigger has been recognized (risk trigger: an indication that a risk has occurred or is about to occur).
- Risk responses have been implemented as planned.
- Risk responses are effective (if not, a new response is necessary).
- Assumptions are still valid.
- Risks have occurred that were not previously identified and need to be addressed now.
- Proper policies and procedures are being followed.

A risk management plan can be monitored in several ways. Not all of these methods are useful in every procurement and all available methods are not included:

- Risk audits
- Periodic reviews of the risk log
- Technical performance metrics reviews
- Additional risk response planning

As you can see, these methods to monitor the risk management plan include regular reviews of the risk log. Review the risk log *every time* you look at the procurement plan and you will stay ahead of the curve—or in this case, ahead of the risk.

Figure 7-9 shows a completed risk log. Below the risk log title are column headings:

Risk: the identified risk
Probability: how likely this risk is to occur
Impact: how much damage will be done if this risk does occur
Response: the detailed action(s) to be undertaken in order to avoid, mitigate, or tolerate the risk
Action: the individual assigned responsibility (name or title of a specific individual)

Risk Log				
Risk	**Probability**	**Impact**	**Response**	**Action**
Requested completion date not workable	High	Very high	Negotiate	Procurement lead
Necessary personnel not available to meet schedule	High	Very high	Negotiate	Procurement lead
Team meetings not attended	Moderate	High	Determine better meeting time and place	Procurement lead
No competitors in market	Moderate	Very high	Find and research competitors in this industry and market	Financial analyst
IBP insists on sole-sourced process	Moderate	Very high	RFS completely filled out and signed; advise management	Procurement lead
Scope of work not detailed enough	High	Very high	Face-to-face (or telephone) interview with SME	Procurement lead
Funding not adequate to provide requested services	Moderate	Very high	Negotiate funding levels	Procurement lead
Funding level does not provide savings	Moderate	Low	Negotiate lower spend levels	Negotiation lead
RFP not delivered on time	High	Very high	Allow enough time for drafting and reviewing RFP	Procurement lead (RFP writer)
RFP responses late	Moderate	High	Allow enough time for questions, responses, and finalizing responses	Procurement lead
RFP responses inadequate	Moderate	Very high	Include extremely detailed scope of work, specifications, draft contract, responses to all RFP questions from suppliers; amend RFP as needed	Procurement lead (RFP writer)
Response evaluation delayed	High	Very high	Negotiate work assignments of team members as necessary	Procurement lead
Top three competitors' oral presentations delayed schedule	Moderate	High	Allow enough time	Procurement lead
Weather adversely impacted oral presentation schedule	Low	High	Allow float time for oral presentation schedule	Procurement lead

Figure 7-9. Risk log with actions.

SUMMARY

As you can see, risk management is an involved and important piece of procurement management. The more complex your procurement, the more involved risk management should be. To be a successful procurement manager, you will need to manage the risks to your procurement—no matter where the risk comes from.

As a successful procurement manager, look for everything that can adversely affect your procurement. Be suspicious. Seek out problems. Positive thinking is for motivating people, but is not appropriate for good procurement management.

After you have identified risks, you will analyze their probability of occurrence and their impact on the procurement. Then you and your team will determine responses to every risk and assign actions to specific people.

In the next chapter, we will look at negotiations and techniques to use for successful outcomes.

This book has free material available for download from the Web Added Value™ resource center at *www.jrosspub.com.*

CHAPTER 8

NEGOTIATIONS

During a negotiation, it would be wise not to take anything personally. If you leave personalities out of it, you will be able to see opportunities more objectively
—Brian Koslow

Negotiations are a form of communication. We negotiate for many things every day. You will negotiate eating out with your family. Your children will negotiate their bedtimes with you. You will negotiate a raise with your boss. You will negotiate the price of a vehicle. As a procurement professional, you will negotiate for goods/services on behalf of your company.

Most people do not think about their everyday negotiations as "real" negotiations. Formal negotiations carry a connotation that intimidates many people. Lots of people even think negotiations are "mind games." These mind games include manipulation of others—often to their detriment. Unfortunately, procurement professionals often believe the same thing. At times they do whatever it takes to avoid conflict—even in negotiations for a contract. Avoiding conflict is not negotiation. It is caving in. Avoiding conflict does not get a good deal for your company and often achieves just the opposite.

In this chapter, we will discuss how good communications skills lead to negotiations that get you the best value for your money.

GOALS

What are the goals of your negotiation? You know the price you want. You know exactly what the goods or services must do. What else is there?

It is rare that we will ever get goods or services for the exact price that we want to pay. So before you begin negotiations, define some other objectives to give you more options.

For example, in *Case Example 2: Janitorial Services* from Chapter 3, you want the services at the price you can pay for them (established in the SOW by the contract spend for the first year: to be as high as $500,000). So your goal is to get the services for less than $500,000. You already have the specifications for the work you need done. What other objectives do you have?

You want the janitorial employees to be checked for criminal records. You want the employees to actually show up and do the work. You want the supplier's employees to be easily identifiable when they are on your property. You want the work guaranteed by the supplier. You want the supplier to use their equipment. You want specific chemicals and other supplies used in your property. Go through the procurement plan and see all of the other objectives that you have in the janitorial services procurement. (The complete plan is downloadable as Web Added Value™ at www.jrosspub.com.)

Each one of these objectives becomes a goal in addition to the pricing of the service. Finding additional objectives is often an opportunity to educate your stakeholders. Share with them all of the objectives in your procurement so that they understand that price is only one goal. This is an easier task if you and the stakeholders have developed the weighted evaluation criteria used in the RFP process. (When you and your stakeholders develop the weighted criteria together, they already know and understand the concept.) See an example of weighted criteria in Appendix C, *RFP for Case Example 2: Janitorial Services.*

Listing all of your goals *before negotiations begin* is the first step in preparing for negotiations. Next, prioritize each goal—is one more important than another? Some goals will have the same priority as others. Usually, however, you will find that one goal has the highest priority and several goals are in the next lower level of priority. Now look at the goals that wind up in the bottom level of the priority list to see if they are actually necessary. If some of these goals can be dropped during negotiations, you will have choices available that will make your deal more valuable for your company.

INFORMATION

During the RFP process, you received information on the supplier's company. Your financial analyst, or you, did the research into the company's finances. You had the opportunity to ask questions during the supplier's oral presentation. What else do you need?

After you have a list of priorities for negotiations, you need more information about the people who will be negotiating for the supplier. You need to know *exactly* with whom you will be negotiating. Ask for names and titles of everyone who will be involved in the negotiation. Find out who will have the final decision authority in the supplier's company. Who will actually sign the contract? Ask for resumes for everyone on the supplier's negotiation team. You might not get them, but asking shows that you are not a run-of-the-mill negotiator.

Being very careful to *never* allow even a glimmer of impropriety, ask the main negotiator to lunch. You pay for lunch—*never* allow a potential supplier to pay for anything. Bring someone from your negotiations team and invite at least one other person from the supplier's team. Meeting during lunch is a good way to get to know each other before formal negotiations start. Ask lots of questions about the supplier's negotiation team including work histories, degrees, positions in the company, etc. Your goal here is to learn as much as possible about the other people and find commonalities. Bonding over food is traditional in most cultures around the world.

If it is not possible to meet over lunch, or even face-to-face, arrange a telephone call. A video telephone call is ideal because you get to see the other person's face as you talk. The goal is the same—to learn as much as possible about the other team.

Although you had enough financial information on the potential supplier's company to have chosen them, you need still more financial information. Make sure you or your financial analyst take a broader view of the industry your supplier is in. Are there imminent materials shortages? Does your supplier have reliable suppliers? Are there political situations that could adversely affect your supplier or the supplier's supply chain? Think about the supplier's business and ask yourself what could adversely impact it. Then investigate those issues to get a good idea of the risks. After that, you can ask questions of your supplier's team to get the information that you need in order to negotiate.

As discussed earlier, ask questions either during the supplier's oral presentation or before you begin negotiations. These questions are better asked of an executive of the supplier's company than a sales person. The executive will probably be more familiar with the internal workings of the company. Some questions to ask include:

- How will working with your company make my business more profitable?
- What are the biggest operational challenges that your company faces now?

- What changes are you seeing in your industry in the near future?
- How are you preparing for those changes?
- Are there any questions that I haven't asked that I should have?

You should now have enough information about your supplier's business, industry, and personnel to develop a negotiation strategy.

STRATEGIES

Although many experienced negotiators have one specific strategy that they always use, there are actually several different strategies for negotiations. One is the hardball strategy. In the hardball strategy, one side demands that everything be exactly as they want it. Hardball negotiators use manipulation and confrontation in order to prevail. The underlying idea is that the negotiation produces a winner—and a loser.

Another strategy is the softball strategy. In the softball strategy, one side gives in to the demands of the other side in order to reduce confrontation and conflict. Again, this strategy is based on the idea that there will be a winner and a loser. Although the softball strategy is the polar opposite of the hardball strategy, it is surprising how many procurement professionals use it. Why? In our culture, conflict is seen as negative. Many people avoid it at all costs, both in professional life and in personal life.

Most of the other negotiation strategies will fall somewhere within the boundaries of the hardball and softball strategies. "Good cop, bad cop" is one of those strategies. In the good-cop, bad-cop strategy, one person on the negotiation team acts like a bully—demanding concessions, yelling if they do not get them, etc. Another person on the bully's team then steps in, asks the bully to leave the room for a minute to "cool off," and apologizes to the other team. The good cop usually says something like, "We can get some of this agreed to before he comes back." The other team is relieved and wants to conclude the negotiations before the bad cop comes back. Of course, all of this was planned before the meeting started so the bad cop has no plans to return to the negotiations. Although these strategies work to one degree or another, none of them is truly successful in getting the best value for your company.

In their book, *Getting to Yes: Negotiating Agreement Without Giving In*, Penguin (1981), by Roger Fisher and William Ury (reissued in 1991 with Bruce Patton), the idea of *negotiation on the merits*, or principled negotiations, is presented. This strategy is also known as win-win. Fisher and Ury urge negotiators to "change the game." Basically, they describe a strategy that focuses on coming up with solutions that give mutual gain. Often that means developing an idea that is new in order to solve an issue between two parties (the companies in our example).

Think about our negotiation and the win-win strategy. If the supplier does not accept your company's terms and conditions, would you be able to find a way—together with the supplier—to address the specific issue that the supplier has? Depending on the issue, one common area to look at is *indemnification.* Lawyers insist on certain language in the contract to protect your company from liability created by the supplier. Because most indemnification clauses are general, it makes sense that the supplier's attorney will not accept the language in your company's contract. Are there ways to work with both attorneys to find more specific language that still protects your company *and* does not put the supplier's company at higher risk? By putting your heads together, you can find solutions.

Negotiation on the merits uses collaboration as a major part of the strategy. Collaboration does not mean violating ethics or giving away business secrets. Collaboration means that you and the supplier's negotiator share information that is pertinent to the work you want to do together. This information includes what the supplier needs, e.g., a 20% profit margin, a guarantee of work, or fast payment terms, as well as what your company needs, e.g., quality, reliability, pricing, etc.

Collaboration also means that you and the supplier's negotiation team brainstorm options for all issues that are in disagreement. Unique solutions are easier to find with several brains working on them. As usual with brainstorming, anything is acceptable in the first round—it gets all kinds of ideas on the table. The next step is to go through the ideas and discard those that will not work. This step is also done together with the supplier's team. The final step is to come to a decision on the best solution. Again, this is done with both your team and the supplier's team. You will repeat this collaboration for every issue where disagreement exists.

Although it seems to take more time for the negotiation, brainstorming actually *saves* time. When negotiations are based on positions, as in hardball strategies, negotiations move slowly because each side gives the other side time to reconsider and back down. Softball negotiations proceed the fastest—and get the worst results for you and your company. In negotiations, be prepared to take the time required for brainstorming with your team and with the supplier's team. Negotiation on the merits will give both your company and the supplier's company the best results.

Negotiation on the merits uses a specific method:

- Separate the people from the problem.
- Focus on interests, not positions.

- Invent options for mutual gains.
- Insist on using objective criteria.

Separating the people from the problem means to focus on the issue, not the people involved in the negotiations. Do not take anything personally.

You might be wondering how to deal with a team that is not using the win-win strategy. Several tactics can be used to refocus the negotiations. First, focus on what you need to do: concentrate on the issues, not the positions. Often doing this is the game changer that gets the supplier's team to also focus on the issues.

If focusing on what you need to do does not work by itself, then focus on what the supplier's team can do—come up with options. *Caution*: Be careful not to push back when the supplier's negotiators take a firm position. Do not criticize their position or reject it outright. Do not defend your own proposal or make it a position (a hard stand). If the supplier's negotiators attack you, do not defend yourself and do not attack them. These are all reactions that you can control. By refusing to react the way the supplier's negotiators expect you to, you surprise them. So what do you do instead of pushing back? Ignore their attack and focus on your strategy—coming up with options based on the interests of both parties.

If neither of these tactics works, the final choice is to include a mutually agreed upon third-party mediator. This person (or a team) needs to be trained to focus on interests, options, and criteria. A mediator is not directly involved in the deal, so the mediator can more easily separate the people from the issue. The mediator can also direct the discussion to interests and options more effectively than either party involved in the negotiations can. The mediator can get to the basis of the position taken so that solutions can be found.

Getting a third party mediator can be costly and time consuming. The only time most companies use this approach is when the company is risking so much that failure is not an option.

Let's talk about *positions* versus *interests*. Using *Case Example 2: Janitorial Services*, one position the supplier might take is that the janitorial staff will work no more than four hours per weekday. Instead of addressing that position directly, ask questions about it:

- How did you come up with four hours per weekday?
- Is that how long it usually takes your team to complete work in a facility of this size and type?
- Exactly what work does that include?
- What happens if an inexperienced employee is on the team assigned to our facility?

During your discussion, you can ask more questions as they arise. Perhaps the supplier is basing this time on experience with similar facilities or perhaps it is based on something completely different. You need to know. As you conclude the discussion, ask the supplier for options to this commitment of an exact number of hours worked per day. Asking for options may spark another discussion on the pricing model for the contract—time and materials or fixed price. The decision will be based on the interests of each company. Your company's interest is in how much money it will spend in one year for these services. The supplier's interest is in how much profit it needs to make on this contract in one year.

Our discussion on negotiation strategy will be incomplete if we leave the topic of negotiations at only two parties. It is rare that there are only two parties in a negotiation. The larger negotiation effort will be between your company and the supplier company. Within that effort, however, will be the negotiations between you and the procurement owner, SME, end users, etc. In other words, you and your stakeholders will have your own negotiations within the procurement. Using the same win-win strategy in these negotiations will work. Find out what the basis is for the position the other person (or people) is taking and together seek options for solutions.

TECHNIQUES

Several techniques are involved in using any negotiation strategy. In this chapter, we will only use techniques that are successful in the win-win strategy.

Take control of negotiations from the beginning. You had control during the RFX process (Request for Proposal, Request for Quote, Request for Information, etc.). You told the potential suppliers exactly what you needed and when you needed it. You also told them the criteria for success. The negotiation still needs you to direct it, but with less rigidity. At this point, communication is two-way (or more). You need to listen as much, or more, than you talk. You need to set up the negotiation meetings. As always when more than one person is involved, you need everyone to consult their calendars and find mutually agreeable dates and times. (Finding mutually agreeable dates and times becomes more complicated when people are in different time zones or across the date line—different days because of the large difference in time.)

Provide the agenda. The next step is to provide an agenda. As simple as that sounds, the party that provides the agenda leads the negotiation. If you allow the supplier to send out the agenda, issues that are important to you may be overlooked. When you send the agenda, be aware that the supplier may have different issues from yours. Make sure to allow enough time for the supplier to thoroughly review the agenda, make comments/changes, and get back to you in time to publish the agenda at least one day before the negotiations begin.

Open the meeting. On the day of the meeting, make sure you open the meeting. Doing this automatically makes you the leader in the negotiations at this point. Do all the usual meeting proprieties —have each person introduce themselves, let everyone know how much time is allotted to this meeting, go over the agenda quickly—then begin with the first item. Leading the meeting means that you will be the person who directs people back to the issue at hand, or the next agenda item, so that time is not wasted. Be careful when directing the discussion back to an issue at hand, however, because valuable discussion is never a waste of time. More meetings can be scheduled if needed to finalize the negotiations.

Determine the best method for including all negotiators. Business in our world makes it difficult to get everyone involved in a negotiation in one room for face-to-face discussions. Web-based meetings with video and screen visibility are the next best choice. Seeing faces and body language during negotiations is important for most of us. Negotiating over the telephone in a conference call is the next choice. The fewer people involved in a negotiation, the easier it is to use other methods of communication such as email, texting, etc.

Two other negotiating techniques are often talked about, but rarely used: silence and walk-away. Using either of these techniques is very difficult.

Silence. Asking a question and then shutting up completely until you get an answer is hard for most of us to do, but this is the starting point for active listening—focusing on what the person is saying and repeating it back. Often the other person will also be silent for a moment. Resist the urge to fill in the space with more information about your question or to ask more questions. The silence technique takes practice. When done correctly, it gets amazing results. Often you will discover the basis (or the interest) for the position that has been taken.

Walk-away. Walking away means that you will no longer negotiate ***at all*** with the supplier. Sometimes the supplier's negotiation team will come back to the table with a better deal, but most often they will not. So what do you need to do before you use the walk-away technique? You must have a backup plan for what you will do after walking away. Your walk-away plan might not be as desirable. It might be more costly. It might be harder to "sell" to management. Before walking away, be sure your backup plan is doable and that you are prepared to implement it.

Now let's look back at *Case Example 1: Shopping for a Car* from Chapter 1. The family had decided to buy a car. They had also decided exactly what make and model they wanted. There had been a discussion about the options that they wanted, so they knew enough basic information in order to negotiate. The only area left to decide was which car dealer they would buy from. If, during the price negotiation, the salesperson at a dealership would not meet the price they wanted, they would walk out of the dealership. Then they would go to another dealer with the same make and model of car and start the price negotiation all over again. Depending on the number of dealerships in their area, this family would continue the price negotiation process several times until they got the price they wanted. (Later in this chapter we will see how the price negotiations went.)

In a business, however, things are not always that simple or clear cut. Sometimes there is only one supplier for what you need. When that happens, you have to negotiate with this supplier. You do not have the option of walking away because you do not have a fallback plan. When there is only one supplier, you will need to be very good with the other techniques we discussed earlier in order to negotiate the best value for your company.

CASE EXAMPLE 1 DISSECTION

If you think that procurement negotiations begin *after* the RFX process, think about it again. Negotiation preparation involves all of the steps that Bill and Sheila took to buy a car. Look for the areas where the family did well and where they could have improved. Let's now dissect *Case Example 1: Shopping for a Car* from Chapter 1.

Bill and Sheila needed to buy a vehicle for their sixteen-year-old daughter, Abby. Their decision to buy a vehicle took quite some time—their daughter's safety was first in their minds. Now that the decision to buy the vehicle had been reached, they started looking at different makes and models. The first requirement, safety, ruled out several models. Abby would not be getting a Ford Mustang, a Dodge Charger, a Chevrolet Corvette, and many other vehicles. Next they looked at body styles—SUV, minivan, sedan, and pickup. They could not see a sixteen-year-old girl driving a minivan or a SUV. That left sedan or pickup. They did not need a pickup because Bill already drove one. So a sedan it would be.

From this paragraph, we see that Bill and Sheila made a decision to make a purchase. They went through the process of deciding what they needed and what they wanted. The prevailing need was safety in a vehicle. The secondary need was body style. Both of these needs were influenced by wants: they wanted their daughter to have a car, and they wanted it to be appropriately stylish for their culture. We could argue that a sixteen-year-old girl does not need her own vehicle at all. That would address both safety and style. But that decision has already been made, just as these types of decisions are often made before procurement is brought in to the process.

Doing their research online, Bill and Sheila started with a trusted site. This site had reports on all types of vehicles. The reports included safety, reliability, fuel consumption, and comfort as the metrics, along with the technical specifications for each vehicle. The site also provided guidance on pricing of each vehicle and which vehicles provided the best value for the money.

Here Bill and Sheila did their due diligence. Finding out as much information as possible about the product they wanted to buy is an important step in any purchase. It was just as important that they trusted the information that was provided during their research.

After they narrowed down the choices, Bill and Sheila visited car dealerships. They still had to decide if they would buy a new sedan or a used sedan, so they went to both types of dealers. They also looked in the local newspaper for ads for both new and used vehicles. With ongoing conversations between each other, and with their daughter, they decided to buy a new car. The major factors influencing their decision were safety, reliability, and value. With car loan interest rates very low, and prices for new vehicles quite reasonable, they decided that this new car would last their daughter at least through college—and probably several more years after that.

This is the point where Bill and Sheila got first-hand experience with the product. Although getting first-hand experience is not always possible in business, and rarely possible with services, it is still a good idea for the team to see and experience a product before it is purchased. For example, request a tour of the plant where the product is made. Of course, if the product is one that your company buys often, then getting first-hand experience is not necessary every time a purchase is made.

Bill and Sheila also realized that they needed to make more decisions before they were ready to buy a car. These decisions involved the quality and reliability of the product. All of the factors they considered—safety, quality, reliability—contributed to the value of the product. Note that they did not think about price yet.

Still looking for the best possible value, Bill thought about a hybrid car. Sure it would save on gas costs over the life of the vehicle, but what would that life be? Five years? Ten years? More? What about repairing or replacing the batteries? Bill decided to do research to find out about hybrids. This is some of what he found online:

> **Pros:** *great gas mileage (ranges from about 42 to over 60 miles per gallon); very quiet while running on batteries; good reliability; good durability;*

great braking; good interior style; smooth ride; good cargo capacity; good power train performance

Cons: *sluggish handling (steering); high price; slow acceleration; too quiet (cannot hear engine running); not enough leg room; poor driving position reduces visibility; not recommended for towing; high maintenance costs*

With these findings, Bill talked with Sheila and Abby and they all decided to do test drives. The conflicting ratings of the quietness and power train performance would be decided during the drives, as well as the driving position and comfort level for Abby.

Having completed the first round of in-person visits to see products that they would consider buying, Bill and Sheila did more research. This is analogous to the RFP process used in procurement. Finding out what options are available for the goods or services that you need is the goal of an RFP or RFI. In our case study, Bill and Sheila discovered an option that they had not considered before. With conflicting information about a hybrid vehicle, they decided to take test drives to find out if any of these observations would affect their purchase. In a procurement, you may find information from the RFP or RFI about the range of services provided or the quality of materials that influences the pricing—information that gives you options that you might not have known about before.

They decided to test drive a Toyota Prius first. At the dealership, there was only one Prius available. All three went on the test drive, with Abby driving out of the dealership. The salesman rode in the back seat and answered questions as she drove. Bill and Sheila found the Prius to be very different from the vehicles that they had driven all their lives. It was very quiet without the gas engine running. They had to agree with the online comments that the steering was less responsive than they were used to, but Abby did not have any problems with it. Secretly Sheila was very happy that the car did not have the pep that sports cars have—Abby would be safer. When they arrived back at the dealership, the salesman invited them into the office to talk about the car.

Now the family got direct experience with the product that they are considering for purchase. Each person had a slightly different conclusion about the experience, but overall they were happy with it. At this point, we have to wonder if they are ready to make the purchase.

Before they went to the dealership, all three had decided that they would do the test drive only. They did not want to buy the car right now. There were other cars to look at and test drive before their decision could be made.

There is our answer. The family had made the decision not to buy the car right now. As a team, this is a crucial point in the negotiation. If *even one* of them forgets this decision, or changes their mind without consulting the others, the negotiation moves to the next step without the requisite planning.

Inside the dealership office, the salesman pointed out that there was only the one Prius at the dealership. He said that they never kept a Prius on the lot for more than two days, and this one had arrived the day before. No other dealers had a Prius on their lots right now either. If they wanted a Prius without a wait, they would need to make a decision now.

Bill and Sheila looked at each other, then at Abby, and Bill stood. Sheila asked, "What kind of deal can we get on this Prius?"

The salesman responded, "Do you have a trade in?"

"No. And we're not ready to proceed with this right now, are we?" Bill said as he looked at Sheila.

"But, honey, we're here now and we all like the car. Does it hurt to find out more?" Sheila looked at the salesman.

Bill sat down. Abby touched her mother's arm and said, "Mom, we need to go. We're looking at some other cars now, remember?"

Sheila looked surprised and then gathered her belongings. She stood up and extended her hand to the salesman. "Perhaps you can give us a card. We'll call you when we make a decision."

Mistake number one: going inside the dealership with the salesman
Mistake number two: Sheila reacting to the pressure from the salesman
Mistake number three: Bill sitting down
Saving moment: Abby reminding her mother that they had decided to test drive other cars

What could this family have done better? The simple answer is that they could have avoided each of the mistakes that they made. (When a decision is made about how to proceed with the negotiations, it needs to be honored by every member of the team.)

The salesman stood and shook hands with Sheila and Bill. Then he handed Sheila his business card. "I hope you folks hurry with your decision. That Prius won't be here tomorrow."

The comment by the salesman is a pressure tactic that we expect from sales people. Even when the information is true, the fact that this particular car would not be available for long should have no impact on the decision to buy it. Another Prius will be available, either from another dealership or by ordering it from the manufacturer.

After two weeks of test drives and getting answers to their questions, the family was ready to make a decision. They decided that despite the high initial price of the Toyota Prius, it was the best choice for their daughter.

Now the family is one step closer to making the purchase. They have a solid decision about the car they will buy. So far, this family has followed all the best practices for buying a vehicle. The only stumbling block was when one member of the team either forgot about their decision not to buy anything on that trip or she caved in to sales pressure.

They called the salesman at the Toyota dealership to find out if he had a Prius on the lot. He did not, but suggested that they could order one and it would be there within three weeks. They agreed with his suggestion and went to the dealership to negotiate. The salesman met all three of them at the door of the dealership and escorted them to his office. After bringing in an extra chair, the salesman sat behind his desk.

It could be argued here that Bill and Sheila made a mistake by bringing the entire family to this crucial negotiation meeting. If all three of them are not on the same page, this meeting could go very badly for them. Their goal is to get the best value for the lowest price. Unless the entire team knows, understands, and agrees with the strategy here, the end result could easily be too high a price.

The salesman started the negotiation. "For the model you folks looked at, the Prius C, which trim did you decide on?"

Bill answered, "We want the C 3."

"Uhh!" Everyone looked at Abby, the source of the noise. Abby rolled her eyes.

"That's what you and Mom want. I want the C 2." Abby said and crossed her arms.

"What do you mean, you want the C 2? We discussed this and decided on the C 3." Bill squinted his eyes, but maintained his calm.

"You mean you and Mom decided. I couldn't get a word in edgewise," said Abby.

The mistake here is that not all of the members of the team had agreed to the strategy for this meeting. It is apparent that Abby was not happy with the trim that her parents had decided on. The way to avoid this mistake was for Bill and Sheila to encourage Abby to speak up before they went to the dealership.

"Okay," the salesman interrupted. "We can look at both models again and see all the options. Here are the brochures." He handed Bill two glossy brochures.

In this instance, the salesman shines in using the win-win strategy. He focuses on the interest of the family, not on either position that was taken. Bill's position was the C 3 trim and Abby's position was the C 2 trim. The salesman helps the other party (the family) to focus on their interests, too, by handing them information on all of the options available.

Sheila took the brochures from Bill and laid them on the desk so that all three of them could see. She opened them up side by side.

"Honey," she said, "we just want the safest car for you. That's our main concern."

"Yeah, but I want something that's fun. Something that my friends will like." Abby said as she scooted forward in her chair to see the brochures. "See, the C 2 has so much more fun stuff. And it's safe, isn't it?" She looked at the salesman.

While Abby did something that is very common, what she did is not good practice in a negotiation. She brought in the other party to bolster her position, which shows that she has "dug in" and needs more focus on what is needed as opposed to what is wanted in this purchase. This scenario is a great example of a negotiation within a negotiation. When one party feels unheard, that party often takes a position that will be difficult to move from. Part of the win-win strategy is to listen to *all* parties—meaning use active listening so that everyone is heard.

"Of course it's safe," he answered. "It's a Toyota." The three adults smiled at that.

"Okay, let's go through it all again," Bill conceded.

They went through the various base and option specifications. They compared how the two models were alike and how they differed. The salesman answered questions as they came up. The three members of the family discussed the pros and cons of each model.

At this point, the best negotiator at the table is the salesman. He is not supporting any position, but is looking at options for solutions. He is giving the other team plenty of time to make a decision.

And they did not reach a conclusion. Parents wanted the C 3 and teenager wanted the C 2. At this point the salesman spoke up.

"If she were my teenager, I'd go with the C 3. It does have more safety features ... now let me talk," he said and held up his hand, "and fewer entertainment features. Those features can be a distraction—especially with friends in the car."

When negotiating with a sales person, we must understand that time is money. Every minute spent with you is a minute that could be spent finalizing a sale. In this negotiation, one party (the family) had come to a loggerhead. They were no closer to a final decision even after taking quite a bit of time. In a win-win strategy, the salesman could have suggested that they take a break and meet tomorrow, but because he is in a situation where a sales commission is at stake, he chose to support one specific position—which changes the negotiation from win-win to more of a hardball strategy.

Abby crossed her arms, sat back in her chair, and looked away from the adults. It was a full power huff.

Now Abby has made the negotiation a full-on hardball negotiation between herself and her parents—there will be a winner and a loser within her own negotiation team.

Bill and Sheila looked at each other for a few seconds, and then Bill spoke. "Honey, we really want your first car to be as safe as possible. That includes reliability, which Toyota has, and safety features. We also want to spend as little as possible to get those things. But you'll have this car for a long time, we hope, and you need to be happy with it. So we'll get the Prius C 2."

Bill and Sheila's response to Abby's hardball strategy was to completely cave in. This is how many negotiations are conducted in business, too. By caving in, Bill and Sheila will not get the best value for their family. But they will get peace at home. (You decide how much that is worth.)

No one has ever seen a happier teenage girl. Abby jumped up and hugged her parents. Then she kept on jumping and clapping her hands. "Thank you, thank you, thank you. I'll take really good care of it and I'll be careful. I promise!"

"Okay, okay," the salesman was grinning. "Why don't you go out to the waiting area while your folks and I finalize this?" He rose and walked around his desk to open the door for her. As he seated himself again, the salesman started typing on the computer. "So, you want the Prius C 2. We need to get specific with the options that you want. Here's the list again and we'll go through it, item by item. Okay?"

"Sure." Bill sat back and let Sheila look at the brochure.

Of course the happy reaction from Abby made everyone smile. Was that the goal of this negotiation? No, it was not. The goal was to get the safest, best-quality, and most reliable car that they could. In this part of the negotiation, the salesman removed the person who might make things difficult during the rest of it. As you can see, throughout this negotiation the salesman has taken the lead. (Do you think the lead will change during the talks about price?)

CASE EXAMPLE 1 PRICE NEGOTIATION DIALOGUE

Did you notice something missing in our discussion of Case Example 1? Where was the price negotiation? We will include that now. Look for who takes the lead in this part of the negotiations, who takes a firm stand, and how the overall negotiation worked out. Was this a win-win negotiation?

After they decided on the options for the new car, it was time to talk about price. The salesman opened the discussion. Let's continue with the dialogue.

"Do you have a trade in?"

"No. We talked about that last time we met. What's the price with these options?" Bill asked.

"The sticker price is $22,060 for this model. With all the options you chose, it comes to $26,020."

Bill and Sheila looked at each other, then at the salesman.

"That's too much for this car. We did some research and thought it would be about $19,000," Bill said.

"Wow, that's low for this model. Where did you do your research?" the salesman responded.

"That doesn't matter. What can you do for us? We can't pay that much," replied Bill.

"How much can you afford in monthly payments?" the salesman asked.

"We don't budget that way. We need to talk about the total price of the vehicle," Bill responded.

"Okay. How much can you afford to pay for it?" the salesman asked.

"Like I said, we thought it'd be about $19,000. That's what we budgeted," replied Bill.

"Well, let me take this to my manager. We'll put our heads together and come up with something. I'll be just a few minutes." With that, the salesman got out of his chair and walked out of the office, leaving the door open.

"I can't believe they want that much!" Sheila said and looked at Bill.

"Shh! He might be just outside waiting for us to say something," Bill whispered.

"Now you're just paranoid, Bill." Sheila smiled and looked away.

"No, I'm not. Sales folks do stuff like that all the time. You know the price we researched is their invoice cost, right?" Bill asked.

"Right," answered Sheila.

"So," Bill said, "we'll have to pay more, but it should be much less than $26,000."

Sheila sighed and shrugged her shoulders. They sat in silence until the salesman returned.

"Well, my manager won't budge. The Prius is selling so fast that we can't keep them on the lot. You know that. That's why we have to order one for you. Part of the increase in the cost to you is that we have to pay more to get it from another dealership. We all have to make money to stay in business." The salesman sat back in his chair.

"Again, that's more than we can pay. We were thinking we could go as high as $20,000." Bill also sat back in his chair.

"Well, Toyota has a great financing program right now. If you can put 10% down, Toyota will finance the car for 0%. Of course, that depends on your credit score." The salesman cocked his head to the left.

"Can you give us a minute to talk about this? It's so much more money than we expected, we might have to walk away from the deal," Bill said.

"Sure." The salesman left the room, again leaving the door open behind him.

Bill motioned for Sheila to be quiet and then went to the door and looked around.

"Okay, we can talk. He's not there." Bill watched Sheila suppress a smile.

"Well, Bill, it sounds like they won't take any off of the car. Abby's heart is set on this car. She didn't like any of the others nearly as much. And we've been here for a long time. What if we take the deal? Can we come up with $2,602 for the down payment?"asked Sheila.

"Yeah, we can make the down payment. No problem. And I think our credit score is good enough to get the 0% interest on the loan. But the loan will be $23,418. That's a pretty hefty monthly payment. Probably for 60 months," Bill said as he sat down.

"I guess it's your decision, honey. Abby really wants this car."

"And we'll have to either pay the fees and taxes up front or add them to the loan. That makes everything even more expensive." Bill dropped his head. Sheila sat in silence, but stretched her hand out to Bill. He took it.

"Whatever decision you make, I'll back it," she said. Bill raised his head and smiled at her.

"I appreciate that. Let's go ahead and buy this thing. At least the decision will be made and we can move on."

"If you're sure," Sheila replied with a smile.

"Yes. I'll go find the salesman and we'll get this done." Bill got out of his chair and left the room.

Abby poked her head into the office. "Why are we still here, Mom?"

"Oh, honey. Your dad just decided that we're actually buying this car for you. Now we have to do all the paperwork. It's still going to be a little while."

"I thought that decision had been made—hours ago. What happened?" Abby asked.

"We have to pay more than we thought we would. But your dad's willing to do that so that you have the car you want. Maybe a little appreciation is in order."

Just then Bill and the salesman came around the corner toward the office. Abby ran up to her dad, threw her arms around his neck, and said, "Thank you, Daddy. Thank you, thank you, thank you."

The salesman grinned and said, "Then I guess you're going to accept our offer." Bill nodded yes with a smile.

What do you think about the way the negotiations about pricing went? Who got what they wanted and who did not? Was this negotiation a win-win for all the parties? Did anyone cave in under pressure from one or more of the parties? Who was the lead in these negotiations? What tactics were used to conclude this negotiation? These are the questions to ask yourself every time you participate in a negotiation. When you are the lead negotiator, it is even more important to ask these questions.

In our example pricing negotiation, the final outcome was a deal that everyone agreed to. The car salesman, Abby, and Sheila got what they wanted. The salesman got a sale, Abby got the new car she wanted, and Sheila made her daughter happy. Did Bill get what he wanted? It appears that Bill caved under the pressure from the other three parties. But if Bill's ultimate goal was to get his daughter a safe, reliable car that she likes, did he get what he wanted, too? Yes. If Bill's ultimate goal was to pay as little as possible for a car for Abby, then he did not get what he wanted.

The salesman appears to have had the winning technique in this negotiation. Note that he changed tactics as the need arose in order to get what he wanted. The salesman stayed in the lead during these negotiations. Bill and Sheila could have broken that strategy by calling it a day and returning to the dealership closer to the end of the month when all salespeople want to make a vehicle sale in order to meet their quotas. Bill could even have called ahead to make sure this salesman was not at the dealership so he could start the negotiations over with another salesperson.

The final analysis is up to you. Decide which techniques and strategies could have worked better for this family. Then pay attention the next time you are in a negotiation. The way to learn is by doing, so practice win-win techniques every chance you get. Excellent negotiations lead to great success.

SUMMARY

In this chapter we discussed negotiation. Negotiation is a specialized form of communication. Not limited to business, we use negotiations in everyday life. In our personal lives, we negotiate for the goods/products that we buy. We negotiate within our families about who will do chores. In our work lives, we negotiate daily work priorities. Even in volunteer activities, we negotiate what we will actually do and our schedule for doing it. Supply chain professionals, of course, negotiate procurements.

To negotiate, there must be at least one goal to achieve. We talked about the information that you need in order to successfully negotiate for your goal(s). You need to know about the company and the members of the team who you will negotiate with. It is very important that you understand the industry that your supplier works in so that you know more about his business. It is with this information that you can discern the interests of your supplier in order to negotiate with a win-win strategy.

Although there are many strategies that can be used in negotiations, the win-win strategy gives you the best chance at getting the value that your company needs. Described in detail in their book *Getting to Yes: Negotiating Agreement Without Giving In, Penguin* (1981), by Roger Fisher and William Ury (reissued in 1991 with Bruce Patton), the win-win strategy is called negotiation on the merits or principled negotiations. The method used in a win-win strategy has four steps:

- Separate the people from the problem.
- Focus on interests, not positions.
- Invent options for mutual gains.
- Insist on using objective criteria.

We also discussed some techniques that can be used in negotiations. They include taking control of the negotiations, silence, and walking away. The silence and walking away techniques are often talked about, but are very difficult to actually do.

Finally, we looked at *Case Example 1: Shopping for a Car* from Chapter 1. We looked at what was done well and what was not done well in this part of the negotiation process. *Case Example 1 Price Negotiation Dialogue* concluded the case study by taking us through the price negotiation.

In the next chapter, we will go through the process of closing a procurement.

This book has free material available for download from the Web Added Value™ resource center at *www.jrosspub.com*.

CHAPTER 9

SIGNING THE CONTRACT AND CLOSING THE PROCUREMENT

After you have completed negotiations, the next step is to document the agreed-upon terms, the SOW, and all other items that were negotiated with the supplier. When you have received the documented agreement from the supplier, draft the contract. Nothing in this chapter (or book) is intended as legal advice. Everything is general information. An attorney licensed to practice law in your jurisdiction must address specific legal concerns.

DRAFT CONTRACT

Drafting the contract depends on the policies and procedures of your company. We will now discuss contracts although *in no way will any legal advice be offered.*

If you work for a small firm, there may not be any policies or procedures in place. In that case, you can find contract templates for many types of agreements online. It would be wise, however, for you to consult an attorney if you are not trained in contracts because the law can be complicated depending on your industry and the supplier's industry.

If you work for a larger company, or a governmental entity, you will probably have policies and procedures already in place. Become familiar with them. If checklists are available, use them. Contracts are the area of supply chain management that can either bring value to your company or bring legal woes and costs.

Note: Although purchase orders are a form of contract, we will not discuss them. If your company does not have one, purchase order templates are available online. *Caution*: Take care to fully review and understand all of the legal ramifications of any purchase order template before you use it.

Parts of a Contract

A contract has many parts. In general, there are the specifics of the goods or services you are procuring, legal terms and conditions, and the signatures. At the beginning of a contract, you will have a contract number and the title of the contract. (If your company does not keep a log of contract numbers, ask your boss how you should develop one.) The title includes the supplier's name and usually the goods or services for which the contract is required, for example: Contract 131031 Janitorial Services with 24-Hour Professional Janitorial Service.

After the contract number and title are the following:

Specifics of the goods or services:
- Identity of the parties
- Addresses of the parties
- Purpose and background of the contract
- Assumptions for the contract
- Restrictions, if any
- Pricing model and actual price
- Duties of each party
- Rights of each party
- Start date and end date of contract
- Deliverable dates, if any
- Deliverables quantities, if any
- Time is of the essence
- Contract renewal or extension
- Payment terms
- Payment due dates
- Shipping and handling charges, if any
- Taxes, if any
- Interest, if any
- Late fees, if any

Terms and conditions:
- Ownership of intellectual property
- Representations and warranties
- Disclaimers
- Liability
- Indemnification
- Insurance

Confidentiality provision
Termination of contract
Liquidated damages
Default
Arbitration clause, if any
Waiver
Assignment
Severability
Notice
Entire agreement
Jurisdiction

Signatures:

Signature of party
Printed name of party (a requirement that depends on jurisdiction)
Title of party
Date signed

Not all of the items listed will be appropriate in every contract, and some contracts may need terms that are not listed. The provisions listed are generally included in contracts, and all are important enough to seriously consider before deciding not to include them.

If you are unfamiliar with any of these concepts, please consult a person who has more experience. That person could be inside or outside your company. Other sources of information include workshops and seminars which may be found by doing an online search; the professional society for supply chain management for your industry which has information on many types of training about contracts; and the ISM which is an excellent resource for all supply chain training as well as templates. An attorney who regularly does commercial contracts is also an excellent resource.

Reviews

After you have drafted the contract, including the appropriate terms and conditions as well as the SOW and specific information necessary, it is time for reviews. Your company may have procedures in place for getting the draft contract reviewed. If you are in a small company, you may have to decide who needs to look over the contract before it is signed. The most important idea in getting the draft contract reviewed is that everything that needs to be stated in writing is included. Frequently another person will think of things that need to be there that you never thought about. Also a fresh pair of eyes can find typos that change the meaning of the language in the draft contract.

At a minimum, a more experienced procurement professional should read the contract. A more experienced procurement professional might have questions about it. Usually questions mean that you need to add more information to make sure everything is there and is clear. A better way to have the draft contract reviewed is to have legal, your supervisor, the department manager/executive, and the procurement owner review it. Each of these people will look for different things in the contract. This level of review is still no guarantee that every issue or risk has been addressed, but it is certain to ensure that most have been. (In the case that something important has been left out, you will have the remedy of amending the contract in the future—usually with the agreement of all parties and in writing.)

In medium-size and large companies, using a checklist is appropriate to make sure you have all of the reviews required. Figure 9-1 shows a minimum review requirement for a medium-size company.

Signatures

After all of the reviews have been completed and you have incorporated comments as appropriate, you need to get all of the signatures required by your company. Again, your company may have procedures for obtaining all required signatures for a contract. Often, in medium-size and large companies, you will need several approval signatures before the final signature on the contract. This requirement is usually dependent on the amount of the contract (capital expenditure) and the risk to the company. The higher the cost, or the greater the risk, the more approval signatures you will need to get. Usually there is a separate sheet for approval signatures that will be filed with the executed contract. (Most contracts will require only one signature per party, although sometimes there will be more than one signature per party.)

Figure 9-2 shows a sample checklist for obtaining approval signatures that will then become the permanent, written record of the signatures. Using a checklist ensures that no signature is overlooked.

A contract is not a legal document until *all* parties sign it (known as *a fully executed contract*, which is legally binding). When you have all the approval signatures and the signed contract from your company, you will send the contract to the supplier for signature.

Contract Review Checklist for Janitorial Services Contract, Contract Number 131031					
Area Reviewed	**Completed**	**Title**	**Person (Print)**	**Initials**	**Date**
Entire contract		Strategic Sourcing Manager	Donna Johnson		
Entire contract		Director of Procurement	Robert Golden		
Identity and address of all parties		Corporate Attorney	Samantha Grey		
Purpose and background		Corporate Attorney	Samantha Grey		
Assumptions		Corporate Attorney	Samantha Grey		
Restrictions		Corporate Attorney	Samantha Grey		
Duties of each party		Corporate Attorney	Samantha Grey		
Rights of each party		Corporate Attorney	Samantha Grey		
Start date and end date		Corporate Attorney	Samantha Grey		
Deliverable dates and quantities		Corporate Attorney	Samantha Grey		
Time is of the essence		Corporate Attorney	Samantha Grey		
Renewal or extension		Corporate Attorney	Samantha Grey		
Payment terms including due dates		Corporate Attorney	Samantha Grey		
Shipping and handling		Corporate Attorney	Samantha Grey		
Taxes and interest		Corporate Attorney	Samantha Grey		
Late fees		Corporate Attorney	Samantha Grey		
Intellectual property ownership		Corporate Attorney	Samantha Grey		
Representations and warranties		Corporate Attorney	Samantha Grey		

Figure 9-1. Contract review checklist for Case Example 2: Janitorial Services.

Contract Review Checklist for Janitorial Services Contract, Contract Number 131031					
Area Reviewed	**Completed**	**Title**	**Person (Print)**	**Initials**	**Date**
Disclaimers		Corporate Attorney	Samantha Grey		
Liability and indemnification		Corporate Attorney	Samantha Grey		
Insurance requirements		Corporate Attorney	Samantha Grey		
Confidentiality		Corporate Attorney	Samantha Grey		
Termination		Corporate Attorney	Samantha Grey		
Confidentiality		Corporate Attorney	Samantha Grey		
Liquidated damages		Corporate Attorney	Samantha Grey		
Default		Corporate Attorney	Samantha Grey		
Arbitration		Corporate Attorney	Samantha Grey		
Waiver		Corporate Attorney	Samantha Grey		
Assignment		Corporate Attorney	Samantha Grey		
Severability		Corporate Attorney	Samantha Grey		
Notice		Corporate Attorney	Samantha Grey		
Entire agreement		Corporate Attorney	Samantha Grey		
Jurisdiction		Corporate Attorney	Samantha Grey		
Signatures/date		Corporate Attorney	Samantha Grey		
SOW, terms, exhibits		Facilities Manager	Bill Green		
Entire contract		Vice President of Operations	John Q. Public		

Figure 9-1. Contract review checklist for Case Example 2: Janitorial Services (continued).

Contract Signature Checklist
Janitorial Services Contract, Contract Number 131031

Title	Name (Print)	Signature	Date
Strategic Sourcing Manager	Donna Johnson		
Director of Procurement	Robert Golden		
Corporate Attorney	Samantha Grey		
Facilities Manager	Bill Green		
Vice President of Operations	John Q. Public		

Note: Before signing this approval sheet, ensure that all comments from previous reviews have been added, as appropriate. Signing this sheet gives approval of the contract as it is.

Figure 9-2. Checklist for final contract signatures.

EXECUTED CONTRACT

When you receive the signed and dated contract from the supplier, your contract has been executed. The purpose of the contract (goods or services) will commence on the start date specified within the agreement—that could be the delivery of materials or products or the start of services.

You now need to file the executed contract with everyone who needs it. Of course, your supplier has to have the executed contract. Usually the supplier needs an original, just as your company does. You file the company's original in the contract file. You and everyone else who needs the contract will get a copy. As stated earlier for reviews and signatures, depending on the size of your company or agency, you may have an exact procedure to follow for filing the contract. If not, the following people need a copy of the executed contract:

- You
- The procurement owner
- Any person who deals with the supplier on a daily basis
- Legal
- Accounts payable
- The contract administrator (if not you)

In very small companies, you and the bookkeeper may be the only ones who need a copy of the contract. Check with your boss to make sure. No matter what, you need to keep a copy of every contract if you were part of the procurement team. Even if you did not lead a particular procurement, you still need a copy for your records. This is the only way to be certain that you can refer to any given contract at any time. Having a copy of the contracts also helps you keep track of the work that you have done (good at performance reviews and for updating resumes—not that these two activities go together all the time).

DEBRIEF UNSUCCESSFUL SUPPLIERS

Now that the agreement (the contract) has been executed and filed correctly, you can debrief unsuccessful suppliers that responded to your RFX. Not all companies do this. For some, there are concerns about the legal ramifications of telling suppliers why they did not get the work. Most government agencies and industries that are highly regulated, however, do have formal debriefs. For these industries and agencies, this is the final step in ensuring fair competition for the work.

Preliminary notifications. Many procurement professionals provide a preliminary notification to unsuccessful suppliers immediately after the RFX is complete and the short list of suppliers to be invited for oral presentations has been decided. *Caution*: Think very carefully before you do notifications at this time. If the competition resulting from the RFX is close—similar pricing for similar goods or services—then you are probably safe to do notifications to unsuccessful suppliers now. If, however, variations in either pricing or other important areas of the RFX are wide, then you may want to wait. Why? At times when the short-listed suppliers are unable to meet all of your company's requirements, you will need to invite the next group of suppliers in for oral presentations and questions. Most procurement professionals believe that it is better to invite suppliers from the next group when the potential suppliers do not yet know that their companies were originally out of the running. You have a better position for negotiation when these suppliers have no idea that you are desperate. When you keep your options open, your negotiating position is also better with the supplier that is chosen by your team. This supplier will usually be ready to work with you when they know that you have other suppliers waiting in the wings. Competition leads to better value for your company.

Debrief requests. Some companies allow unsuccessful suppliers to request a debriefing after they receive notification that the company is going with another supplier. Being able to request a debriefing allows unsuccessful suppliers to decide if it is important for them to hear why they were not chosen for the work. If allowing unsuccessful suppliers to request a debriefing is the way things are done in your company, then there will be a statement in the RFX about it so that all suppliers will know how to make a request. Usually there is also a specific amount of time allowed after notification for suppliers to make their requests.

Debrief meetings. When the deadline for debriefings has been met, arrange an individual meeting with each supplier making a request. At this meeting, you can speak directly about their particular proposal without giving out confidential information to the other suppliers. *Important*: You need to receive the names of all the people from the supplier who will be attending the debriefing meeting. During each debriefing meeting, also be careful not to disclose information that is confidential to your company or to the successful supplier. Think about the possible ramifications of all of the information that you plan to discuss. Can it harm the chosen supplier's strategy for getting work? Can it compromise your company's competitive strategies?

Information shared at debrief meetings. Naturally unsuccessful suppliers will want to know specifics about the winning proposal. They will ask questions. Again, guard against revealing information that you know needs to be protected. Some areas of information that are appropriate to reveal at debriefs include:

- Supplier's pricing was not competitive (but *do not* reveal any other supplier's pricing).
- Supplier would be overly dependent on business from your company.
- Supplier is unable to provide adequate materials, products, or services as requested.
- Supplier is unable to meet insurance requirements.
- Supplier's response was received after the deadline in the RFX.
- Supplier's response to the RFX was incomplete.

In the case of the last two reasons for an unsuccessful proposal—missing the deadline or an incomplete response—notify these suppliers as soon as the RFX has closed. Include the reason in your written notification, which allows these suppliers to understand that they must meet deadlines and supply complete information in order to qualify for getting work with your company in the future.

Information not shared at debrief meetings. Several areas of information *should not* be shared with unsuccessful suppliers, including where the supplier was listed after the weighted evaluations were complete, details of the winning proposal, and the merits or technical standings of competitors. Additional areas to not disclose include:

- Trade secrets (your company's or any supplier's company)
- Privileged or confidential information
- Pricing of any competitor
- Profit margins (your company's or any supplier's company)
- RFX weighted evaluation results

Complaints after debrief meetings. Most government agencies and large companies have a procedure for an unhappy supplier to express dissatisfaction with a debriefing. If your company does not have a procedure, tell the supplier to submit the pertinent issues in writing. Then make an appointment with the appropriate management personnel at your company. Often that will be your boss. Sometimes it will be someone above that level. Alternatively, just tell the unhappy supplier that the decision has been made and it is final. There is no appeal. Before you say that, however, make sure your boss agrees and will back you up. Suppliers have been known to make calls to all levels of management when they are unhappy and concerned about a procurement decision.

LESSONS LEARNED

Lessons learned is a project management term that is in wide use. Lessons learned means that everything about a project is recorded so that future projects can be managed better. In procurement, the contract file usually contains *only* the executed contract, exhibits, amendments, etc. The contract file therefore may not convey important information about all procurement activity. Creating a way to easily convey the good and the bad from each procurement activity by developing a lessons learned file will be worth the time and effort. Although lessons learned information may not be stored in the contract file, it can be stored on a shared drive so that all of the procurement staff can have access to it.

One of the great concerns about being completely honest in a lessons learned database is that you will be telling everyone about your mistakes. And that is true. But you will also be showcasing your successes to everyone. Doing both is the only way to pass on your knowledge and hard-won wisdom. It is also the best way to avoid mistakes in the future and utilize best practices as proven in the real world.

Put together lessons learned by debriefing your entire procurement team when the contract has been executed. After a little time passes between the effort and the debriefing, team members will realize that some things were done well and that some were not. Meet with the whole team at once or meet with each individual or do both. Meeting with the whole team at once can do the same thing that brainstorming does—inspire more participation and ideas from each other. Meeting with individuals, however, allows for more direct and honest discussion about the procurement process. Conducting both types of meetings takes more time, but it nets you more information than either type of meeting alone.

During either a team meeting or an individual meeting, your goal is to find out two things:

- What went right?
- What went wrong?

Before either type of meeting, compile a list of what you think went right and wrong. This list will be the starting point for your discussion if your team cannot think of anything. (It is surprising how few people think in this way—a method known as *strategic thinking*. Strategic thinking is useful in all areas of life.)

After you discuss what went right and wrong in the procurement, ask for ideas on improving the process in the future. Some things that went right might be improved, and some things that went wrong might have room for improvement or even need to be dropped. At the very least, get ideas for ways to fix the things that went wrong.

An important part of a lessons learned file is the schedule. You documented the actual schedule versus the planned schedule during the monitoring and control process of the procurement. Where were the delays, if any? What can be done to change these delays? What can be done to improve future estimated schedules?

Another important part of lessons learned is reviewing past procurements. (If there is no file for lessons learned, or any other documentation about successes and problems, looking at the contract files can give you a lot of information.) Even with limited time, reviewing similar procurements is wise. Compare your results to them. Understand, however, that savings is not the only metric to look for. Saving money is important to everyone, but gaining value is the key to making a company successful. Did similar past procurements provide as much, or more, value as your procurement?

Lessons learned are an important key to continuous improvement in procurements.

SUMMARY

In this chapter we discussed everything that needs to be done after negotiations are completed. You need to:

- Draft the contract
- Have it reviewed
- Get signatures from your company
- Get signatures from the supplier
- File the contract
- Make sure everyone who needs it has a copy of the contract
- Keep your own copy of the contract
- Develop a lessons learned file or database

Closing the procurement is the final step in a procurement. Your job is done. Or is it? In the next chapter, we will discuss contract administration.

This book has free material available for download from the Web Added Value™ resource center at *www.jrosspub.com.*

CHAPTER 10

CONTRACT ADMINISTRATION

In Chapter 6 (*Communications*), you were asked if contract execution and file closeout were the end of the procurement communication process. In Chapter 9 (*Signing the Contract and Closing the Procurement*), you were asked if your job was done when you closed the procurement. The short answer to both questions is *yes*. When the contract has been executed and the file has been closed out, including lessons learned, the procurement is technically finished—because the next step, contract administration, is a *process*.

Administering a contract means managing the contract. To manage a contract, several processes need to be completed. As we have learned throughout this book, a process is not a project. Because contract administration is a process, it is separate from a procurement. We will discuss those processes in this chapter.

IS CONTRACT ADMINISTRATION YOUR JOB?

Not all procurement professionals are tasked with contract administration. Depending on your company (or agency), you may be responsible for strategic sourcing only or you may be responsible for purchase orders only. So is contract administration part of your job?

Even if contract administration is not part of your responsibilities, you are still the expert on this contract. You have more knowledge about the terms and conditions than anyone else in your company. The person who will manage the day-to-day efforts under this contract will become very familiar with those terms that apply to the work, but he will likely be unfamiliar with the negotiations effort and the relationship that you built during the procurement. You will therefore need to be ready to answer questions while day-to-day work is done under this contract—from both your own people and the supplier's people. That is the main reason to always have a copy of the complete contract at your desk, as well as all notes, diaries, correspondence, etc. that you kept during the procurement.

You also need to continue to foster the working relationship between your company and the supplier. Schedule a time to talk with everyone in your company who deals with this contract. Ask how things are going. Be prepared to provide information and, when necessary, advice. (Of course, you *never* provide legal advice unless you are an attorney, but you can give general business advice and relationship advice.) Sometimes a small disagreement will turn into a full-blown feud between people. You can be a mediator in some situations. During preparation of the contract, you developed the atmosphere that the supplier's people expect when they do business with your company. It is in your company's best interest that cordial working relationships flourish.

By checking in with the supplier's people occasionally, you show that you are still interested in the working relationship. *Important*: The caution here is to make sure that people in your company know that you will be talking with the supplier from time to time. Territorial issues can develop very suddenly if a person thinks you are checking up on them. Make it clear that your intent is only to be sure the supplier is happy with the way the work is going.

Sometimes the supplier will be able to talk more openly with you about any concerns that they have about the work. Although finding yourself in the middle of a disagreement can be easy in situations such as this, getting everything out in the open and having direct discussions about solutions will pave the way to a better working relationship for everyone. Not every issue needs to escalate to legal action.

Even if contract administration is not your job, keep a calendar. Let the appropriate business unit know when it is time to decide about the next contract in plenty of time to implement the decision on how to proceed. By giving the business unit a heads up in time to make an informed decision, you have made yourself part of their team. (They, of course, will have to decide how to move forward and will ask for your advice or information because you made yourself part of the team.) Choices for your business unit partners to make include:

- To exercise an option year (extension of the existing contract with agreed-upon differences from original contract that were negotiated into original contract)
- To pursue the competitive process (find another supplier through the RFX process; a procurement)

- To terminate this contract and bring the work back inside the company
- To terminate this contract with no further action (if goods or services are no longer needed)

Other choices may be available depending on the goods or services and your industry.

If, however, contract administration is your job, remember that it is not a project. Contract administration is a *process*. Create a regular routine. Every billing period, usually one to three months, review invoices. Talk with people in your company who are working directly with the supplier. Make sure that these people have received everything the invoice shows. Ask questions as you review the invoices. You may need to question both your people and the supplier's people in order to get good answers. Do not stop asking questions until the answers are clear or changes to an incorrect invoice have been made. *Remember*: It is your job to ensure that your company gets the value you negotiated for.

CONTRACT ADMINISTRATION REQUIREMENTS

We will now discuss some of the requirements for contract administration. (These requirements may apply to your company, or agency, or they may not.) Be sure to learn about the policies and procedures at your company *before* starting the process of managing a contract.

Certain requirements are basic to contract administration. The following list is aimed at either the procurement lead who will be the contract administrator or the administrator who was not the procurement lead. Your company may have more, or fewer, requirements than listed. If your company does not have any procedures for contract administration, this is good basic list to use:

- Submit pricing for new contract to accounting (accounts payable).
- Submit pricing updates if extension of contract.
- Submit pricing updates if existing products/services or supplier.
- Add contract file to contract system (if procurement lead did not).
- Distribute executed contract (if procurement lead did not).
- Review invoices when they are received (before payment is made).
- Document supplier performance (discussed later in chapter).
- Document cost savings (discussed later in chapter).
- Create and distribute contract notices as required.

- Create and distribute amendments/addendums (discussed later in chapter).
- Monitor contract expiration dates (discussed later in chapter).
- Create and distribute contract termination notices if required (discussed later in chapter).
- Maintain contract files.

Again, because this list may be incomplete compared with your company (or agency) procedures, check with your boss to find out if you need to include additional procedures.

Document Supplier Performance

Over time, it has become the job of the contract administrator to manage supplier performance. We often call the criteria for supplier performance a *scorecard*. Measuring supplier performance has become very important because outsourcing is a normal business model. Your suppliers have a direct effect on your company's bottom line. Just as you need to know how well each employee in your company is performing, you need to know how well each supplier is performing. This area of supply chain is called Supplier Performance Management (SPM).

Years ago, supplier scorecards were used only in manufacturing and only for vendors who supplied materials. Because of the change to outsourcing more business support services, scorecards are now being used for all suppliers in all industries. Another reason to manage supplier performance is the globalization of businesses and supply chains. Your company may have branches all over the world. Even if it does not, your suppliers can be located anywhere in the world. And if that still is not the case for your company, your suppliers' suppliers are all over the world. No matter where in your supply chain it appears, globalization is part of everyday business.

Along with more suppliers comes an increased complexity in managing them. When a company had only one supplier for products, handling that relationship was easy. The products supplied were fundamental to the company's success, and the company's business was fundamental to the supplier's success. Now a medium-sized company will likely have several suppliers—for both goods and services—and will therefore have a responsibility to manage *each* relationship in order to survive and flourish. Sometimes a supplier has much larger customers/clients, so their reliance on your company's business with them is small. While that can be a good thing for the supplier, it can also put your company at the bottom of the supplier's priority list and make managing the relationship more complex.

Outsourcing for services has brought an increased realization that suppliers are not only a cost, but also a strategic input to a company's bottom line. Managing the relationship becomes even more important when a company's existence relies on it. A contract administrator has a key role in managing the strategic relationships with suppliers.

Creating a supplier performance scorecard is only one part of managing the supplier relationship. The scorecard has been touted as the best, or only, way, but there are other important factors in managing performance. Just as you know that your performance evaluation is incomplete if only the number of contracts that you complete, or the amount of savings you negotiated over the year, is taken into account, a supplier's performance has intangible measurements also. Because measuring intangibles is so difficult, most people do not even try. (We will not discuss intangibles in this chapter. Resources for learning more about supplier performance management can be found by searching on the Internet for Supplier Performance Management, by following blogs, and by taking courses. *Sourcing Innovation*, a blog that has information on SPM, as well as all things supply chain, can be found at http://blog.sourcinginnovation.com. A course offered by the Next Level Purchasing Association is free at the time of this writing to members of the association. The association can be found at http://www.nextlevelpurchasing.com.)

One way to create a supplier scorecard is to start with the weighted criteria that were used to select the supplier in the RFX process. These metrics are important to your company and are already in a prioritized order from the weighting. A best practice is to get input from the supplier on the performance evaluation. The supplier will have areas of performance that you and your team might not have thought about.

If the contract contains terms that provide for bonuses or faster payment, these terms should go on the supplier performance scorecard as well. The supplier will always claim the bonus or faster payment, so your company needs to have an objective way to measure the supplier's compliance with the contract terms.

After you have agreement from your people and the supplier's people on the criteria to be used for the performance scorecard, put it together in a document and distribute it. Some scorecards are on text documents such as MS Word, while others are on spreadsheets such as MS Excel. More important than the format used is that the scorecard includes all of the criteria for measuring the supplier's performance.

Figure 10-1 shows how a scorecard can be done in a spreadsheet. The spreadsheet shows a possible scorecard for *Case Example 2: Janitorial Services.*

Supplier Scorecard for Janitorial Services, 24-Hour Professional Janitor Services				
Date evaluated:				
Requirement	**Exceeds Requirement**	**Meets Requirement**	**Fails to Meet Requirement**	**Comments**
Offices (Monday – Friday evening)				
Restrooms				
Clean				
Sanitize				
Stock				
Trash cans				
Empty				
Clean				
Remove trash to designated areas				
Vacuum				
Common areas				
Cubicles				
Offices				
Spot clean carpet stains				
Spot dust horizontal surfaces (do not move papers or other items on desks)				
Sweep and/or mop floors in common areas				
Clean and disinfect break room surfaces				
Clean and disinfect drinking fountains				
Clean and disinfect lobby furniture				
Report maintenance problems to facilities manager				
Offices (quarterly services)				
Deep clean all surfaces in common areas				

Figure 10-1. Example of a supplier performance scorecard for Case Example 2: Janitorial Services.

Supplier Scorecard for Janitorial Services, 24-Hour Professional Janitor Services				
Date evaluated:				
Requirement	**Exceeds Requirement**	**Meets Requirement**	**Fails to Meet Requirement**	**Comments**
Offices (quarterly services)				
Shelves				
Fire extinguishers and/or cabinets for them				
Signs				
Clocks				
Strip and wax all floors				
Deep clean/disinfect all surfaces in restrooms				
Offices (semi-annual)				
Clean carpet				
Common areas				
Cubicles				
Offices				
Retail Store (Monday – Saturday evening)				
Restrooms				
Clean				
Sanitize				
Stock				
Trash cans				
Empty				
Clean				
Remove trash to designated areas				
Spot dust horizontal surfaces (do not move papers or other items)				
Sweep and/or mop floors in common areas				
Clean and disinfect drinking fountains				
Report maintenance problems to facilities manager				

Figure 10-1. Example of a supplier performance scorecard for Case Example 2: Janitorial Services (continued).

Supplier Scorecard for Janitorial Services, 24-Hour Professional Janitor Services				
Date evaluated:				
Requirement	**Exceeds Requirement**	**Meets Requirement**	**Fails to Meet Requirement**	**Comments**
Retail Store (quarterly services)				
Deep clean all surfaces in common areas				
Shelves				
Fire extinguishers and/or cabinets for them				
Signs				
Clocks				
Strip and wax all floors				
Deep clean/disinfect all surfaces in restrooms				
Warehouse (Monday - Saturday evening)				
Restrooms				
Clean				
Sanitize				
Stock				
Trash cans				
Empty				
Clean				
Remove trash to designated areas				
Spot dust horizontal surfaces (do not move papers or other items)				
Sweep and/or mop floors in common areas				
Clean and disinfect drinking fountains				
Report maintenance problems to facilities manager				

Figure 10-1. Example of a supplier performance scorecard for Case Example 2: Janitorial Services (continued).

Supplier Scorecard for Janitorial Services, 24-Hour Professional Janitor Services				
Date evaluated:				
Requirement	**Exceeds Requirement**	**Meets Requirement**	**Fails to Meet Requirement**	**Comments**
Warehouse (quarterly services)				
Deep clean all surfaces in common areas				
Shelves				
Fire extinguishers and/ or cabinets for them				
Signs				
Clocks				
Strip and wax all floors				
Deep clean/disinfect all surfaces in restrooms				
Employee signing in and out				
Supervisor master key management				
Alarm system management				
Use approved supplies/ materials				
Background investigations performed				
Documentation of citizenship/right to work in U.S.				
Employees understand English				
Employees able to read all labels, descriptions, and instructions for all materials used				
Project management effectiveness				
Insurance requirements				
Commercial general liability				
Worker's compenstion				
Employers' Liability				
Automobile				

Figure 10-1. Example of a supplier performance scorecard for Case Example 2: Janitorial Services (continued).

Document Cost Savings

Cost savings are another important metric for contracts. Unless the contract saves the company money, the contract is not valuable. Measuring cost savings is a contentious subject within the procurement profession. There is no best way to measure cost savings because the metric used depends on the accounting system and the perspectives in your company (or agency). If your company is small, cost savings will be measured against actual spend in the past year or years. This measurement is simple and straightforward. If your company is large, or is an agency within any governmental entity, however, there will be formulas that take into account many factors—not just a direct comparison of previous costs. Check with your boss to find out how cost savings are determined in your company. If no method is in place, suggest using the most simple and straightforward method—a direct comparison with past spend.

When you determine how to measure cost savings, you then need to document them. This documentation may be done as often as every billing cycle for the contract or it may done only once per quarter or once per year. Again, check with your boss. If no procedure is in place for documenting cost savings, the simplest way to do it is once per fiscal year. (If your company reports financials every quarter, then it makes sense to document cost savings every quarter.) Cost savings has become an important performance evaluation metric for procurement professionals. So document it.

Place the documented cost savings in the contract file to ensure that the data is available for review at any time. The availability of cost savings information is very important when making the decision to renew or compete the contract.

Prepare Necessary Contract Amendments/Addendums

Sometimes situations change and a contract needs to be changed to reflect them. Changes to an existing contract are called *amendments*. Additions to an existing contract are called *addendums*.

Amendments and addendums are treated in the same way as the original contract. You will draft the amendment or addendum when it becomes necessary. Ensure that the supplier reviews it and makes comments. Developing an amendment or addendum may require some negotiating with the supplier, so be prepared.

After the amendment or addendum is agreed to by the supplier, reviews by all of the appropriate people in your company, as well as a legal review, are required. Use the same type of checklist for reviewing amendments and addendums as you used for the original contract. After the reviews are completed and signed off on at your company, obtain approval signatures. Again, use the same type of approval signature form for an amendment or addendum as you used for the original contract. Then get the final signature(s) from the appropriate person in your company and in the supplier's company. After all signatures are obtained, the amendment or addendum is executed and becomes part of the original contract.

File originals of the amendment or addendum with the supplier and in your contract file. Ensure that everyone who needs a copy gets one.

Monitor Contract Expiration Date

Even though the procurement lead for this contract will be monitoring the contract expiration date, the contract administrator also needs to monitor this date. Alternatively, the procurement lead might not monitor the date or the contract could be assigned to a different procurement professional or team. In any of these scenarios, contract expiration dates are just one more piece of information that can fall through the cracks, so stay on top of monitoring them.

To facilitate monitoring dates, create a contract calendar that shows all of the important dates in the contract. Dates such as delivery of goods/services, invoicing, and contract expiration should be noted. The administrator may need to put other dates from the contract into the calendar depending on the specific contract.

Create a "tickler" file to remind you when the contract will expire. One way to do that is to put this event in the calendar several months before the expiration date. Say something like "Contract ABC expires on 5-28-14." Putting this notation in the calendar will alert you to the fact that you need to let the person who makes decisions about this contract know that the contract needs to be addressed.

Also notify the owner of the contract, as well as procurement and anyone else who makes a decision about the future of this contract, that the contract will expire in *X* months. The timing of when the notification goes out depends on the term of the contract, how long it is in effect, and if a decision to compete the contract might need to be made. Some companies require a three-month notice, while others need at least six months. A very large or complex procurement might need a year or more. Check with your boss.

Terminate the Contract When Necessary

Sometimes a contract needs to be terminated. When a contract is terminated, the contract administrator documents the termination, including the *exact* clause in the contract that allows for the termination, obtains legal and management reviews, and then sends out a notice to the supplier with copies going to the contract owner and procurement. Reasons for termination include: convenience, breach or cause, as well as specific clauses for other types of termination.

Convenience. *Termination for convenience* is a clause that should be included in every contract. A termination for convenience clause means that the balance of a contract can be terminated by your company at its convenience, but never for a supplier's convenience. Although this clause places high risk on a supplier, it protects your company from spending money when it cannot afford to. (*Note*: The termination for convenience clause is a clause that might be dropped during a negotiation, so make sure it is included in your draft contract.)

Breach or cause. *Termination for breach or cause* is a clause that is included in every contract. Termination for breach or cause requires documentation beyond quoting only the clause. Termination for breach or cause is similar to firing an employee—the records must reflect exactly what happened and why the event (or events) is considered a breach of the agreement. Termination for breach or cause can be slightly different from each other, but both need the same level of documentation. Talk with an attorney before drafting a notification to the supplier of termination for breach or for cause because of the possible ramifications of wording these notifications poorly.

Other terminations. Your contract may contain clauses for other types of termination. Be sure you understand them.

Because termination of a contract requires documentation, reviews, and notification, use the same type of review and signature checklists as for amendments and addendums. *Important*: Do not notify a supplier of termination until all approval signatures are in place. When the notification is sent to the supplier, expect to hear from them. Unless the termination is an amiable parting of the ways, the supplier will probably be angry. People in your company who work with the supplier's people everyday will refer these angry people to you. Have an approach ready for dealing with angry suppliers. No one likes conflict, but being prepared for it helps.

After the notification of termination has been sent to the supplier, put an original copy in the contract file. Send copies to the appropriate people in your company (or agency).

SUMMARY

In this chapter, we discussed contract administration. Differing from a procurement, contract administration is a *process*, not a *project*. Some procurement professionals manage the contract; others do not. This chapter addressed both circumstances.

All of the requirements for administrating a contract were listed:

- Submit pricing for new contract.
- Submit pricing updates for existing contract or supplier.
- Add contract file to contract system.
- Distribute executed contract.
- Review invoices when they are received.
- Document supplier performance.
- Document cost savings.
- Create and distribute contract notices as required.
- Create and distribute amendments/addendums.
- Monitor contract expiration dates.
- Create and distribute contract termination notices if required.
- Maintain contract files.

Your company or agency may have many more requirements for contract administration. Make sure you know all of them.

In the next chapter, we will review some final, and important, information for procurement professionals.

This book has free material available for download from the Web Added Value™ resource center at *www.jrosspub.com.*

CHAPTER 11

FINAL WORDS

In this book, many project management techniques and skills have been introduced into the area of procurement. Not all project management techniques, however, have been discussed because they do not apply to the majority of procurements. This book has presented only the fundamental ideas that supply chain professionals can use to start managing their work differently—more successfully. The most important aspects of the areas covered in this book will now be pointed out, some software resources will be provided, and books to read to continue learning about project management techniques, prioritization, communications, and negotiations will be recommended.

COMMUNICATION

It can never be said or written too often that good communication brings great results. Communication is the foundation for getting cooperation, discovering new ideas, and leading any effort. One way to think about communication is that you are either *teaching* something to someone or *learning* something from someone else. To motivate another person to cooperate with you, you need to let them know exactly what you want to achieve—that means teaching them. When you get that person's cooperation, you have the opportunity to learn from them so that your goal will be reached.

Good communication starts with good listening. People will usually tell you what they need, as well as what they want. All you have to do is hear them. Good listening is often called *active listening.* Active listening requires work on the listener's part. The listener focuses on the speaker and, in their own words, repeats what the speaker said. In this way, the speaker then has the opportunity to correct any misunderstanding, and the listener actually understands what the speaker is communicating.

Not all communication is done verbally, of course. Writing requires taking more care in how things are said so that there is a minimum of misunderstanding. Even the simplest written messages can be misunderstood and result in hurt feelings and anger. How often has a personal text message either confused you or made you uneasy? In business, minimizing confusion and staying away from emotional issues is particularly important. Focus on the issue, not the person, especially if your message is less than pleasant.

Even in communication that is as fact-based as a business report, confusion can result. Many books, courses, workshops, and seminars are aimed at business writing. Most professionals work on improving their written communications during their entire careers.

KNOW YOUR COMMODITY

As a procurement professional, you need to know and understand the commodity (or commodities) that you buy. Writing a contract for a fleet of vehicles is very different from writing a contract for mental health services. If you do not know your commodity, sales people can easily take advantage of you. You will not get the best value because you do not know what that is. You will not know what is most important in your negotiation and what is not.

Even when you do know your commodity, do not rely on sales representatives to tell you what your company needs. Do not use a supplier's RFX template. Although using a shortcut is tempting, a supplier's RFX is directed at getting the supplier everything that the supplier wants. A supplier's RFX does not address your company's needs at all. As a shortcut, you can take any type of valuable information from a supplier's template and include it in your own RFX, but be careful here—know exactly what that information means to your company as well as to the supplier. This is all part of knowing your commodity.

KNOW YOUR BUSINESS AND INDUSTRY

It is vital to your ability to contribute to your company that you know the company's business and the industry it is in. The business that your company is in dictates much of what you do and how you do it. A highly regulated business, such as electric utilities or telecommunications, has strict requirements in procurements. A business that is not tightly regulated, such as some manufacturing or most service companies, gives you more flexibility. (You, of course, will always provide a legal and ethical procurement no matter who you work for.)

If you work for a governmental agency, at any level, you are under strict rules and laws for procurements. Although these rules and laws may seem to be restrictive, when you know all of them you can—within legal and ethical boundaries—find areas for creativity.

Very likely your company has competitors within its industry. Get to know who the competitors are and what they do. Often, your company has experts who are watching the competition and know it well. Learn from these people. Taking one of these experts to lunch can be the fastest and easiest way to establish a good working relationship. These experts have information that is vital to how you do your job. Get to know them.

If your company does not have experts watching the competition, you will have to do the research on your own. Start with information on a competing company from a source such as Hoover's (www.hoovers.com). Go to the competitor's website and get a copy of the most recent annual report (usually found on the page for investors). Set up a search that will bring you media information about this company daily. Use the company's name and the names of the board of directors as well as senior executives to get information. Go to professional society meetings, such as ISM, and mingle with supply chain professionals from the competition. Because they are professionals, no one will talk about confidential information or strategies, but you can talk to them about professional topics, such as procurement techniques, and exchange information. Finding out how other people are procuring the same, or similar, goods and services is enlightening. They teach you and you teach them. Communication is a good thing.

PROJECT MANAGEMENT SOFTWARE

There are many sources for project management software. Some companies come and go, as well. This chapter will not recommend or endorse any software product over another. The list of programs for project management is not exhaustive. It is only a list of the most commonly used programs. You must determine which software best fits your needs.

The first step in determining which software program you will use is to find out what software other people in your company use. Learning a program is easier when other users are readily available to answer questions. The next step is to find out if there are enough licenses to allow the program to be loaded onto your computer or for you to use the program on a server. The final step is to learn how to use the software as a tool in managing your procurement. Commonly used programs include:

Microsoft Project. Microsoft Project is used for medium-to-large projects. Most procurements can easily be put into MS Project. If your company has licenses for MS Project, you can learn how to use it with practice. Many workshops and seminars are available that will show you what you need to know in order to use it for procurements.

Microsoft Excel. Microsoft Excel is used for small projects. MS Excel is not aimed at managing projects, but it can be manipulated in ways that produce the schedule and budget in tabular format. Microsoft Excel can also produce a Gantt chart, but doing so is not straightforward. If you need a network diagram or other visual reports, MS Excel is not the software for doing it. By using MS Excel, MS Word, and MS PowerPoint together, however, you can create a network diagram and other visual reports. Actually you can use any spreadsheet, word processor, and presentation software together to create the schedule, budget, Gantt chart, and network diagram.

Primavera. Primavera is used for large projects such as highway construction projects and other large construction projects. Primavera is project management software that is continually improved based on feedback from project managers in the field. For a small- or medium-sized project, Primavera is unwieldy. It takes significant time and effort to learn to use it effectively. Once learned, however, it is a powerful tool in managing very large projects.

Web-based programs. These programs are used for a variety of projects. Because Web-based programs are reached through a browser, they offer the advantage of not having to buy desktop software and the accompanying licensing and upgrading requirements. With Web-based programs, however, there are concerns associated with the security of your data and the reliability of the servers that the software company uses. Bandwidth could also be a concern if data movement needs to be fast. Find out where the actual data is stored. You need to have local copies of everything, whether they are electronic or hard copy. Check out a Web-based project management software company as well as its software. Web-based companies are an area where the companies come and go quickly. You do not need to be in the middle of an important procurement when a project management software company goes belly up. Most Web-based companies will give you a free trial of their software. Take advantage of this free trial by having either a real procurement ready for entry or making up a small procurement for the purposes of testing the software. Be sure the reports that can be generated include everything that you need now and reports that you may need in the future. A short list of paid Web-based project management software includes:

Basecamp (http://basecamp.com)
ProjectManager (http://www.projectmanager.com)
AceProject (http://www.aceproject.com)

This author has not used any of these programs and has no opinion of their value.

Open-source Web-based programs. These programs are usually free. *Open source* means that the source code is available to any programmer, and often many programmers collaborate on it. Collaboration by many programmers allows a program to get the best input from experts at writing software. Some open-source Web-based programs include:

Codendi: a collaborative development platform offered by Xerox used mostly for managing software projects

Redmine: an application using Ruby on Rails framework that includes a project calendar and Gantt charts

ProjectPier: a self-hosted php application for managing projects (Self-hosted means that the software is downloaded to your server. If you have a *WordPress* blog, it is self-hosted if you downloaded it into your domain.)

Collabtive: an open-source alternative to proprietary programs such as Basecamp and ActiveCollab

This author has not used any of these and cannot make a recommendation on any.

REFERENCE BOOKS

Three books are recommended. These books are on the author's shelf of daily reference materials. These books can serve as your entire education in these areas or as jumping off points to continue to learn:

The Complete Idiot's Guide to Project Management, 2nd Edition, Macmillan USA/Alpha (2000), by Sunny and Kim Baker

The 7 Habits of Highly Effective People, by Simon & Schuster (2004), by Stephen R. Covey

Getting to Yes: Negotiating Agreement Without Giving In, Penguin (1981), by Roger Fisher and William Ury (reissued in 1991 with Bruce Patton)

You can find many more books on these and similar subjects by doing Internet searches.

Finally, here's to you and your future. May it be everything you want it to be.

This book has free material available for download from the Web Added Value™ resource center at *www.jrosspub.com.*

APPENDIX A

LIST OF TABLES AND FIGURES

Chapter 10. Contract Administration

Appendix B. Examples of a Complete RFPS, Schedule, and Budget

This book has free material available for download from the Web Added Value™ resource center at *www.jrosspub.com.*

APPENDIX B

EXAMPLES OF A COMPLETE RFPS, SCHEDULE, AND BUDGET

Abbreviated versions of Exhibits 2-3, 4-8, and 5-2 are displayed in Chapters 2 (Figure 2-3), 4 (Figure 4-8), and 5 (Figure 5-2), respectively, to facilitate learning without hampering the flow of material or the reading experience. The full versions are displayed in this appendix.

REQUEST FOR PROCUREMENT SERVICES	
DATE OF REQUEST	May 3, 2013
REQUESTOR NAME	John Q. Public
SHIP TO ADDRESS OR LOCATION OF WORK BEING PERFORMED	XYZ Company 1325 Texas Blvd. Dallas, TX 75032
REQUESTOR PHONE NUMBER	972-555-1234
REQUESTOR FAX NUMBER	972-555-1235

COMPLETE DESCRIPTION OF PROCUREMENT

(Indicate if New Contract, Revised Contract, Purchase Order, or Other type of procurement.)

EXISTING/EXPECTED CONTRACT AMOUNT SPENT PER YEAR in $	New competition for existing contract for janitorial services Annual spend $500,000

DATE CONTRACT REQUIRED

CONTRACT REQUIRED DATE	October 31, 2013

SUGGESTED VENDORS OR SOLE-SOURCE JUSTIFICATION

(Add additional vendors on an attached sheet with all contact information requested below.)

NAME	24-Hour Professional Janitorial Service (see attached for more vendors)
ADDRESS	955 W. Ralph Hall Pkwy. Rockwall, TX 75032
CONTACT NAME	Jane Doe
PHONE NUMBER	972-770-9325
FAX NUMBER	972-770-9326

SOLE-SOURCE JUSTIFICATION

(Must include market data if only supplier of goods or services.)

N/A

Exhibit 2-3. RFPS for Case Example 2: Janitorial Services.

SCOPE OF SERVICE

(Detailed and complete description of services required, personnel qualifications, etc.)

XYZ Company is seeking Janitorial Services for its multiple-use office and warehouse building located at 1325 Texas Blvd., Dallas, TX.

Quality cleaning is required, including full performance of all specified daily service on the first official working day of the contract term. All work will be performed at times as specified and agreed upon by both parties. All cleaning personnel are prohibited from disturbing papers on desks or shelves, opening desk drawers or cabinets, or using telephone or office equipment located in the XYZ Company building.

All contract personnel are required to sign in/out upon arrival and departure of work site. Form is located at the front desk.

All contract personnel are required to know, understand, and perform security protocols, including arming and disarming alarm systems, unlocking and locking doors, etc.

All contract personnel are required to undergo a background check, including credit check, criminal record, sexual offender record, etc. before the first official working day of the contract term. Every new contract employee will be screened to the same level before the first day of work on the XYZ Company property.

REQUESTOR APPROVAL

NAME (Type or Print)	SIGNATURE	DATE
John Q. Public		5-3-13

Exhibit 2-3. RFPS for Case Example 2: Janitorial Services (continued).

WBS	Task Description	Predecessor	Owner	Role	Start Date	Finish Date	Effort (Hours)
0.0	**Procurement for Janitorial Services**		**DS**	**SSM**	**05/03/13**	**10/31/13**	**321.75**
1.0	**Receive RFPS**		**DS**	**SSM, DP**	**05/03/13**	**05/10/13**	**7.50**
1.1	Brainstorm	1.0	DS, RG	SSM, DP	05/07/13	05/07/13	1.25
1.1.2	Strategy	1.0	DS, RG	SSM, DP	05/07/13	05/07/13	0.25
1.1.2.1	Mutual non-disclosure agreement	1.0	DS, RG	SSM, DP	05/07/13	05/07/13	0.25
1.1.2.2	Contract type	1.0	DS, RG	SSM, DP	05/07/13	05/07/13	0.25
1.1.2.3	Length of agreement	1.0	DS, RG	SSM, DP	05/07/13	05/07/13	0.25
1.1.2.4	Sourcing approach	1.0	DS, RG	SSM, DP	05/07/13	05/07/13	0.25
1.2	Review current and historical supplier contracts	1.0	DS, RG	SSM, DP	05/06/13	05/06/13	2.00
1.3	Identify all stakeholders	1.0	DS, RG	SSM, DP	05/06/13	05/06/13	1.00
1.4	Establish the procurement team	1.0	DS, RG	SSM, DP	05/07/13	05/10/13	1.00
1.4.1	Decide what skills are required	1.0	DS, RG	SSM, DP	05/07/13	05/07/13	0.20
1.4.2	Find out who has these skills	1.4.1	DS, RG	SSM, DP	05/07/13	05/07/13	0.20
1.4.3	Find out availability of these people	1.4.2	DS, RG	SSM, DP	05/07/13	05/07/13	0.20
1.4.4	Get these people assigned to procurement team	1.4.3	DS, RG, JB, BG, JQP, SG	SSM, DP, FA, SME, Owner, Attorney	05/07/13	05/10/13	0.20
1.4.5	Define roles and responsibilities	1.0	DS	SSM	05/07/13	05/07/13	0.20

WBS	Task Description	Predecessor	Owner	Role	Start Date	Finish Date	Effort (Hours)
1.5	Silent period with existing supplier	1.0	DS, RG, JB, BG, JQP, SG	SSM, DP, FA, SME, Owner, Attorney	05/03/13	10/31/13	0.25
1.6	Establish a high-level schedule	1.1.2	DS	SSM	05/07/13	05/10/13	2.00
2.0	**Kick-Off Meeting**	**1.6**	**DS**	**SSM**	**05/13/13**	**05/17/13**	**6.00**
2.1	Decide on date for meeting	2.0	DS	SSM	05/13/13	05/13/13	0.25
2.2	Reserve meeting room	2.0	DS	SSM	05/13/13	05/13/13	0.25
2.3	Create agenda	2.0	DS	SSM	05/13/13	05/13/13	0.50
2.4	Send out agenda	2.0	DS	SSM	05/13/13	05/13/13	0.50
2.4.1	Receive comments/additons to agenda	2.4	DS	SSM	05/14/13	05/14/13	0.50
2.4.2	Resend amended agenda	2.4.1	DS	SSM	05/15/13	05/15/13	0.50
2.5	**Hold meeting**	**2.4**	**DS, JB, BG, JQP**	**SSM, FA, SME, Owner**	**05/17/13**	**05/17/13**	**1.50**
2.6	Develop action list and/or meeting minutes	2.5	DS	SSM	05/17/13	05/17/13	0.50
2.7	Send out action list/minutes	2.6	DS	SSM	05/17/13	05/17/13	0.50
2.7.1	Receive comments/additions to action list/minutes	2.7	DS	SSM	05/17/13	05/17/13	0.50
2.7.2	Resend action list/minutes	2.7.1	DS	SSM	05/20/13	05/20/13	0.50

Exhibit 4-8. Schedule for Case Example 2: Janitorial Services.

WBS	Task Description	Predecessor	Owner	Role	Start Date	Finish Date	Effort (Hours)
3.0	**Procurement Plan**	**1.0**	**DS**	**SSM**	**05/20/13**	**05/24/13**	**27.75**
3.1	Finalize procurement strategy	1.1.2	DS, JQP	SSM, Owner	05/20/13	05/20/13	0.50
3.1.1	Review strategy with team members	3.1	DS, JB, BG, JQP	SSM, FA, SME, Owner	05/23/13	05/23/13	1.00
3.2	Develop procurement WBS	1.0	DS, BG		05/20/13	05/20/13	6.00
3.2.1	Review WBS with team members	3.2	DS, RG, JB, BG, JQP, SG	SSM, DP, FA, SME, Owner, Attorney	05/23/13	05/23/13	1.00
3.3	Develop procurement schedule	1.4	DS, JQP		05/21/13	05/21/13	4.00
3.3.1	Review schedule with team members	3.2	DS, RG, JB, BG, JQP, SG	SSM, DP, FA, SME, Owner, Attorney	05/23/13	05/23/13	1.00
3.4	Develop procurement budget	1.4	N/A				
3.4.1	Review budget with team members	3.4	N/A				
3.5	Develop procurement communications plan	1.4	DS	SSM	05/22/13	05/22/13	2.00
3.5.1	Review communications plan with team members	3.5	DS, RG, JB, BG, JQP, SG	SSM, DP, FA, SME, Owner, Attorney	05/23/13	05/23/13	1.00
3.6	Develop procurement risk plan	1.4	DS, JB, BG	SSM, FA, SME	05/22/13	05/22/13	2.00
3.6.1	Review risk plan with team members	3.6	DS, RG, JB, BG, JQP, SG	SSM, DP, FA, SME, Owner, Attorney	05/23/13	05/23/13	1.00

WBS	Task Description	Predecessor	Owner	Role	Start Date	Finish Date	Effort (Hours)
3.7	Review procurement plan with entire team	3.2, 3.3, 3.4, 3.5, 3.6	DS, RG, JB, BG, JQP, SG	SSM, DP, FA, SME, Owner, Attorney	05/23/13	05/23/13	4.00
3.8	Finalize procurement plan	3.6.1		SSM, DP, FA, SME, Owner, Attorney	05/24/13	05/24/13	4.00
3.9	Distribute procurement plan	3 80			05/24/13	05/24/13	0.25
4.0	**Solicitation**	**3.0**	**DS**	**SSM**	**05/28/13**	**06/10/13**	**73.75**
4.1	Silent period with potential suppliers and existing supplier	3.8	DS, RG, JB, BG, JQP, SG	SSM, DP, FA, SME, Owner, Attorney	05/03/13	10/31/13	0.25
4.2	Draft RFP	3.8	DS	SSM	05/28/13	06/07/13	73.50
	Memorial Day holiday				**05/27/13**	**05/27/13**	
4.2.1	RFP Schedule	1.6	DS	SSM	05/28/13	05/28/13	4.00
4.2.1.1	Review with team	4 2.1	DS, JB, BG, JQP	SSM, FA, SME, Owner	05/28/13	05/28/13	2.00
4.2.2	Statement of Work (Scope of Work)	1 4.5	BG, DS	SME, SSM	05/29/13	05/30/13	8.00
4.2.2.1	Review with team	4 2.2	DS, JB, BG, JQP	SSM, FA, SME, Owner	06/04/13	06/04/13	2.00
4.2.3	Determine type of agreement document	[illegible].1	DS, SG	SSM, Attorney	05/30/13	05/30/13	1.00
4.2.3.1	Sample terms and conditions	4.2.3	DS	SSM	05/30/13	05/30/13	2.00
4.2.4	Develop pricing model	1.2	JB, DS, BG	FA, SSM, SME	05/30/13	05/30/13	1.00

Exhibit 4-8. Schedule for Case Example 2: Janitorial Services (continued).

WBS	Task Description	Predecessor	Owner	Role	Start Date	Finish Date	Effort (Hours)
4.2.5	RFP General Instructions	4.2.1	DS	SSM	05/31/13	05/31/13	4.00
4.2.6	Mutual non-disclosure agreement	4.2.3	DS	SSM	05/31/13	05/31/13	2.00
4.2.7	Proposal signature page	4.2.3	DS	SSM	05/31/13	05/31/13	0.50
4.2.8	Develop weighted evaluation criteria	4.2.2	DS, BG	SSM, SME	06/03/13	06/03/13	8.00
4.2.8.1	Review with evaluation team	4.2.8	DS, JB, BG, JQP	SSM, FA, SME, Owner	06/04/13	06/04/13	2.00
4.2.9	MWDBE certification	4.2.3	DS	SSM	06/04/13	06/04/13	0.50
4.2.10	HUB certification	4.2.3	DS	SSM	06/04/13	06/04/13	0.50
4.2.11	Form W-9	4.2.3	DS	SSM	06/04/13	06/04/13	0.50
4.3	Review entire RFP with team	4.2	DS, JB, BG, JQP	SSM, FA, SME, Owner	06/05/13	06/05/13	1.00
4.3.1	Make changes as required	4.3	DS	SSM	06/06/13	06/06/13	2.00
4.3.2	Distribute to team for final review	4.3.1	DS	SSM	06/06/13	06/06/13	0.25
4.4	Commodity strategy	3.0	JB	FA	05/28/13	05/31/13	22.25
4.4.1	Industry/commodity profile analysis	3.0	JB	FA	05/28/13	05/28/13	4.00
4.4.2	Purchasing profile	4.4.1	JB	FA	05/28/13	05/28/13	2.00
4.4.3	Supplier financial analysis	4.4.2	JB	FA	05/28/13	05/29/13	8.00
4.4.4	Total cost of ownership	4.4.3	JB	FA	05/30/13	05/30/13	4.00
4.4.5	Determine qualified supplier bid list	4.4.4	JB, DS	FA, SSM	05/30/13	05/30/13	2.00
4.4.5.1	Contact names and information	4.4.5	JB	FA	05/31/13	05/31/13	2.00
4.4.5.2	Send all information to SSM	4.4.5.1	JB	FA	05/31/13	05/31/13	0.25

WBS	Task Description	Predecessor	Owner	Role	Start Date	Finish Date	Effort (Hours)
4.5	Finalize RFP	4.3, 4.4	DS	SSM	06/06/13	06/07/13	8.00
4.6	**Send RFP out**	**4.5**	**DS**	**SSM**	**06/10/13**	**06/10/13**	**2.00**
5.0	**RFP Process**	**4.6**	**DS**	**SSM**	**06/10/13**	**06/28/13**	**12.25**
5.1	RFP silent period with potential suppliers and existing supplier	4.6	DS	SSM	06/10/13	10/31/13	0.25
5.2	Receive questions on RFP	5.1	DS	SSM	06/10/13	06/19/13	2.00
5.2.1	Assemble questions and answers	5.2	DS	SSM	06/20/13	06/21/13	8.00
5.2.2	Send out assembled questions and answers to all participants	5 2.1	DS	SSM	06/24/13	06/24/13	2.00
6.0	**Proposal Analysis**	**5.0**	**DS**	**SSM**	**06/28/13**	**08/02/13**	**92.50**
6.1	**Receive proposals**	**5.2.2**	**DS**	**SSM**	**06/28/13**	**06/28/13**	**8.00**
6.1.1	Reject all proposals that are not signed	6.1	DS	SSM	07/01/13	07/01/13	4.00
6.1.2	Reject all proposals submitted after the deadline	6.1	DS	SSM	07/01/13	07/01/13	4.00
6.2	Distribute all acceptable proposals to evaluation team	6.1	DS	SSM	07/02/13	07/02/13	4.00
6.3	Team evaluates all proposals indepen-dently	6.2	DS, JB, BG, JQP	SSM, FA, SME, Owner	07/02/13	07/10/13	20.00
	4th of July holiday				**07/04/13**	**07/04/13**	
6.4	Team returns all evaluations	6.3	DS	SSM	07/11/13	07/11/13	2.00

Exhibit 4-8. Schedule for Case Example 2: Janitorial Services (continued).

WBS	Task Description	Predecessor	Owner	Role	Start Date	Finish Date	Effort (Hours)
6.5	Review and collate all evaluations	6.4	DS	SSM	07/11/13	07/12/13	8.00
6.6	Distribute collated evaluations to team	6.5	DS	SSM	07/15/13	07/15/13	2.00
6.7	Evaluation team meets to decide on top proposals	6.6	DS, JB, BG, JQP	SSM, FA, SME, Owner	07/16/13	07/16/13	6.00
6.8	Collect questions on proposals for short-listed potential suppliers	6.7	DS	SSM	07/16/13	07/16/13	2.00
6.9	Notify short list	6.7	DS	SSM	07/17/13	07/17/13	2.00
6.10	Schedule oral presentations	6.9	DS	SSM	07/17/13	07/19/13	5.00
6.10.1	Verify date and time with each company	6.10	DS	SSM	07/17/13	07/18/13	4.00
6.10.2	Reserve meeting room	6.10	DS	SSM	07/17/13	07/17/13	0.50
6.10.3	Notify evaluation team	6.10	DS	SSM	07/17/13	07/18/13	0.50
6.11	**Oral presentations**	**6.10.2**	**DS**	**SSM**	**07/31/13**	**08/01/13**	**16.50**
6.11.1	Make sure someone greets presenters	6.10.2	DS	SSM	07/19/13	07/19/13	1.00
6.11.2	Make sure equipment is ready and working	6.10.2	DS	SSM	07/30/13	07/30/13	1.00
6.11.3	Make sure refreshments are ready	6.10.2	DS	SSM	07/30/13	07/31/13	0.50
6.11.4	Questions	6.8	DS	SSM	07/19/13	07/26/13	7.00
6.11.4.1	Prepared and who will ask each one	6.8	DS, JB, BG, JQP	SSM, FA, SME, Owner	07/19/13	07/26/13	4.00
6.11.5.1	As presentation is given	6.11.4.1	DS, JB, BG, JQP	SSM, FA, SME, Owner	07/31/13	08/01/13	1.50
6.12	Thank yous and walking presenters out	6.11	DS	SSM	07/31/13	08/01/13	1.50
6.13	**Meeting to decide on contract awardee**	**6.11**	**DS, JB, BG, JQP**	**SSM, FA, SME, Owner**	**08/02/13**	**08/02/13**	**4.00**

WBS	Task Description	Predecessor	Owner	Role	Start Date	Finish Date	Effort (Hours)
7.0	**Negotiations**	**6.13**	**DS**	**SSM**	**07/19/13**	**08/19/13**	**34.00**
7.1	Develop negotiation strategy	4.6	DS, JB, BG	SSM, FA, SME	07/19/13	08/02/13	8.00
7.1.1	Where negotiation takes place	4.6	DS, JB, BG	SSM, FA, SME	07/19/13	08/02/13	4.00
7.1.2	Win-win or hard ball	4.6	DS, JB, BG	SSM, FA, SME	07/19/13	08/02/13	4.00
7.2	Identify negotiation team	4.6	DS, JB, BG	SSM, FA, SME	07/19/13	08/02/13	1.00
7.2.1	Fully identify and communicate roles	7.2	DS	SSM	07/19/13	08/02/13	1.00
7.3	**Conduct negotiations**	**7.1**	**DS, JB, BG**	**SSM, FA, SME**	**08/05/13**	**08/16/13**	**8.00**
7.3.1	Finalize deal including terms and conditions	7.3	DS	SSM	08/19/13	08/19/13	8.00
8.0	**Contract Finalization**	**7.3**	**DS**	**SSM**	**07/19/13**	**09/09/13**	**62.00**
8.1	Draft contract	7.3.1	DS	SSM	07/19/13	08/02/13	12.00
8.1.1	Review contract	8.1	RG, SG	DP, Attorney	08/20/13	08/23/13	8.00
8.2	Obtain approval signatures	8.1.1	DS	SSM	08/26/13	08/30/13	40.00
	Labor Day holiday				**09/02/13**	**09/02/13**	
8.3	**Execute contract**	**8.2**	**DS**	**SSM**	**09/09/13**	**10/31/13**	**2.00**
9.0	**Notification of Unsuccessful Suppliers**	**8.3**	**DS**	**SSM**	**09/10/13**	**09/12/13**	**6.00**
9.1	Preliminary notification	8.3	DS	SSM	09/10/13	09/11/13	4.00
9.2	Formal debriefing	9.1	DS	SSM	09/12/13	09/12/13	2.00
10.0	**Contract Administration**	**8.3**	**DS**	**SSM**	**09/09/13**	**End of contract term**	**N/A**

Exhibit 4-8. Schedule for Case Example 2: Janitorial Services (continued).

	A	B	C	D	E	F
1	**Procurement Team**					
2		**Name**	**Role**	**Direct Labor Cost ($)**	**Indirect Labor Cost ($)**	**Total per Hour ($)**
3		Donna Smith (DS)	SSM	39.22	12.94	52.16
4		Robert Golden (RG)	DP	47.89	15.80	63.69
5		James Brown (JB)	FA	20.64	6.81	27.45
6		Bill Green (BG)	SME	31.39	10.36	41.75
7		John Q. Public (JQP)	Owner	88.97	29.36	118.33
8		Samantha Grey (SG)	Attorney	74.84	24.70	99.54

10	**WBS**	**Task Description**	**Owner**	**Role**	**Effort (Hours)**	**Labor Costs**
11	**0.0**	**Procurement for Janitorial Services**	**DS**	**SSM**	**321.75**	**$34,558.46**
12	**1.0**	**Receive RFPS**	**DS**	**SSM, DP**	**7.50**	**$813.23**
13	1.1	Brainstorm	DS, RG	SSM, DP	1.25	$144.81
14	1.1.2	Strategy	DS, RG	SSM, DP	0.25	$28.96
15	1.1.2.1	Mutual non-disclosure agreement	DS, RG	SSM, DP	0.25	$28.96
16	1.1.2.2	Contract type	DS, RG	SSM, DP	0.25	$28.96
17	1.1.2.3	Length of agreement	DS, RG	SSM, DP	0.25	$28.96
18	1.1.2.4	Sourcing Approach	DS, RG	SSM, DP	0.25	$28.96
19	1.2	Review current and historical supplier contracts	DS, RG	SSM, DP	2.00	$231.69
20	1.3	Identify all stakeholders	DS, RG	SSM, DP	1.00	$115.85
21	1.4	Establish the procurement team	DS, RG	SSM, DP	1.00	$115.85
22	1.4.1	Decide what skills are required	DS, RG	SSM, DP	0.20	$23.17
23	1.4.2	Find out who has these skills	DS, RG	SSM, DP	0.20	$23.17
24	1.4.3	Find out availability of these people	DS, RG	SSM, DP	0.20	$23.17

Exhibit 5-2. Budget for Case Example 2: Janitorial Services. SSM, Strategic Sourcing Manager; DP, Director of Procurement; FA, Financial Analyst; SME, Subject Matter Expert.

	A	B	C	D	E	F
10	**WBS**	**Task Description**	**Owner**	**Role**	**Effort (Hours)**	**Labor Costs**
25	1.4.4	Get these people assigned to procurement team	DS, RG, JB, BG, JQP, SG	SSM, DP, FA, SME, Owner, Attorney	0.20	$80.58
26	1.4.5	Define roles and responsibilities	DS	SSM	0.20	$10.43
27	1.5	Silent period with existing supplier	DS, RG, JB, BG, JQP, SG	SSM, DP, FA, SME, Owner, Attorney	0.25	$100.73
28	1.6	Establish a high-level achedule	DS	SSM	2.00	$104.31
29	**2.0**	**Kick-Off Meeting**	**DS**	**SSM**	**6.00**	**$594.24**
30	2.1	Decide on date for meeting	DS	SSM	0.25	$13.04
31	2.2	Reserve meeting room	DS	SSM	0.25	$13.04
32	2.3	Create agenda	DS	SSM	0.50	$26.08
33	2.4	Send out agenda	DS	SSM	0.50	$26.08
34	2.4.1	Receive comments/ additons to agenda	DS	SSM	0.50	$26.08
35	2.4.2	Resend amended agenda	DS	SSM	0.50	$26.08
36	**2.5**	**Hold meeting**	**DS, JB, BG, JQP**	**SSM, FA, SME, Owner**	**1.50**	**$359.53**
37	2.6	Develop action list and/ or meeting minutes	DS	SSM	0.50	$26.08
38	2.7	Send out action list/ minutes	DS	SSM	0.50	$26.08
39	2.7.1	Receive comments/ additions to action list/minutes	DS	SSM	0.50	$26.08
40	2.7.2	Resend action list/ minutes	DS	SSM	0.50	$26.08

Exhibit 5-2. Budget for Case Example 2: Janitorial Services (continued).

	A	B	C	D	E	F
10	**WBS**	**Task Description**	**Owner**	**Role**	**Effort (Hours)**	**Labor Costs**
41	**3.0**	**Procurement Plan**	**DS**	**SSM**	**27.75**	**$7,296.90**
42	3.1	Finalize procurement strategy	DS, JQP	SSM, Owner	0.50	$85.24
43	3.1.1	Review strategy with team members	DS, JB, BG, JQP	SSM, FA, SME, Owner	1.00	$239.69
44	3.2	Develop procurement WBS	DS, BG	SSM, SME	6.00	$563.43
45	3.2.1	Review WBS with team members	DS, RG, JB, BG, JQP, SG	SSM, DP, FA, SME, Owner, Attorney	1.00	$402.92
46	3.3	Develop procurement schedule	DS, JQP	SSM, Owner	4.00	$1,213.50
47	3.3.1	Review schedule with team members	DS, RG, JB, BG, JQP, SG	SSM, DP, FA, SME, Owner, Attorney	1.00	$402.92
48	3.4	Develop procurement budget	N/A			
49	3.4.1	Review budget with team members	N/A			
50	3.5	Develop procurement communications plan	DS	SSM	2.00	$104.31
51	3.5.1	Review communications plan with team members	DS, RG, JB, BG, JQP, SG	SSM, DP, FA, SME, Owner, Attorney	1.00	$402.92
52	3.6	Develop procurement risk plan	DS, JB, BG	SSM, FA, SME	2.00	$242.71
53	3.6.1	Review risk plan with team members	DS, RG, JB, BG, JQP, SG	SSM, DP, FA, SME, Owner, Attorney	1.00	$402.92
54	3.7	Review procurement plan with entire team	DS, RG, JB, BG, JQP, SG	SSM, DP, FA, SME, Owner, Attorney	4.00	$1,611.66

Exhibit 5-2. Budget for Case Example 2: Janitorial Services (continued).

	A	B	C	D	E	F
10	**WBS**	**Task Description**	**Owner**	**Role**	**Effort (Hours)**	**Labor Costs**
55	3.8	Finalize procurement plan		SSM, DP, FA, SME, Owner, Attorney	4.00	$1,611.66
56	3.9	Distribute procurement plan		SSM	0.25	$13.04
57	**4.0**	**Solicitation**	**DS**	**SSM**	**73.75**	**$6,367.38**
58	4.1	Silent period with potential suppliers and existing supplier	DS, RG, JB, BG, JQP, SG	SSM, DP, FA, SME, Owner, Attorney	0.25	$100.73
59	4.2	Draft RFP	DS	SSM	41.25	$5,030.00
60		**Memorial Day holiday**				
61	4.2.1	RFP Schedule	DS	SSM	4.00	$208.63
62	4.2.1.1	Review with team	DS, JB, BG, JQP	SSM, FA, SME, Owner	2.00	$479.37
63	4.2.2	Statement of Work (Scope of Work)	BG, DS	SME, SSM	8.00	$751.24
64	4.2.2.1	Review with team	DS, JB, BG, JQP	SSM, FA, SME, Owner	2.00	$479.37
65	4.2.3	Determine type of agreement document	DS, SG	SSM, Attorney	1.00	$151.70
66	4.2.3.1	Sample terms and conditions	DS	SSM	2.00	$104.31
67	4.2.4	Develop pricing model	JB, DS, BG	FA, SSM, SME	1.00	$121.36
68	4.2.5	RFP general instructions	DS	SSM	4.00	$208.63
69	4.2.6	Mutual non-disclosure agreement	DS	SSM	2.00	$104.31
70	4.2.7	Proposal signature page	DS	SSM	0.50	$26.08
71	4.2.8	Develop weighted evaluation criteria	DS, BG	SSM, SME	8.00	$1,480.35
72	4.2.8.1	Review with evaluation team	DS, JB, BG, JQP	SSM, FA, SME, Owner	2.00	$479.37

Exhibit 5-2. Budget for Case Example 2: Janitorial Services (continued).

	A	B	C	D	E	F
10	**WBS**	**Task Description**	**Owner**	**Role**	**Effort (Hours)**	**Labor Costs**
73	4.2.9	MWDBE Certification	DS	SSM	0.50	$26.08
74	4.2.10	HUB Certification	DS	SSM	0.50	$26.08
75	4.2.11	Form W-9	DS	SSM	0.50	$26.08
76	4.3	Review entire RFP with team	DS, JB, BG, JQP	SSM, FA, SME, Owner	1.00	$239.69
77	4.3.1	Make changes as required	DS	SSM	2.00	$104.31
78	4.3.2	Distribute to team for final review	DS	SSM	0.25	$13.04
79	4.4	Commodity strategy	JB	FA	22.25	$715.08
80	4.4.1	Industry/commodity profile analysis	JB	FA	4.00	$109.80
81	4.4.2	Purchasing profile	JB	FA	2.00	$54.90
82	4.4.3	Supplier financial analysis	JB	FA	8.00	$219.60
83	4.4.4	Total cost of ownership	JB	FA	4.00	$109.80
84	4.4.5	Determine qualified supplier bid list	JB, DS	FA, SSM	2.00	$159.21
85	4.4.5.1	Contact names and information	JB	FA	2.00	$54.90
86	4.4.5.2	Send all information to SSM	JB	FA	0.25	$6.86
87	4.5	Finalize RFP	DS	SSM	8.00	$417.25
88	**4.6**	**Send RFP out**	**DS**	**SSM**	**2.00**	**$104.31**
89	**5.0**	**RFP Process**	**DS**	**SSM**	**12.25**	**$638.92**
90	5.1	RFP silent period with potential suppliers and existing supplier	DS	SSM	0.25	$13.04
91	5.2	Receive questions on RFP	DS	SSM	2.00	$104.31
92	5.2.1	Assemble questions and answers	DS	SSM	8.00	$417.25
93	5.2.2	Send out assembled questions and answers to all participants	DS	SSM	2.00	$104.31

Exhibit 5-2. Budget for Case Example 2: Janitorial Services (continued).

	A	B	C	D	E	F
10	**WBS**	**Task Description**	**Owner**	**Role**	**Effort (Hours)**	**Labor Costs**
94	**6.0**	**Proposal Analysis**	**DS**	**SSM**	**72.00**	**$7,432.63**
95	**6.1**	**Receive proposals**	**DS**	**SSM**	**8.00**	**$417.25**
96	6.1.1	Reject all proposals that are not signed	DS	SSM	4.00	$208.63
97	6.1.2	Reject all proposals submitted after the deadline	DS	SSM	4.00	$208.63
98	6.2	Distribute all acceptable proposals to evaluation team	DS	SSM	4.00	$208.63
99	6.3	Team evaluates all proposals independently	DS, JB, BG, JQP	SSM, FA, SME, Owner	20.00	$4,793.72
100		**4th of July holiday**				
101	6.4	Team returns all evaluations	DS	SSM	2.00	$104.31
102	6.5	Review and collate all evaluations	DS	SSM	8.00	$417.25
103	6.6	Distribute collated evaluations to team	DS	SSM	2.00	$104.31
104	6.7	Evaluation team meets to decide on top proposals	DS, JB, BG, JQP	SSM, FA, SME, Owner	6.00	$239.69
105	6.8	Collect questions on proposals for short listed potential suppliers	DS	SSM	2.00	$104.31
106	6.9	Notify short list	DS	SSM	2.00	$104.31
107	6.10	Schedule oral presentations	DS	SSM	5.00	$260.78
108	6.10.1	Verify date and time with each company	DS	SSM	4.00	$208.63
109	6.10.2	Reserve meeting room	DS	SSM	0.50	$26.08
110	6.10.3	Notify evaluation team	DS	SSM	0.50	$26.08
111	**6.11**	**Oral presentations**	**DS**	**SSM**	**20.50**	**$2,850.74**
112	6.11.1	Make sure someone greets presenters	DS	SSM	1.00	$52.16

Exhibit 5-2. Budget for Case Example 2: Janitorial Services (continued).

	A	B	C	D	E	F
10	**WBS**	**Task Description**	**Owner**	**Role**	**Effort (Hours)**	**Labor Costs**
113	6.11.2	Make sure equipment is ready and working	DS	SSM	1.00	$52.16
114	6.11.3	Make sure refreshments are ready	DS	SSM	0.50	$26.08
115	6.11.4	Questions	DS	SSM	7.00	$365.10
116	6.11.4.1	Prepared and who will ask each one	DS, JB, BG, JQP	SSM, FA, SME, Owner	4.00	$958.74
117	6.11.5.1	As presentation is given	DS, JB, BG, JQP	SSM, FA, SME, Owner	1.50	$359.53
118	6.12	Thank yous and walking presenters out	DS	SSM	1.50	$78.24
119	**6.13**	**Meeting to decide on contract awardee**	**DS, JB, BG, JQP**	**SSM, FA, SME, Owner**	**4.00**	**$958.74**
120	**7.0**	**Negotiations**	**DS**	**SSM**	**34.00**	**$3,503.29**
121	7.1	Develop negotiation strategy	DS, JB, BG	SSM, FA, SME	8.00	$970.84
122	7.1.1	Where negotiation takes place	DS, JB, BG	SSM, FA, SME	4.00	$485.42
123	7.1.2	Win-win or hard ball	DS, JB, BG	SSM, FA, SME	4.00	$485.42
124	7.2	Identify negotiation team	DS, JB, BG	SSM, FA, SME	1.00	$121.36
125	7.2.1	Fully identify and communicate roles	DS	SSM	1.00	$52.16
126	**7.3**	**Conduct negotiations**	**DS, JB, BG**	**SSM, FA, SME**	**8.00**	**$970.84**
127	7.3.1	Finalize deal including terms and conditions	DS	SSM	8.00	$417.25
128	**8.0**	**Contract Finalization**	**DS**	**SSM**	**62.00**	**$4,748.18**
129	8.1	Draft contract	DS	SSM	12.00	$625.88
130	8.1.1	Review contract	RG, SG	DP, Attorney	8.00	$1,305.83
131	8.2	Obtain approval signatures	DS	SSM	40.00	$2,086.27

Exhibit 5-2. Budget for Case Example 2: Janitorial Services (continued).

	A	B	C	D	E	F
10	**WBS**	**Task Description**	**Owner**	**Role**	**Effort (Hours)**	**Labor Costs**
132		**Labor Day holiday**				
133	**8.3**	**Execute contract**	**DS**	**SSM**	**2.00**	**$104.31**
134	**9.0**	**Notification of Unsuccessful Suppliers**	**DS**	**SSM**	**6.00**	**$312.94**
135	9.1	Preliminary notification	DS	SSM	4.00	$208.63
136	9.2	Formal debriefing	DS	SSM	2.00	$104.31
	10.0	**Contract Administration**	**DS**	**SSM**	**N/A**	

Exhibit 5-2. Budget for Case Example 2: Janitorial Services (continued).

This book has free material available for download from the Web Added Value™ resource center at *www.jrosspub.com.*

APPENDIX C

RFP FOR CASE EXAMPLE 2: JANITORIAL SERVICES

REQUEST FOR PROPOSAL FOR JANITORIAL SERVICES

RFP # 130602

XYZ Company
Purchasing Department
1325 Texas Blvd.
Dallas, TX 75032

INVITATION

XYZ Company is accepting proposals from vendors providing Janitorial Services.

XYZ Company invites your firm to submit a proposal. If you are interested in submitting a proposal, please follow the General Instructions and Requirements outlined in the enclosed Request for Proposal.

Vendors will pay particular attention to all instructions, requirements, and deadlines indicated in the attached documents. Late or incomplete proposals will not be accepted.

In accepting proposals, XYZ Company reserves the right to reject any and all proposals, to waive formalities and reasonable irregularities in submitted documents, and to waive any requirements in order to accept any proposal deemed to be in the best interest of XYZ Company. XYZ Company is not obligated to accept the lowest priced proposal.

XYZ Company will not release the names of the participants to this Request for Proposals at any time. Participants will be notified of the next step after the XYZ Company evaluation team has evaluated the proposals. An award determination will be made and approved by XYZ Company executives, and Vendor(s) will be notified.

We greatly appreciate your efforts and look forward to reviewing your proposal.

Donna Smith, MBA, CPSM
Strategic Sourcing Manager
XYZ Company

TABLE OF CONTENTS

SECTION I - OVERVIEW

Background and Objectives

XYZ Company is the importer, distributor, and retailer for an international brand of tea. It has 50,000 square feet of mixed-use property: 10,000 square feet is used for offices, 25,000 square feet is a warehouse, and 15,000 square feet is a small retail store.

XYZ Company invites interested and qualified companies, herein after referred to as "Contractors," "Providers," or "Vendors," to submit proposals for Janitorial Services in response to this solicitation.

XYZ Company has fixed pricing budgets and all pricing quoted/proposed should remain fixed for the duration of the contract. Our goal is to employ best practices and cost effectiveness.

SECTION II - REQUEST FOR PROPOSAL (RFP) TIMELINE OF EVENTS

Event	Date
Request for Proposal Packet Issue Date	June 10, 2013
Mandatory Pre-Proposal Conference	June 14, 2013
Mandatory Site Visit	June 14, 2013
Receive Questions from Prospective Vendors	June 19, 2013
Distribute Answers to Questions	June 24, 2013
Submit Final Proposal	June 28, 2013
Anticipated Oral Presentations	July 31, 2013 and August 1, 2013
Anticipated Award Date	Contingent on Executive Approval

SECTION III - GENERAL INSTRUCTIONS

A. Questions

Deadline for Questions from Providers: June 19, 2013, by 4:30 p.m. CDT

Deadline for Response to Questions: June 24, 2013, by 4:30 p.m. CDT

All questions concerning the RFP specifications must be submitted in writing and emailed to the Strategic Sourcing Manager, listed below. To ensure receipt of all questions in a timely manner, the preferred method is via email.

Donna Smith, Strategic Sourcing Manager
Email: dsmith@xyz.com

B. Submittal Procedure

A person or officer of the company submitting the proposal, who is authorized to enter into contractual agreements on behalf of the company, must sign the proposal, subject to all conditions and specifications attached hereto, in INK.

Proposals received unsigned will be deemed non-responsive and will not be accepted.

Deadline to submit "Final Proposal" is June 28, 2013, by 4:30 p.m. CDT. The original proposal, signed in ink, five (5) additional photocopies, and an electronic copy (CD-ROM) should be submitted in a SEALED ENVELOPE and delivered to:

XYZ Company
ATTN: Donna Smith, Purchasing Department
1325 Texas Blvd.
Dallas, TX 75032

Label the outside of the sealed envelope: Janitorial Services

No proposal will be accepted after the stated deadline.

Respondents may mail or personally deliver their proposals to the Purchasing Department of XYZ Company at the above address. XYZ Company will not be responsible for any proposal(s) that is (are) lost in the mail or not delivered to the Purchasing Department by the stated deadline for any reason.

Proposals shall include all documentation as requested in this Request for Proposal.

C. Non-Discrimination Policy Statement

XYZ Company does not discriminate against any individual or Vendor with respect to his/her compensation, terms, conditions, or award of contract because of race, color, religion, sex, national origin, age, disability, political affiliation, or limit, segregate, or classify candidates for award of contract in any way which would deprive or tend to deprive any individual or company of business opportunities or otherwise adversely affect status as a Vendor because of race, color, religion, sex, national origin, age, disability, or political affiliation.

D. Immigration Reform and Control Act of 1986

By submitting their proposals, Vendors certify that they do not, and will not, during the performance of this contract, employ illegal alien workers or otherwise violate the provisions of the federal Immigration Reform and Control Act of 1986.

E. References and Experience

All Vendors are required to submit, with their proposal, a comprehensive list of references. Vendors are required to provide a minimum of three (3) references where Vendor has provided janitorial services (within the last six months) that pertain to the technical requirements of this RFP. References shall include company name, address, telephone number, fax number, contact person, and email address. Vendors must agree to authorize clients to furnish any information required by XYZ Company to verify references provided, and for determining the quality and timeliness of previous work performed.

Vendor shall submit with their proposal documentation of past performance in projects of similar magnitude, and resulting customer satisfaction particularly in the areas of professionalism, contract performance, quality of the personnel, responsiveness and flexibility, etc.

F. Proposal Guarantee/Award Procedure

It is anticipated that a recommendation for award for this proposal will be made no more than thirty (30) days after the proposal due date. All Vendors are required to guarantee their proposals as an irrevocable offer valid for one hundred twenty (120) days after the proposal due date. XYZ Company, in its sole and absolute discretion, shall have the right to award an agreement for any or all items/services listed in each proposal, shall have the right to reject any and all proposals as it deems to be in its best interests, to waive formalities and reasonable irregularities in submitted documents, shall not be bound to accept the lowest priced proposal, and shall be allowed to accept the total proposal of any one vendor.

G. Permits

Any and all permits as required by authorities having jurisdiction (local, state, county, and/or federal) are the total responsibility of the Vendor.

H. Financial Information

Vendor must submit a copy of their last AUDITED financial statement. A letter from Vendor's CPA is an acceptable alternative for Non-Public companies, and must include a statement that financial solvency is adequate to meet expenditures for at least one year.

I. Payments

Vendor is to submit properly completed invoice(s) to the address specified in the contract. To ensure prompt payment, each invoice should indicate purchase order number, discount terms, and include Vendor's name and return remittance address.

J. Price Adjustments

Vendor will be required to honor its proposed prices for the term of the contract period.

K. Minority/Women and/or Disadvantaged Business Enterprises (M/W/DBE)

XYZ Company shall make a good faith effort to utilize Minority/Women and/or Disadvantaged Business Enterprises (M/W/DBEs) in contracts for services. Please submit proof of M/W/DBE certification.

L. Direct or Indirect Assignment

The successful Vendor will not be permitted to directly or indirectly assign rights and duties under the contract without express written approval by XYZ Company.

M. Form W-9

Vendors are to complete Form W-9 and submit with their proposal documents. The form can be found and downloaded at: http://www.irs.gov/pub/irs-pdf/fw9.pdf.

SECTION IV – PROPOSAL STIPULATIONS AND REQUIREMENTS

A. Modification or Withdrawal of Proposals

Any proposal may be modified or withdrawn prior to the deadline, provided such modification or withdrawal is submitted prior to the deadline. Any modification received after the deadline shall be deemed late and will not be considered.

B. Offer and Acceptance Period

All proposals must be an irrevocable offer valid for one hundred twenty (120) days after the proposal due date.

C. Late Proposals

Proposals received after the stated deadline shall be deemed late and will not be considered.

D. Irregularities in Proposals

Except as otherwise stated in this RFP, evaluation of all proposals will be based solely upon information contained in the Vendor's response to this RFP. XYZ Company shall not be held responsible for errors, omissions, or oversights in any Vendor's response to this RFP. XYZ Company may waive technical irregularities that do not alter the price or quality of the services.

XYZ Company shall have the right to reject proposals containing a statement, representation, warranty, or certification that is determined by XYZ Company and its counsel to be materially false, incorrect, misleading, or incomplete. Additionally, any errors, omissions, or oversights of a material nature may constitute grounds for rejection of any proposal.

The inability of a Vendor to provide one or more of the required components or specified features or capabilities required by this RFP does not, in and of itself, preclude acceptance by XYZ Company of the proposal. All proposals will be evaluated as a whole and in the best interest of XYZ Company.

E. Oral Presentations

Any Vendor that submits a proposal in response to this RFP may be required to make an oral presentation for further clarification upon XYZ Company's request.

F. Amendments to the Proposal

If it becomes necessary to revise any part of this RFP package, or if additional information is necessary to clarify any provision, the revision and/or additional information will be provided to each Vendor via fax or e-mail.

G. Availability of the Proposal

No proposal shall be open to public inspection. Each Vendor must request confidentiality for its proposal, in part or in its entirety, to ensure that information is not inadvertently disbursed.

H. Retention of Proposals

All proposals submitted to XYZ Company shall become the property of XYZ Company and shall not be returned. Proposals that do not result in an award of contract will be shredded by XYZ Company.

I. Notice of Non-Participation Form

Vendors must respond to the proposal request whether they can or cannot provide the products, supplies, and/or services listed in the RFP. Fill out Attachment C (Notice of Non-Participation Form) and return it to the above address.

J. Incurred Expenses

XYZ Company shall not be responsible for expenses incurred by a Vendor in the preparation and submission of a proposal. This provision also includes any costs involved in providing an oral presentation of the proposal.

K. Deviation Form

Each response to this RFP shall contain a Deviation Form that states the Vendor's commitment to the provisions of this RFP and Sample Contract. An individual authorized to execute contracts must sign the Deviation Form. Any exceptions taken to the terms and conditions identified in this RFP package, including the Sample Contract, must be expressly stated in the Deviation Form. See Attachment B.

L. Subcontractors

All provisions and/or stipulations within this RFP package also apply to any authorized subcontractors.

M. Term of Contract

The intent of the RFP is to award this contract to the qualified Vendor who can provide, and meet, all specified requirements of this RFP. The contract shall commence with an award date for a one (1) year base period with three (3) one-year renewal options at the sole discretion of XYZ Company. Award of renewal option years will be based upon satisfactory performance, which will be reviewed on an annual basis.

N. Licensure

Vendor shall submit, with its proposal, a copy of any license(s), certification(s), registration(s), permit(s), etc. as required by authorities having jurisdiction – local, state, county, and/or federal.

O. Pricing

Each vendor shall provide responses to this RFP on the "Proposal Reply" page with total pricing. See Section VIII.

P. Conflict of Interest Provision

The XYZ Company organizational conflict of interest provision is applicable, in that vendors who participate in the development of draft specifications, requirements, statements of work, and/or the RFP for a proposed procurement shall be excluded from submitting a proposal to compete for the award of such procurement.

SECTION V – INSURANCE REQUIREMENTS

A. Policies, Coverages, and Endorsements

Vendor agrees to maintain, or to cause its personnel providing services under this Agreement to maintain, at its sole cost and expense or the cost and expense of its personnel, the following insurance policies, with the specified coverages and limits, to protect and insure XYZ Company and Vendor against any claim for damages arising in connection with Vendor's responsibilities or the responsibilities of Vendor's personnel under this Agreement and all extensions and amendments thereto.

1. Commercial General Liability	
General Aggregate	$2,000,000
Each Occurrence	$1,000,000
2. Workers' Compensation and Employers' Liability If Applicable	
Medical and Indemnity	Statutory Requirements
Bodily Injury by Accident	$500,000 Each Accident
Bodily Injury by Disease	$500,000 Each Employee
Bodily Injury by Disease	$500,000 Policy Limit
Employers Liability	$500,000
3. Automobile Liability	
Includes Hired and Non-Owned Automobiles	$2,000,000 Combined Single Limit

A CURRENT "CERTIFICATE OF INSURANCE" MUST ACCOMPANY ALL PROPOSALS.

B. Insured Parties

All policies shall contain a provision naming XYZ Company (and its officers, agents, and employees) as Additional Insured parties on the original policy and all renewals or replacements during the term of this Agreement.

C. Subrogation

All policies must contain a Waiver of Subrogation endorsement to the effect that the issuer waives any claim or right in the nature of subrogation to recover against XYZ Company, its officers, agents, or employees.

D. Proof of Insurance

The policies, coverages, and endorsements required by this provision shall be shown on a Certificate of Insurance on which XYZ Company must be listed as the Certificate Holder and which should be furnished to XYZ Company prior to the commencement of this Agreement. All such insurance shall be secured and maintained with an insurance company, or companies, licensed to do business in the State of Texas. XYZ Company may withhold payments under the terms of this Agreement until the Vendor furnishes XYZ Company copies of all Certificates of Insurance from the insurance carrier, or carriers, showing that such insurance is in full force and effect.

E. Cancellation

New Certificates of Insurance shall be furnished to XYZ Company at the renewal date of all policies named on these Certificates. Vendor shall give XYZ Company thirty (30) days prior written notice of any proposed cancellation of any of the above-described insurance policies.

F. Indemnification

To the extent permitted under the Constitution and the laws of the State of Texas, Vendor hereby agrees to indemnify and hold harmless XYZ Company and all of its directors, officers, employees, and agents from all suits, actions, claims, or costs of any character, type, or description brought or made on account of any injuries, death, or damage received or sustained by any person or persons or property arising out of, or occasioned by, any acts or negligence of Vendor or Vendor's personnel, if any, or its agents or employees whether occurring during the performance of the services hereunder or in the execution of the performance of any of its duties under this agreement.

SECTION VI – PROPOSAL EVALUATION PROCESS

Not all evaluation factors are equal in importance and each factor is weighted in accordance with its importance to XYZ Company. Each item has been assessed a percentage upon which the final score will be determined. A total of 100 percentage points for the following items will be considered a perfect score.

The following will be significant factors in evaluating proposals, but the evaluation will not be limited to these items when making a final decision:

A.	Overall Program Concept	25%	Indication that Vendor has a well-defined concept and program structure for all components of service desired by XYZ Company, including equipment, availability, and start-up time.
B.	Understanding	20%	Indication that Vendor understands the nature of XYZ Company's services and constraints in providing those services, and that Vendor has thoroughly analyzed XYZ Company's needs and requirements.
C.	Financial Condition	15%	As evidenced by the financial information requested from each vendor, indication that Vendor is financially stable and able to provide related services in their entirety.
D.	History and Description of Firm	10%	Indication from brief history and description of Vendor's firm that it has the number of employees necessary to satisfactorily provide services described in RFP and that its areas of specialization match RFP requirements.
E.	Credentials of Staff	10%	Indication from Vendor's description of any special expertise the firm has in providing janitorial services to firms similar to XYZ Company.
F.	References	10%	Results from investigating references furnished by Vendor as requested in this RFP package. Issues that will be addressed include contract performance, quality of personnel, responsiveness, etc.
G.	Cost	10%	Cost will become a determining factor when all other conditions are equal. Final cost may be negotiated with the successful Vendor.

SECTION VII - SPECIALIZED SERVICES TO BE PERFORMED

Scope of Services:

XYZ Company is seeking Janitorial Services at 1325 Texas Blvd.

Janitorial Specifications

General Information

A. Work Scheduling and Reporting: Quality cleaning is required, including full performance of all specified daily services on the first official working day of the contract period. All work will be performed at times as specified and agreed upon by Vendor and XYZ Company. All cleaning personnel are prohibited from disturbing papers on desks or shelves, opening desk drawers or cabinets, or using telephone or office equipment provided for XYZ Company use. Instructions pertaining to conduct and other regulations, as required by XYZ Company, must be followed.

All contract personnel are required to sign in/out upon arrival and departure of work site (Contractor Sign-in Log, Attachment E). Sign-in log is located in the janitorial closet in each part of the facility (office, retail space, warehouse).

Qualified Vendors who are notified of short-listing are required to:

1. After review of proposals:
   a. Submit for approval by XYZ Company samples of, and a list indicating the manufacturer, brand name, and intended use of, each of the supplies and materials proposed for use in the performance of the work.
   b. Provide a tour of their facility for designated XYZ Company staff.
   c. Supply all employee safety and operational training materials utilized by the contractor to designated XYZ Company staff.
   d. Provide to XYZ Company information regarding Vendor's hiring process, criteria, and procedures.
2. Two weeks prior to the contract starting date, successful Vendor will:
   a. Meet with XYZ Company staff to review the total workload and cleaning methods as proposed by Vendor.
   b. Provide a list, for the approval of XYZ Company, indicating staff and contact information (staff and supervisory) by space type in the facility (office, retail, warehouse). If there is a change to schedule or staff, notify XYZ Company designated representative at least 24 hours in advance.
   c. Provide a proposed schedule, for the approval of XYZ Company, identifying by performance date, all weekly, quarterly, and semi-annual requirements, as detailed in this specification.

   d. Submit, in writing to XYZ Company, the names of at least two (2) representatives, one of which must be authorized to act for Vendor in every detail concerning the requirements as described in this specification.
3. During contract period:
   a. Update listing of staff by location, including cell phone numbers.
   b. Work with XYZ Company designated representative to schedule special services.
   c. During the night of the last day of the contract, fill all soap and paper product dispensers to full capacity. Soap and paper stocks for dispensers shall remain and not be removed at the end of the last official day of the contract.
4. In the event of an emergency condition at the facility, e.g., flooding, assist as necessary to perform the cleanup. For after-hours emergencies, Vendor will provide assistance within one hour of notification by XYZ Company representative. Vendor will not be penalized for scheduled work not performed while performing emergency assistance.

B. Facility Security: Facility master key will be provided to Vendor supervisor only. Vendor will be liable for all costs associated with re-keying, re-issuance, or programming of keys, access cards, and security codes which result from the loss or compromising of keys, access cards, or security codes by contractor's personnel.

Vendor's supervisors will be trained on the use of alarm systems. Supervisors will be responsible for training cleaning personnel on the use of alarm systems.

Vendor's employees will be responsible for securing all offices, gates, and exterior entrances/exits upon completion of contracted services unless otherwise directed by the designated XYZ Company representative. Vendor's employees shall immediately communicate to XYZ Company representative any inability to secure by code, alarm, or mechanical lock any office, gate, or door. Failure to secure all exterior entrances/exits and/or gates will result in a $50.00 charge per occurrence. Repeated failure to maintain a secure facility when providing janitorial services will be cause for termination of the contract.

Vendor will also be responsible for payment of any fines incurred by the owner due to false alarms at a facility not properly secured.

Repeated failure to maintain a secure facility when providing janitorial services shall serve as cause for termination of contract.

C. Supplies and Materials: Vendor will furnish all supplies and materials necessary for the performance of the contract. Any changes to the items on the XYZ Company list of approved supplies and materials must be submitted in writing to the XYZ Company representative and approved prior to use in the XYZ Company property. Vendor must maintain within each janitorial closet a list of Material Safety Data Sheets (MSDS) for each product used by Vendor. Vendor will not use any material that XYZ Company determines unsuitable for the purpose intended, or that is harmful to any part of the building, contents, or equipment.

Electricity and hot/cold water will be available, at no charge, to Vendor from existing outlets for use with contractor's equipment.

D. Equipment: Vendor will provide all necessary cleaning equipment, including power-driven floor scrubbing machines, waxing and polishing machines, industrial-type vacuum cleaners, all necessary motor trucks, etc. to successfully perform the work agreed to in the contract. The XYZ Company representative will approve all equipment before it is used in the property. Equipment deemed to be of improper type or design, or inadequate for the purpose intended, will be replaced by the contractor.

E. Storage Provisions: XYZ Company will provide storage space for supplies used daily.

Vendor Qualifications

A. Vendor Personnel:

1. Project Manager (PM) – The PM is responsible for the scheduling and management of work to be performed as detailed in this specification. Therefore, the PM must have, prior to employment as PM on this job, at least three (3) of the last five (5) years work experience in the management of custodial type operations for buildings of the approximate size and similar characteristics of the building in this specification. **Each vendor shall include as part of the submitted proposal a detailed resume of the intended PM.**
2. Supervisory Employees – All supervisory personnel engaged in fulfilling the requirements of this specification shall have, prior to assuming a supervisory capacity for the job described herein, experience in custodial type work. Supervisory personnel shall be available during the hours of service and must be provided with cell phones by Vendor. Names and cell phone numbers must be provided to XYZ Company's designated representative, and updated when changes are made. All supervisory personnel must be fluent in both verbal and written communication in the English language.
3. Production Employees – Vendor shall employ only qualified personnel who are skilled in the performance of janitorial work and shall screen all employees, requiring satisfactory references. Production employees

shall be available during the hours of service and must be provided with a cell phone. All employees of Vendor shall be neatly attired in uniforms supplied by Vendor while working at XYZ Company. Vendor personnel assigned to this contract will be furnished identification badges by XYZ Company and must properly display the furnished identification badge. The minimum uniform will consist of an outer garment with Vendor's name located on the chest. No shorts or open-toe shoes allowed.

B. **Miscellaneous:** Vendor's employees must have a good working knowledge of the principles and techniques of the machines, equipment, and cleaning products used in building maintenance, as well as a good working knowledge of safety procedures. Vendor shall be responsible for instructing its employees in safe work habits and requirements:

1. Vendor employees are allowed to use break rooms at XYZ Company.
2. Vendor will pay for criminal background investigations for all personnel assigned to work at XYZ Company property for the term of the contract.
3. All production employees substituted by Vendor, on either a temporary or permanent basis, will be taken to the facility by their immediate supervisor, introduced to XYZ Company designated representative, and instructed by Vendor's supervisor on duties to be performed as well as securing of facility.
4. XYZ Company may require the removal of a contractor employee from the XYZ Company site without cause. This may be immediate and at XYZ Company's sole discretion.
5. Vendor shall be required at his/her own expense to conduct a criminal background investigation and TB testing (skin test and/or check X-ray as required) for all personnel assigned to work at the facility under this contract.
6. All persons employed by Vendor shall be U.S. citizens or possess papers showing that they are legal aliens.
7. All personnel assigned to the XYZ Company facility shall be able to understand the English language.
8. All personnel must be able to understand labels, descriptions, and instructions for all materials used at the XYZ Company facility. Project managers and supervisors are required to understand and speak English fluently.
9. Emergency situations are exempted from the ban on using XYZ Company telephones.
10. No one is to accompany Vendor's employees to XYZ Company property who is not employed by Vendor and assigned to work in the property.

C. Trash bags removed from cans/receptacles will not be placed on carpet.

Schedule of Cleaning Services

A. Offices

1. Monday through Friday evening services consisting of:
    - i. Clean, sanitize, and stock restrooms as needed.
    - ii. Empty trash cans.
    - iii. Clean trash cans as needed.
    - iv. Remove trash to designated disposal area.
    - v. Vacuum common areas.
    - vi. Vacuum cubicles and offices.
    - vii. Spot treat carpet stains.
    - viii. Spot dust horizontal surfaces without moving papers or other items on desks.
    - ix. Sweep and/or mop floors in common areas.
    - x. Clean and disinfect break room surfaces.
    - xi. Clean and disinfect drinking fountains.
    - xii. Clean and disinfect lobby furniture.
    - xiii. Report maintenance problems to XYZ Company facilities manager.

2. Quarterly services consisting of deep cleaning all surfaces in common areas including shelves, fire extinguishers and/or cabinets for them, signs, clocks, etc.; stripping and waxing all floors; deep cleaning/disinfecting all surfaces in restrooms

3. Semi-annual services consisting of carpet cleaning in all common areas and cubicles/offices

B. Retail Store

1. Monday through Saturday evening services consisting of:
    - i. Clean, sanitize, and stock restrooms as needed.
    - ii. Empty trash cans.
    - iii. Clean trash cans as needed.
    - iv. Remove trash to designated disposal area.
    - v. Vacuum common areas.
    - vi. Vacuum cubicles and offices.
    - vii. Spot treat carpet stains.
    - viii. Spot dust horizontal surfaces without moving papers or other items on desks.
    - ix. Sweep and/or mop floors in common areas.
    - x. Clean and disinfect break room surfaces.
    - xi. Clean and disinfect drinking fountains.

xii. Clean and disinfect lobby furniture.
xiii. Report maintenance problems to XYZ Company facilities manager.

2. Quarterly services consisting of deep cleaning all surfaces such as shelves, fire extinguishers and/or cabinets for them, signs, clocks, etc.; stripping and waxing all floors; deep cleaning/disinfecting all surfaces in restrooms

3. Semi-annual services consisting of carpet cleaning in all common areas and cubicles/offices

C. **Warehouse**

1. Monday through Saturday evening services consisting of:
   i. Clean, sanitize, and stock restrooms as needed.
   ii. Empty trash cans.
   iii. Clean trash cans as needed.
   iv. Remove trash to designated disposal area.
   v. Vacuum common areas.
   vi. Vacuum cubicles and offices.
   vii. Spot treat carpet stains.
   viii. Spot dust horizontal surfaces without moving papers or other items on desks.
   ix. Sweep and/or mop floors in common areas.
   x. Clean and disinfect break room surfaces.
   xi. Clean and disinfect drinking fountains.
   xii. Clean and disinfect lobby furniture.
   xiii. Report maintenance problems to XYZ Company facilities manager.

2. Quarterly services consisting of deep cleaning fire extinguishers and/or cabinets for them, signs, clocks, etc.; stripping and waxing floors; deep cleaning/disinfecting all surfaces in restrooms

Quality of Work

Services performed as required by this specification shall be subject to inspection and approval by XYZ Company. Vendor's supervisory and production employees shall be proactive in efforts to keep XYZ Company facilities clean and comfortable for XYZ Company customers and staff. Production employees shall take initiative in identifying, reporting, and correcting all readily recognizable custodial and maintenance conditions, especially spot cleaning of spills, flooring, walls, glass surfaces, restrooms, and lobbies.

Failure to adequately perform services will result in notification of Vendor's supervisor upon first occurrence. Subsequent occurrences will result in notification of Vendor's PM. If performance issues are not corrected, XYZ Company may request that the production employee(s) be replaced.

Payment Adjustment Information

A. Deduction for non-performance – It is the objective of XYZ Company to obtain complete and satisfactory performance in accordance with the requirements of this specification. Failure to perform Quarterly and Semi-Annual Services will result in a deduction of payment equal to the cost charged to provide these services.
B. Failure of contractor to resolve performance issues shall serve as cause for termination of contract.

SECTION VIII – PROPOSAL REPLY PAGE

The intent of this RFP is to award the contract to the qualified vendor who can provide and meet all specified requirements of this request for proposal. The contract shall commence with a tentative award date for a one (1) year base period with three (3) one-year renewal options at the sole discretion of XYZ Company based upon satisfactory performance, which will be reviewed on an annual basis.

For Contract Period – Initial (One Year) Ending 2014

Space Type	Cleanable Area	Evening Services		Quarterly Services		Semi-Annual Services		Annual Totals
	Sq Ft	Sq Ft Unit Cost ($)	Monthly Cost ($)	Per Quarter Cost ($)	Annual Cost ($)	Per Semi-Annual Cost	Annual Cost ($)	Total Annual Cost ($)
Office	10,000							
Retail	15,000							
Warehouse	25,000							
Subtotals	50,000							

For Contract Period – Option Year 1 (One Year) Ending 2015

Space Type	Cleanable Area	Evening Services		Quarterly Services		Semi-Annual Services		Annual Totals
	Sq Ft	Sq Ft Unit Cost ($)	Monthly Cost ($)	Per Quarter Cost ($)	Annual Cost ($)	Per Semi-Annual Cost	Annual Cost ($)	Total Annual Cost ($)
Office	10,000							
Retail	15,000							
Warehouse	25,000							
Subtotals	50,000							

For Contract Period – Option Year 2 (One Year) Ending 2016

Space Type	Cleanable Area	Evening Services		Quarterly Services		Semi-Annual Services		Annual Totals
	Sq Ft	Sq Ft Unit Cost ($)	Monthly Cost ($)	Per Quarter Cost ($)	Annual Cost ($)	Per Semi-Annual Cost	Annual Cost ($)	Total Annual Cost ($)
Office	10,000							
Retail	15,000							
Warehouse	25,000							
Subtotals	50,000							

For Contract Period – Option Year 3 (One Year) Ending 2017

Space Type	Cleanable Area	Evening Services		Quarterly Services		Semi-Annual Services		Annual Totals
	Sq Ft	Sq Ft Unit Cost ($)	Monthly Cost ($)	Per Quarter Cost ($)	Annual Cost ($)	Per Semi-Annual Cost	Annual Cost ($)	Total Annual Cost ($)
Office	10,000							
Retail	15,000							
Warehouse	25,000							
Subtotals	50,000							

SECTION IX - PROPOSAL CONTENTS

Title Page: All proposals must include the following information:

- Name of Vendor
- RFP number listed on this package
- Mailing address
- Contact name
- Telephone number
- Fax number
- Email address

Table of Contents: All proposals must include the following information:

- Clear identification of information by section and page
- List of at least three (3) references, including contact person, telephone number, fax number, and email address
- Identification of all services provided

Proposal: All proposals must:

- Be typed
- Provide a brief history of company and ownership, date business started, current total number of employees, and include any special accommodations/services that could be provided
- Provide a description of services available under this proposal
- Bear the original signature of a principal or authorized officer of the interested party
- Make provision to meet and comply with all applicable laws and regulatory criteria
- Submit along with the proposal any additional descriptive information about services that might be helpful
- Be submitted with one (1) original and five (5) copies and an electronic copy (CD-ROM), mailed or delivered in a sealed envelope to XYZ Company

Additional documents to be submitted:

- One (1) copy of the most recent AUDITED financial statement (A letter from a CPA is an acceptable alternative for non-public companies, but must include a statement that financial solvency is adequate to meet expenditures for at least one year.)
- Documentation of experience addressing professionalism, contract performance, quality of personnel, responsiveness and flexibility, etc. to achieve overall customer satisfaction
- Proof of insurance

- Proof of Historically Underutilized Business (HUB) State Certificate and/or City of Dallas M/W/DBE Certificate
- If your firm is not certified, a statement if you intend to subcontract or affiliate with a certified firm and what percentage of work will be given to them
- Deviation Form (Attachment B)
- Notice of Non-Participation Form (Attachment C)
- Completed Form W-9 (Attachment D)
- Policy and Procedure for criminal background checks of vendor's employees or subcontractor employees who would gain entrance to, or provide services to, XYZ Company's property

****PLEASE INCLUDE ANY ADDITIONAL DESCRIPTIVE LITERATURE THAT MIGHT BE OF ASSISTANCE IN THE DECISION-MAKING PROCESS. ****

SECTION X – SIGNATURE PAGE

XYZ Company, in its sole and absolute discretion, shall have the right to award contracts for any or all services listed in each proposal, shall have the right to reject any and all proposals, shall not be bound to accept the lowest priced proposal, and shall be allowed to accept the total proposal of any one vendor.

This submission is guaranteed as an irrevocable offer valid for one hundred twenty (120) days after the proposal opening date.

Authorized Signature	Vendor/Provider's Name
Typed or Printed Name	Number and Street Address
Title	City, State, Zip Code
Telephone Number	Fax Number
Email Address	

This proposal will ONLY be accepted if this page is signed by an authorized representative.

SECTION XI – ATTACHMENTS

A. Sample Contract

B. Deviation Form

C. Notice of Non-Participation Form

D. Form W-9 – Request for Taxpayer Identification Number and Certification

E. Contractor Sign-In Log

Note to reader: This sample contract is *not* legal advice. It can be used as a template to draft an agreement for an attorney's review. Do *not* rely on the legal terms and conditions used in this sample contract. Your company, agency, industry, or jurisdiction may use different language. Do *not* include this note in a RFP.

ATTACHMENT A – SAMPLE CONTRACT

A sample contract is included for your review. Any exceptions to terms and/or conditions must be identified in the Deviation Form Attachment (Attachment B).

Contract ID No.: ________________

STANDARD SUPPORT SERVICES CONTRACT

THIS AGREEMENT is made and entered into this __________, 2013, by and between XYZ Company, at 1325 Texas Blvd., Dallas, TX 75032, a company ("Company"), and _________ ("Contractor") with offices at __________, for the purpose of providing janitorial services as specified in this agreement.

RECITALS

WHEREAS, the Company desires that Contractor provide janitorial services under the terms and conditions set forth in this Agreement;

WHEREAS, each of the parties is committed to the delivery of services in an effective, cost efficient, and quality manner; and

WHEREAS, this Agreement sets forth the terms and conditions evidencing the Agreement of the parties hereto;

NOW THEREFORE, in consideration of the mutual covenants, rights, and obligations set forth herein, the benefits to be derived therefrom, and other good and valuable consideration, the receipt and sufficiency of which are acknowledged, the parties agree as follows:

I. PERSONNEL

The Company staff member authorized to approve billing is Donna Smith. The Company staff member responsible for overseeing this Agreement is Donna Smith. The Company staff member responsible for day-to-day operations is Bill Green, Facilities Manager.

II. INDEPENDENT CONTRACTOR RELATIONSHIP BETWEEN THE PARTIES

1. **Independent Contractor.** The relationship between the Company and Contractor shall be that of an independent contractor. The parties agree that none of the provisions of this Agreement are intended to create, nor shall be deemed or construed to create, any relationship between the Company and Contractor other than that of independent parties contracting with each other solely for the purpose of effectuating the provisions of this Agreement. It is expressly agreed that Contractor and Contractor's personnel, if any, shall not for any purpose be deemed to be an employee, agent, partner, joint venturer, ostensible or apparent agent, servant, or borrowed servant of the Company. Contractor agrees that he will not hold himself out as an agent of the Company to any persons.

2. **Professional Judgment.** In the performance of all services pursuant to this Agreement, Contractor is at all times acting as an independent contractor engaged in the delivery of a professional service. Contractor and his personnel, if any, shall employ his own means and methods and exercise his own professional judgment in the performance of services pursuant to this Agreement. The sole concern of the Company under this Agreement or otherwise is that, irrespective of the means selected, such services shall be provided in a competent, efficient, and satisfactory manner in compliance with the policies and procedures of the Company and the applicable federal, state, and local laws, rules, and regulations.

III. OBLIGATIONS OF CONTRACTOR

1. **Services.** The specialized support services to be provided by Contractor and the schedule of hours Contractor will deliver such services are set forth in **Exhibit A.** Said schedule and services may be changed only with the mutual written consent of the parties.

2. **Company Approval of Contractor Personnel.** Contractor agrees that any individual or entity selected by him to deliver designated services for Company, including any and all contractors, is subject to approval by Company. The services of any individual to whom Contractor delegates the delivery of designated services are the direct responsibility of Contractor, and Contractor agrees to indemnify and hold harmless Company, its employees, agents, officers, and assigns from any claim or liability arising from the negligent acts or any other acts of Contractor or an individual to whom he delegates the delivery of designated services.

3. **Representations and Warranties.**

   (a) Contractor represents and warrants that, at all times during this Agreement, he will comply with all applicable policies of the Company and all applicable local, state, and federal laws, rules, and regulations now in effect and that become effective during the term of this Agreement. Contractor further agrees to provide services to the Company in a manner consistent with applicable professional standards and consistent with standards of reasonable due care.

   (b) Contractor agrees to perform his services with decorum and in a manner designed to assist in the efficient operation of the Company. Contractor agrees to interact with Company staff in a cooperative manner. The adequacy of the performance of this obligation will be determined at the sole discretion of the Company.

   (c) Contractor represents and warrants that he is not currently an employee of the Company.

4. **Disclosure.** Contractor declares that neither Contractor nor any of its subcontractors or employees rendering services pursuant to this Agreement has been convicted of a criminal act and Contractor will give immediate notification to the Company if such occurs anytime during the term of this Agreement.

5. **Immigration Reform and Control Act.** Contractor agrees to maintain appropriate identification and employment eligibility documents, and to complete a W-9 form, Request for Taxpayer Identification Number and Certification, and to meet requirements of the Immigration Reform and Control Act of 1986.

6. **Required Information for Criminal Conviction Checks.** Contractor shall provide to Company proof that criminal history record checks have been conducted on Contractor/subcontractor's applicants or employees, and that if an applicant or employee of the Contractor/subcontractor has a criminal history relevant to his or her employment, then the Contractor/subcontractor will take appropriate action with respect to the applicant or employee, including terminating or removing the employee from Company property. If Contractor's employee has such a conviction, and Contractor fails to remove such employee, then this contract may be terminated without prior notice.

7. **Access.**

   (a) Contractor agrees that Company and its representatives, including independent financial auditors, shall have access to all facilities, service providers, records, data, and other information under the control of Contractor or its subcontractors as necessary to enable the Company to audit, monitor, and review all financial or programmatic activities and services associated with this Agreement,

(b) Acceptance of funds directly under this contract, or indirectly through a subcontract under this contract, acts as acceptance of the authority of the Company to conduct an audit or investigation in connection with those funds; and

(c) Contractor must provide Company's auditor with access to any information the auditor considers relevant to:

   i. Evaluating Contractor's performance under the contract or subcontract;
   ii. Determining Company's rights or remedies under the contract; and/or
   iii. Evaluating whether the Contractor has acted in the best interest of the Company.

IV. OBLIGATIONS OF THE COMPANY

1. **Payment.**

(a) In consideration of the obligations undertaken by Contractor, the Company agrees to pay Contractor, in accordance with the fee schedule attached as **Exhibit A**, for an amount not to exceed $________.

(b) The payment amount will be based on a monthly invoice which shall reflect the services provided by Contractor and is approved by the Company employee(s) authorized to approve billing(s) as set forth above. Invoices or claim forms for services rendered are to be submitted by the fifth (5) calendar day of the month following that in which the services were rendered.

(c) Invoices or claim forms for services must be received no later than forty-five (45) calendar days after the end of the month in which services were rendered. Invoices or claim forms for services received later than forty-five (45) calendar days after the end of the month in which the services were rendered will not be paid.

(d) Payment shall be made thirty (30) calendar days after receipt of goods, services, or invoice, whichever is latest. Payment may be delayed, adjusted, or withheld, where a deficiency is noted in goods, services, or invoices received. Company retains the right to offset payments for prior invoices paid where a deficiency is noted after payment has been processed.

Invoices shall be submitted in duplicate as follows:

I. Invoices must include a Company purchase order number, which will be indicated on the final, fully executed, copy of the contract.
II. Original and one duplicate, marked "Duplicate," sent to Company staff member authorized to approve billing as set forth above.

(e) Contract Rate Change clause – If a Contractor's contracted rates change during the period of the contract as agreed upon by both parties, the Contractor will be notified in writing and the contract will be amended to reflect such changes.

2. **Staff and Facilities.** The Company agrees to allow Contractor access to its staff and facilities necessary for carrying out the services provided by the Contractor.

V. INSURANCE

1. **Policies, Coverages, and Endorsements.** Contractor agrees to maintain the following insurance policies, with the specified coverages and limits, to protect and insure the Company and Contractor against any claim for damages arising in connection with Contractor's responsibilities or the responsibilities of Contractor's personnel under this Agreement and all extensions and amendments thereto:

1. Commercial General Liability	
General Aggregate	$2,000,000
Each Occurrence	$1,000,000
2. Workers' Compensation and Employers' Liability If Applicable	
Medical and Indemnity	Statutory Requirements
Bodily Injury by Accident	$500,000 Each Accident
Bodily Injury by Disease	$500,000 Each Employee
Bodily Injury by Disease	$500,000 Policy Limit
Employers Liability	$500,000
3. Automobile Liability	
Includes Hired and Non-Owned Automobiles	$2,000,000 Combined Single Limit

2. **Insured Parties.** All Policies shall contain a provision naming the Company (and its officers, agents, and employees) as Additional Insured parties on the original policy and all renewals or replacements during the term of this Agreement.

3. **Subrogation.** All Policies must contain a Waiver of Subrogation endorsement to the effect that the issuer waives any claim or right in the nature of subrogation to recover against the Company, its officers, agents, or employees.

4. **Proof of Insurance.** The policies, coverages, and endorsements required by this provision shall be shown on a Certificate of Insurance on which the Company must be listed as an Additional Insured party and the Certificate Holder, and which should be furnished to the Company prior to the commencement of this Agreement. All such insurance shall be secured and maintained with an insurance company, or companies, licensed to do business in the State of Texas. The Company may withhold payments under the terms of this Agreement until the Contractor furnishes the Company copies of all Certificates of Insurance from the insurance carrier, or carriers, showing that such insurance is in full force and effect.

5. **Cancellation.** New Certificates of Insurance shall be furnished to the Company at the renewal date of all policies named on these Certificates. Contractor shall give the Company thirty (30) days prior written notice of any proposed cancellation of any of the above-described insurance policies.

VI. INDEMNIFICATION

To the extent permitted under the Constitution and the laws of the State of Texas, Contractor hereby agrees to indemnify and hold harmless the Company and all of its directors, officers, employees, and agents from all suits, actions, claims, or cost of any character, type, or description brought or made on account of any injuries, death, or damage received or sustained by any person or persons or property, including but not limited to customers, arising out of or occasioned by any acts or negligence of Contractor or Contractor's personnel, if any, or its agents or employees whether occurring during the performance of the services hereunder or in the execution of the performance of any of its duties under this Agreement.

VII. TERM AND TERMINATION

1. **Term.** This Agreement is effective ________, 2013 to ______________, 2014, unless sooner terminated pursuant to this Agreement.

2. **Renewal Options.** This Agreement may be renewed at the sole discretion of Company for up to three (3) one-year renewal options at rates and placement fees specified in **Exhibit A**.

3. **Immediate Termination.** Company may terminate this Agreement immediately if:

    (a) Company has cause to believe that termination of the Agreement is in the best interests of the health and safety of the employees and customers served under this Agreement.

    (b) Contractor has its applicable license or certification suspended or revoked.

    (c) Contractor submits falsified documents or fraudulent billings or Contractor makes false statements.

    (d) Company may terminate this Agreement immediately upon written notice to Contractor if it is determined by the Company that Contractor will not be able to deliver services in a timely or appropriate manner to meet the business needs of the Company.

4. **Termination upon Default.** Either party may terminate this Agreement after thirty (30) days written notice if the other party is in default of any of the provisions herein and/or any of the provisions in the Request for Proposals (RFP), which is attached hereto and incorporated herein by reference as if set out in full. Such termination shall be ineffective if, within said thirty (30) day period, Contractor cures such default to the satisfaction of the Company. The Company at its sole discretion may extend the period to cure the default for a reasonable time if the Company determines that the Contractor has initiated action to cure the default within the thirty (30) day period. The Company reserves the right to suspend services provided by the Contractor and payment for services not authorized during the thirty (30) day cure period, if at the Company's sole discretion, it is determined that suspension is in the best interest of the Company and/or its customers.

5. **Termination for Convenience.** Due to the need for Company to replace the services being provided by Contractor, this Agreement may be terminated by Contractor, without cause, after one hundred and twenty (120) days written notice to the Company. Company may terminate this Agreement, without cause, after thirty (30) days written notice.

VIII. MISCELLANEOUS

1. **Nondiscrimination.** Each party to this Agreement agrees that no person, on the basis of race, color, national origin, religion, sex, age, handicap, or political affiliation, will be excluded from participation, be denied the benefits of, or be subject to discrimination in the provision of any services hereunder. Without limiting the foregoing, the parties hereto agree to comply with the Civil Rights Act of 1964, the Americans with Disabilities Act of 1990, as amended, and the Civil Rights Act of 1991, as amended.

2. **Business Ethics.** During the course of pursuing contracts, and the course of contract performance, Company will maintain business ethics standards aimed at avoiding real or apparent impropriety, abuse, fraud, waste, or conflicts of interest. No substantial gifts, entertainment, payments, loans, or other considerations beyond that which would be collectively categorized as incidental shall be made to any employees or officials of Company by Contractor employees, directors, officers, and agents. At any time Contractor believes there may have been a violation of this obligation, or any business ethics standard, Contractor shall notify Company of the possible violation.

3. **TB Testing Requirement.** Contractor shall provide to the Company proof that its employees, whose duties place them in Company facilities, whether there is direct or indirect contact with employees and customers, have completed TB testing on an annual basis at the cost of the Contractor. In addition, chest X-ray testing will be required when there is a positive TB result.

4. **Amendment.** Unless otherwise specifically provided herein, this Agreement may be amended or changed only by mutual written consent of an authorized representative of the Company and Contractor.

5. **Entire Agreement.** This Agreement and the documents incorporated herein constitute the sole and only Agreement of the parties hereto and supersede any prior understandings and any prior written or oral Agreements between the parties respecting the subject matter herein.

6. **Assignment.** No assignment of this Agreement or rights or obligations thereunder shall be valid without written consent of the parties.

7. **Additional Requirements.** If Contractor is required to comply with an additional requirement pursuant to compliance with state or federal law, or community standard, regulations, resolutions, settlements, or plans, and compliance results in a material change in Contractor's rights or obligations under the contract or places a significant financial burden on the Contractor, the Contractor may, upon giving sixty (60) days notice of such intention, be entitled to renegotiate the Agreement.

8. **Governing Law and Venue.** This Agreement shall be construed and enforced in accordance with the laws of the State of Texas, and venue shall lie in Rockwall County, Texas.

9. **Captions.** The captions contained herein are for reference purposes only and shall not affect the meaning of this Agreement.

10. **Gender and Number.** The masculine, feminine, or neuter gender, and the singular or plural number, shall be deemed to include the other whenever the context so indicates or requires.

11. **Notices.** Any notice required to be given pursuant to this Agreement shall be in writing and shall be sent, postage prepaid, by certified mail, return receipt requested, to Company or Contractor at the address below. The notice shall be effective on the date of delivery indicated on the return receipt:

    If to Company:
    Donna Smith, MBA, CPSM
    XYZ Company
    Purchasing Department
    1325 Texas Blvd.
    Dallas, TX 75032

    If to Contractor:

    ____

    ____

12. **Remedies.** All rights, powers, and remedies granted either party by any particular term of this Agreement are in addition to, and not in limitation of, any rights, powers, or remedies which it has under any other term of this Agreement, at common law, in equity, by statute, or otherwise, and all such rights, powers, and remedies may be exercised separately or concurrently, in such order and as often as may be deemed expedient by either party. No delay or omission by either party to exercise any right, power, or remedy shall impair such right, power, or remedy or be construed to be a waiver of any breach or default or acquiescence therein. A waiver by either party of any breach or default thereunder shall not constitute a waiver of any subsequent breach or default.

13. **Dispute Resolution.** Any controversy or claim arising out of, or relating to, this contract, or the breach thereof, shall be settled by arbitration administered by the American Arbitration Association in accordance with its Commercial Arbitration Rules, including the Optional Rules for Emergency

Measures of Protection, and judgment on the award rendered by the arbitrator(s) may be entered in any court having jurisdiction thereof.

14. **Severability.** The invalidity or unenforceability of any term or provision hereof shall not affect the validity or enforceability of any other term(s) or provision(s).

15. **Effect of Severable Provision.** In the event that a provision of this Agreement is rendered invalid or unenforceable and its removal has the effect of materially altering the obligations of either the Company or Contractor in such manner as, in the sole judgment of the affected party, (1) will cause serious financial hardship to such party, or (2) will cause such party to act in violation of its corporate Articles or Bylaws, the party so affected shall have the right to terminate this Agreement upon thirty (30) calendar days prior written notice to the other party.

16. **Exhibits.** All Exhibits referred to in this Agreement and attached hereto are incorporated herein by this reference.

The Contractor warrants and assures XYZ Company that it possesses adequate legal authority to enter into this Agreement. The Contractor's governing body, where applicable, has authorized the signatory official(s) to enter this Agreement and bind the Contractor to the terms of this Agreement and any subsequent amendments hereto.

CONTRACTOR	**XYZ COMPANY**
Signature ____________________	Signature ____________________
Name (Printed/Typed): _________	Name (Printed/Typed): _________
Title: ______________________	Title: ______________________
Date: ______________________	Date: ______________________

EXHIBIT A

CONTRACTOR:

CONTRACT ID#:

CONTRACT PERIOD:

SERVICE:

SERVICE DESCRIPTION: Provide janitorial services company wide

PERFORMANCE:

RATE AND RATE DESCRIPTION:

NOT TO EXCEED:

UNITS/ACCOUNT CODE:

PAYMENT DOCUMENTATION: Contractor will submit invoices as rendered.

ATTACHMENT B - DEVIATION FORM

All deviations to this Solicitation (RFP and Sample Contract) must be noted on this sheet. In the absence of any entry on this Deviation Form, the prospective contractor assures XYZ Company of their full agreement and compliance with the specifications, terms, and conditions including all provisions of the Sample Contract.

Each response to this Solicitation shall contain a Deviation Form, which states the prospective contractor's commitment to the provisions of this Solicitation and Sample Contract. An individual authorized to execute contracts must sign the Deviation Form. Any exceptions taken to the terms and conditions identified in this Solicitation Package, including the Sample Contract, must be expressly stated in the Deviation Form (Attachment B).

THIS DEVIATION FORM MUST BE SIGNED BY EACH PROSPECTIVE CONTRACTOR, WHETHER THERE ARE DEVIATIONS LISTED OR NOT, AND SUBMITTED WITH THIS PROPOSAL.

SPEC# Section# or Page#	DEVIATION

_______________ _______________ _______________

Company Name | Authorized Signature | Date

ATTACHMENT C - NOTICE OF NON-PARTICIPATION FORM

Dear Vendor,

Please check the appropriate box below, complete the remainder of this form, and return it PRIOR to the Final Proposal submittal date and time:

___ I/Our Company cannot provide the products, supplies, and/or services listed in this request.

___ I/We have chosen NOT to submit a proposal at this time, but would like to remain on your list for this proposal category. We did not submit a Proposal. Reason(s):

___ REMOVE my/our name from all XYZ Company lists until further notice. Reason(s):

Independent Provider and/or Provider Firm Name: ____________________

Representative: ____
Please print

Address: ____

Phone: ____________________

Fax: ____________________

Email: ____

PLEASE RETURN THIS FORM ONLY TO:
XYZ Company
Purchasing Department
Notice of Non-participation – Janitorial Services
1325 Texas Blvd.
Dallas, TX 75032

Authorized Signature: ______________________________________

Title:______________________________Date:____________________

VENDORS WHO RESPOND TO THIS INVITATION WITH A COMPLETED NOTICE OF NON-PARTICIPATION FORM WILL REMAIN ON OUR MAILING LIST. VENDORS MAKING NO RESPONSE MAY BE REMOVED FROM THAT LISTING.

Thank you for your time and assistance.

ATTACHMENT D – FORM W-9, REQUEST FOR TAXPAYER IDENTIFICATION NUMBER AND CERTIFICATION

Vendor/Providers are to complete the form at the link, below, for W-9, and submit it with proposal.

http://www.irs.gov/pub/irs-pdf/fw9.pdf

ATTACHMENT E – CONTRACTOR SIGN-IN LOG

Contractor Sign-in Log

Date	Time In	Time Out	Printed Name	Company

This book has free material available for download from the Web Added Value™ resource center at *www.jrosspub.com.*

INDEX

D

M

N

O

P